# Indian Writing in English

## A Critical Study

*Edited by*

K.A. Agrawal

ATLANTIC

PUBLISHERS & DISTRIBUTORS (P) LTD

ATLANTIC
PUBLISHERS & DISTRIBUTORS (P) LTD

7/22, Ansari Road, Darya Ganj, New Delhi
Tel.: +91-11-4077 5252, 2327 3880
E-mail: orders@atlanticbooks.com
Web: www.atlanticbooks.com

Published by Atlantic Publishers & Distributors (P) Ltd.

Reprinted in 2018, 2021, 2023, 2025



Printed & bound in India by Atlantic Print Services

# Preface

Indo-Anglian literature is not essentially different in kind and form from other Indian literatures. This literature is a part of it. This literature is a curious phenomenon with a fairly long history of more than one hundred and seventy years. Ever since the publication of the poems of the three poets in Indo-Anglian literature—Henry Louis Vivian Derozio, Kashiprasad Ghose, and Michael Madhusudan Dutt—the Indian English Literature rapidly developed. They wrote in the first part of the nineteenth century. 'Indian Writing in English' has grown considerably in bulk, variety and maturity. It was the first group of poets who were composing poems from the Indian soil. Next came the poets who migrated to the West. But they had their roots in their native land. These poets, Aru Dutt, Toru Dutt, Romesh Chardra Dutt, Hur Chunder Dutt, Govin Chunder Dutt, Omesh Chander Dutt and Greece Chunder Dutt, have written their poems on Indian history, legend and landscape, the picturesque elements of the Christian and Hindu faith and such ideas. The beginning of the 20th century has witnessed the group of poets like Rabindranath Tagore, Sarojini Naidu, Aurobindo Ghose and H.N. Chattopadhyaya who were influenced with Gandhiji and so in their poetry there is increasing political awareness for self-rule and freedom. The poetry of this period vibrates with intense patriotism and political awareness. The last period is from the post-Independence times upto the present day.

'Indian English Fictions' have also enriched Indo-Anglian literature. Indian English fiction falls in the four natural divisions. The beginning of this branch of literature is considered with the publication of Bankim Chandra Chatterjee's *Rajmohan's Wife* in 1864. The other novelists of this period are Raj Laxmi Devi, Kshetrapal Chakrabarti, H. Dutt, Rajam Iyer, A. Madhaviah, S.B. Bannergea, Ghoshal, Mrs. Ghoshal, S.M. Mittra, G. Jogendra Singh, Balkrishna and Sorabji Cornala. The second phase of Indian English fiction is called 'The Gandhian Era.' The fictions of this period have the impact of the Second World War. The main novelists of this period are: Sardar Jogendra Singh, A.S.P. Ayyar, Mrs. Kaveri Bai, A. Subramanayam, S. Nagrajan, Kumar Guru, Sir Hari Singh Gaur, K.S. Venkataramani, Manjeri Isvaran, Adi K. Sett, Prof. Humayun Kabir, G.K. Chettur, Muhammad Habib, Louis Gracias, Joseph Furtado and Dhirendra Nath Paul.

The third phase of 'Indian English Fiction' is from Independence and onward. In the novels of this period there is the echo of Gandhian thoughts. "The Big Three"—Mulk Raj Anand, Raja Rao and R.K. Narayan—are influenced with Gandhian Philosophy. After 1950, the Indian English Fiction's interest moved from the public to the private sphere. They renounced the larger world in favour of the inner man. They engaged themselves in a search for the essence of human living. Bhabani Bhattacharya, Kamala Markandaya, Manohar Malgonkar, Anita Desai, Shashi Deshpande, Arun Joshi and Nayantara Sahgal have contributed Indian English fiction by opening a new vista of human nature, man-woman relationship and socio-political consciousness. The last important stage in this field falls from 1980 and onward. Now the Indian writing fiction has become mature and it received international recognition, mainly through writers of Indian origin who have settled abroad. These creative writers are Salman Rushdie, Vikram Seth, Arundhati Roy, Jhumpa Lahiri, Shauna Singh Baldwin, Amitav Ghosh, Allen Sealy, Upamanya Chatterjee etc. They are writing their fictions on socio-political themes. Their creative works are devoted to the common, poor and down trodden people specially the female world.

The present volume, which is a collection of twenty essays and research papers on Indian English poetry and Indian English fiction, may be seen as a modest attempt to examine some of the Indian poets and novelists writing in English to ascertain their merits and demerits. I take this opportunity to express my gratitude to the learned scholars who very kindly accepted my invitation to contribute their essays/research papers to it. This volume would not have been completed without their kind co-operation. I thank them most heartly for this. I must also express my deep sense of attitude to Dr. K.R. Gupta, Managing Director of M/s Atlantic Publishers and Distributors, New Delhi, for his readily agreeing to my proposal of publishing this volume at the earliest possible.

K.A. AGRAWAL
Editor

# Contents

## SECTION — B
## INDIAN ENGLISH FICTION

# Contributors

**K.A. Agrawal,** Reader, Department of English, Gurukul Kangri University, Haridwar, Uttaranchal.

**N. Sharma,** Formerly Dean, Faculty of Humanities and Professor and Head, Department of English, Gurukul Kangri University, Haridwar, Uttaranchal.

**Rashmi Gaur,** Associate Professor, Department of Humanities and Social Science, Indian Institute of Technology, Roorkee, Uttaranchal.

**S.C. Dwivedi,** Professor, Department of English, Allahabad University, Allahabad, Uttar Pradesh.

**Shubha Tiwari,** Reader, Department of English, A.P.S. University, Rewa, Madhya Pradesh.

**S.D. Sharma,** Professor and Head, Department of Humanities and Social Sciences, Faculty of Basic Sciences and Humanities, G.B. Pant University, Pantnagar, U.S. Nagar.

**A.N. Dwivedi,** Professor, Department of English, Allahabad University, Allahabad, Uttar Pradesh.

**J.P. Tripathi,** Formerly Professor and Head, Department of English, Gorakhpur University, Gorakhpur, Uttar Pradesh.

**M.R. Verma,** Professor and Head, Department of English, Gurukul Kangri University, Haridwar, Uttaranchal.

**Kavita Agrawal,** Formerly Lecturer in English, Kanya Gurukul (PG) College, Gurukul Kangri University, Haridwar, Uttaranchal.

**Shivani Vatsa,** Department of Humanities, Indian Institute of Technology, Roorkee, Uttaranchal.

**O.P. Budholia,** Associate Professor, Department of English, K.R.G. Government (Autonomous) College, Gwalior, Madhya Pradesh.

**Ambuj Kumar Sharma,** Reader, Department of English, Gurukul Kangri University, Haridwar, Uttaranchal.

**Lalji Mishra,** Head, Department of English and Research Studies, K.N. Government Post Graduate College, Gyanpur, Uttar Pradesh.

**Balram S. Sorot,** Reader, Department of English, G.M.N. (PG) College, Ambala Cantt., Haryana.

**Alka Rani Purwar,** Reader and Head, Department of English, D.V. (P.G.) College, Orai, Jalaun, Uttar Pradesh.

**Neelam Singh,** Research Scholar—English (Department of Humanities), Indian Institute of Technology, Roorkee, Uttaranchal.

**Rashmi G.,** Research Scholar—English (Department of Humanities), Indian Institute of Technology, Roorkee, Uttaranchal.

**Shubha Dwivedi,** A freelance writer on contemporary issues in English Literature.

**L.M. Joshi,** Reader, Department of English, Kumaon University, Nainital, Uttaranchal.

**Siddhartha Sharma,** Head, Department of English, Mahatma Gandhi Chitrakoot Gramodaya Vishwavidyalaya, Chitrakoot, Satna, Madhya Pradesh.

SECTION – A

# INDIAN ENGLISH POETRY

# Chapter 1

# Mind and Art of Toru Dutt

*K.A. Agrawal*

Perfection is the most desired ideal in art. It does not come in the twinkling of an eye; instead, it is a matter of constant application and growth. The moment an artist ceases to apply himself wholeheartedly to his work and to 'grow' regularly, his art becomes stale and imperfect. Toru Dutt is a poetic artist who applies herself to her art sincerely and tried to 'grow' from within ceaselessly. It is the desire of application and growth that is so conspicuous in her art. It is this desire that makes her restless to experiment with a number of themes and verse-forms. It is this that explains the great dynamism and substantiality of her poetry.

But the development of art and vision comes with the growth of years. It requires a hard practice, an unflagging fancy, and a mature mind. The reader of Toru Dutt knows that her early poetry suffers from certain shortcomings of meter, rhythm and grammar but they disappear with the greater maturity of her mind. The *Sheaf* has many inversions, archaic words and phrases, and twisted expressions, and also a discordant music here and there, as pointed out by the reviewers of *The Examiner* and *The Englishman,* but the same cannot be said of *Ancient Ballads* and Miscellaneous Poems. If the Sheaf holds out a promise for an upcoming poetess, *Ancient Ballads* is, in a way, the fulfilment of that promise. This naturally leads us to construe that Toru Dutt's art constantly grew and was on trial until it gained in scope and depth towards the close of her life on earth.

The diction that one comes across in Toru's poetry is usually simple, clear and sweet, though this is not literally true in case of some of her translations. Here is an example of her sweet diction:

> What was the meaning—was it love?
> Love at first sight, as poets sing,
> Is then no fiction?[1] (p. 40)

And this is an illustration of her obtuse diction to be found in some of her translations:

> Dante, old Gibelin! when I see only in passing
> The plaster white and dull of this mask so puissant
> That Art has bequeathed us of thy features majestic,
> I cannot help feeling a slight shudder O poet;
> So strongly the band of genius and that of misfortune
> Have imprinted upon them the dark seal of sorrow.[2]
> (p. 147)

But, here, Toru is not her usual self. In many of her translations she writes with a force that seems to have come from within her. In this connection, one may cite, "To Those Who Sleep" by Victor Hugo:

> Lo; He lifts up His hand,
> And the tigers fly howling through deserts of sand,
> And the sea-serpents crawl
> Obedient and meek; He breathes on idols of gold
> In their temples of marble gigantic and old
> And like Dagon they zall:
>
> You are not armed? It matters not,
> Tear out the hinges of the door!
> A hammer has deliverance wrought:
> David has pebbles from the shore, (p. 87)

As an Indo-Anglian author, Toru's main achievement lies in her effective mastery of the medium. She shows in her poetry a fine sense of the English language, a feeling for its rhythm and diction. So remarkable is her treatment of diction and rhythm that she was regarded by many as an Englishman writing under the pseudonym of 'Toru Dutt.' There is elasticity in her verse, which renders it graceful and interesting. The variance of diction according to the need the occasion may be easily found in it; she has, thus, used monosyllabic as well as polysyllabic diction with much success. As an instance of the first variety, we may take up the following from "Sindhu":

> Ah me! what means this?—Hark, a cry,
> A feeble human wail,
> "Oh God!" it said—"I die,—I die,
> Who'll carry home the pail?" (p. 131)

And for the second variety, the following from "Dhruva" may be quoted:

> "Mother, they words of consolation find
> Nor resting-place, nor echo in this heart
> Broken by words, severe, repulsing Love
> That timidly approached to worship." (p. 111)

One really marvels at the vast resourcefulness of Toru's diction. Of course, there are archaisms, inversions, twisting at places, which partly mar the overall effect of her art. Toru does not hesitate to employ even French words and expressions in her poetry: for example, "Va-nu-pieds!" in the poem "On the Fly-Leaf of Erckmann-Chatrian's Novel Entitled, Madame Therese." It must be admitted that she is not conversant with the colloquial turns of modern English.[3]

As in case of diction, Toru's rhythm has received a mixed reaction from critics. It is true that she sometimes succeeds and sometimes fails in capturing the English tunes.

There is, no doubt, must force and fire in Toru's verse, and lyricism touches a high-watermark at times, such as in:

> The doors of every house are hung
> With gay festoons of leaves and flowers;
> And blazing banners broad are flung,
> And trumpets blown from castle towers. (p. 49)

And in:

Past all the houses, past the walls,
        Past gardens gay, and hedgerows trim,
Past fields, where sinuous brooklets small
        With mother silver to the trim
Glance in the sun's expiring light,
        Past frowning hills, past pastures wild,
At last arises on the sight,
        Foliage on foliage densely piled. (p. 49)

In the latter passage, the repetitive use of 'past,' and 'I,' 'g' and 'd' sounds produce a charming rhythm. Toru was at home in the handling of ballads and sonnets, and the reader feels delighted to read them. They are also free from the burdensomeness and dullness of her blank verse. What actually Toru lacked was "mellow sweetness" to perfect her as an English poet, and "of no other Oriental who has ever lived can the same be said."[4] Speaking of her melodies, Anant says that they "were often foreign if not harsh to the English ear," and that they were "the melodies of Bengal, her native land, the melodies which she drank in so often that they now formed part of her very soul."[5] Her lapses in rhythm can be easily traced in *A Sheaf*, at least in some of her renderings, such as in:

They are the watch-dogs, terrible, superb,
Enormous, faithfully that Paris guard.
As at each moment we could be surprised,
As a wild horde is there, as ambush vile
Creeps sometimes even to city walls.
("The Forts of Paris," p. 137)

Nothing to speak of rhyme, there is hardly any rhythm in this extract. Milton produced sonorous and haunting music in his blank verse, but that is totally lacking here.

On the appearance of the *Sheaf*, Toru's versification was found to be 'crude' and 'wooden.' This is how *The Englishman* greeted it: "Miss Dutt's meter often limps, her grammar is not always faultless, and expressions are sometimes quaint or tame." Mr. Gosse also points out that at times "the rules of our prosody are absolutely ignored." Dr. Edward J. Thompson remarks as follows:

> It is easy to feel that, in the work done, she never escaped from the influence of her favourite English poets, such writers as Mrs. Browning, whose work did not furnish satisfactory prosodic models. The meters used by Toru Dutt are nearly always of the simplest, and her use of them is marred by much crudity. Yet against this much be set many signs of haste and lack of opportunity to finish, the punctuation of the *Ballads*, for example, is chaotic.... Yet, even amid the many marks of immaturity and haste, there are signs that she would have escaped before long from many of her prosodic limitations. "Our Casuarina Tree," surely the most remarkable poem ever written in English by a foreigner, shows her already possessed of mastery over the more elaborate and architectural from of verse. In any case, there is enough to show that experience and practice would have brought release from the cramping and elementary forms that she used....[6]

As contrasted to this, Sri Aurobindo has observed: "Toru Dutt was an accomplished verse-builder with a delicate-talent and some outbreaks of genius and she wrote things that were attractive and sometimes something that had a strong energy of language and a rhythmic force."[7] Elsewhere he is said to have remarked that "she has written poetry not as an Indian writing in English but like an English woman."[8] E.F. Oaten, while appreciating Toru's real creative and imaginative power, has taken note of her 'almost faultless technical skill'. Coming to the Sheaf, we find "the meter at least is smooth and suggestive of no labour or hard toil in its making."[9] Such, for instant, is Berat's "My Normandy" or Peyrat's "Roland." This is the last stanza of "My Normandy:"

> There is an age, alas! in life,
> When every idle dream must end,
> An age of introspection, rife
> With memories that cross and blend.
> When such an age arrives for me,

And folds her wing, my Muse, to rest,
May I behold my Normandy,
The favoured land I love the best. (p. 36)

Here one finds the same kind of smooth rhythm and rhyme as in Aru's rendering of "Morning Serenade," which has been oft praised by critics.

As hinted earlier, Toru tried her hand at blank verse too, but not very successfully. In a note to a piece by Louis Bouihet, she says: "Although a Frenchman would faint away at the idea of blank verse, which is not allowed in French poetry, we have not hesitated to render this piece in that form, as well as others."[10] Her lines are all end-stopped, and she is never really happy in blank verse, though a few lines in "The Death of Wolf" and some in the *Ancient Ballads*, especially "The Royal Ascetic and the Hind," "Dhruva" and "Sita," lead us to believe that with more practice she would have been just as much at home in that form as in so many others, notably the sonnet.

Toru seems to have had a great liking for the sonnet form. In *Ancient Ballads* we have two charming sonnets—"Sonnet-Baugmaree" and "Sonnet—The Lotus." Her biographer, Harihar Das, is aware of her partiality to this form. In the Sheaf, there is an original sonnet addressed to her father,—one entitled "A mon Pere."

The *Sheaf* is curiously uneven in merit. There are poems in it which read like bad prose translations, there closeness to the original being their sole worth, but there are others which are real products of genius.

Some distinct verse-forms in *Ancient Ballads* are: the ballad, the blank verse (of which we have already spoken and the octolined stanzas. Toru used the first form in "Savitri," "Jogadhya Uma" and "Sindhu," and last in "Lakshman," "Buttoo" and "Prahlad." She, however, is at her best in handling the balladform. Only one example is being given below to consolidate the statement:

I know in such a world as this
No one can gain his heart's desire,
Or pass the years in perfect bliss;
Like gold we must be tried by fire; (p. 67)

In this quatrain, sense glides along without interruptions. It has a wonderful metrical felicity.

The narrative and descriptive powers of Toru Dutt are best seen in *Ancient Ballads*. She had a rare gift of story telling, of arousing interest and curiosity, of creating suspense, and of drawing character. It may be reasonable said, remarks Dr. Jha, that "had she lived longer she would have attained distinction in narrative verse and in descriptive verse."[11] Toru's narrative skill is beautifully manifested in the way she manages to tell the stories of the past—of Savitri, Sita, Jogadhya Uma, Lakshman, Buttoo, Sindhu, Prahlad, Bharat and Dhurva. But perhaps in descriptive poetry she is even superior. This how Yama, and God of Death, is described:

Upon his head he wore a crown  
That shimmered in the doubtful light;  
His vestment scarlet reached low down.  
His waist, a golden girdle delight.  
His skin was dark as bronze: his face  
Irradiate, and yet severe;  
His eyes had much of love and grace,  
But glowed so bright, they filled with fear. (p. 63)

Toru described Savitri's faint hopes and vivid fears and later her bold encounter with Yama after the death of Satyavan with immaculate skill.

Toru's deep love of Nature and her keen appreciation of natural beauties are visible in all her productions. The *champak* and the lotus and the *kokila* always inspired her song and made her ecstatical. In the presence of natural beauty her heart leapt up with an unspeakable delight, and her lips, like Keats's, quivered in a state of rapture. Here is a beautiful description of the sunset on an Indian lake to be found in "Sindhu:"

Upon the glassy surface fell  
The last beams of the day,  
Like fiery darts, that lengthening swell,  
As breezes wake and play.

Osiers and willows on the edge
And purple buds and red,
Leant down,—and, mid the pale greens edge
The lotus raised its head.
And softly, softly, hour by hour
Light faded, and a veil
Fell over tree, and wave, flower,
On came the twilight pale. (pp. 129-130)

As one reads the ballads, one is struck with the larger space covered by description of Nature; for example:

What glorious trees! The sombre saul
On which the eye delights to rest,
The betel-nut,—a pillar tall,
With feathery branches for a crest,
The light-leaved tamarind spreading wide,
The pale faint-scented bitter need,
The seemul, gorgeous as a bride,
With flowers that have the ruby's gleam,
The Indian fig's pavilion tent
In which whole armies might repose,
With here and there a little rent,
The sunset's beauty to disclose,
The bamboo bough that sway and swing
Neath bulbuls as the south wind blows,
The mango-tope, a close dark ring,
Home of the rooks and clamorous crows,

The Champak, bok, and South-sea pine,
The nagessur with pendant flowers
Like ear-rings,—and the forest vine
That clinging over all, empowers,
The sirish famed in sanscrit song,
Which rural maidens love to wear,
The peepul giant-like and strong,
The bramble with its matted hair,

All these; and thousands, thousands more,
With helmet red, or golden crown,
Or green tiara, rose before
The youth in evening's shadows brown.
("Buttoo," pp. 115-116)

What is quoted here is actually a part of a very long yet charming description of Nature. It is not that the Sheaf has no such descriptions, and this is a pen-picture of the fall of the leaves in the autumn season:

The autumn had bestrewed the vale
With withered leaves,—the woods were left
Bare, and of mystery bereft,
And voiceless was the nightingale;
Sad, almost dying in his dawn,
A sick youth, wandered slow, in tears,
Once more in places far withdrawn
That he had loved in earlier years. (p. 126)

This passage shows that not only the lovely pictures of Nature drew Toru's attention but also the naked and deserted ones, and she gave room to both of them in her poetry.

Toru has sometimes made a fine use of images and symbols in her poetry. It is to be seen in *Ancient Ballads*. Her imagery is often drawn with a masculine vigor and boldness. Though a frail women herself, she displayed a wonderful power in grappling with the sublime and the terrible. Thus, Savitri has:

My daughter, night with ebon wing
Hovers above: the hour is late. (p. 56)

Here the darkness of the night is compared to the black skin of ebony. Another beautiful image is to be found in the following:

She took the soul,
No bigger than the human thumb. (p. 74)

In it an abstract thing has been measured in terms of a concrete thing. This is yet another impressive image in "Savitri:"

I had a pain, as if an asp
Gnawed in my brain (p. 74)

The image of a gnawing 'asp' has been evoked herein to express the intensity of pain. The following passage is also very effective in covering a vivid imagery:

> The shaven stalks of grass,
> Kusha and kasha, by its new teeth clipped,
> Remind me of it, as they stand in lines
> Like pious boys who chant the Saga Veda
> Shorn by their vows of all their wealth of hair.
>
> (p. 104)

The 'shaven stalks of grass' look like some hairless *brahmacharis*, and this is really a masterially stroke of Toru's fertile imagination.

We don't find a systematic network of symbolism in Toru's poetry. Only very rarely has she used symbols. Thus, in "Savitri," the night and its shades are associated with death and distress: in "The Tree of Life," the "tree" becomes a symbol of life, and the 'Angel' of Jesus Christ; and "Our Casuarina Tree" is more than the poetic evocation of a tree,—it is rather recapturing the past, and immortalizing the moments of time so recaptured. In the words of Dr. Iyengar, "The tree is both tree and symbol, and in it are implicated both time and eternity."[12]

Figures of speech are generally used to frequently used to adorn the language and to convey ideas more effectively than in the normal course. Now, Toru has employed them for both purposes.

The figures of speech which Toru has frequently used are simile, metaphor, onomatopoeia, personification, alliteration, and hyperbole. Instances of simile in *Ancient Ballads* are: 'When glided like a music-strain Savitri's presence though the room'; 'Nor melt his lineage like the frost;' 'Tall tree like pillar's;' 'It came as chain less as the wind;' 'he staggers, like a sleepy child,' 'His skin was dark as bronze;' 'The dreadful sword/ Like lightning glanced one moment dire;' 'They lacerate my inmost heart/ And torture me, like poisoned swords;' 'the lion's roar... like a thunder-clap/ Burst in that solitude from a thicket high'; 'Unseen the magic arrow came...like lighting flame/ Sudden and sharp;' and 'the water-lilies spring, like snow enmassed.'

Instances of metaphor in it are: 'His merit still remains a star;' 'The pair look statues, magic-bound;' Savitri 'looked the goddess of the land,' etc. One beautiful instance of onomatopoeia is:

But the good
God's purity there loved to trance,
Mirrored in dawning womanhood. (p. 38)

The frequency of 'd' sound in it gives a sense of hold fear in God-fearing view. Another instance is: 'Whizzing the deadly arrow flew/ Ear-guided, on the game.' A fine example of personification is:

Rang trump, and conch, and piercing fife,
Woke Echo from her bed!
The solemn woods with sounds were rife
As on the pageant sped. (p. 127)

Instances of alliteration are: 'Stern warriors, when they saw her, smiled,/ As mountains smile to see the spring;' 'A stately sable warrior sprang,' etc. Examples of hyperbole are: 'All these, and thousands, thousands more...rose before/ The youth in evening is shadow brown'; 'Hundreds, nay thousands, on they went,' etc.

The *Sheaf* is also not without these figures of speech, but for Toru's original contribution to these areas of literary grace one will have to go *Ancient Ballads*.

Toru was a reserved woman, and she rarely resorted to airing out personal feelings in her verse. But it does not mean that her verse is totally devoid of personal touches. Both of her poetical volumes contain beautiful autobiographical flashes. Thus, in the *Sheaf*, awe have "My Vocation" and "The Death of a Young Girl," among others, this is how Toru writes in the former:

All men have a task,
And to sing is my lot—
No meed from men I ask
But one kindly thought,
My vocation is high—
'Mid the glasses that sing,
Still-still comes that reply,
Chant poor little thing. (pp. 10-11)

Here she hints at her vocation as a poetess. In the latter, we have the following:

She died in earliest womanhood;
Thus dies, and leaves behind no trace,
A bird's song in a leafy wood—
Thus melts a sweet smile from a face. (p. 35)

This entire poem is applicable to the poetess's sister, Aru, who died at the age of twenty, leaving behind no trace of herself.

*Ancient Ballads* has also some poems in which the personal note is clearly articulated. Of such poems, mention may be made of "Jogadhya Uma," "Sita," and Miscellaneous poems (almost all). At the end of "Jogadhya Uma," Toru gives us this stanza:

Absurd may be tale I tell,
Ill-suited to the marching time,
I loved the lips from which it fell,
So let it stand among my rhymes. (p. 100)

In it she forwards the reason for her love of this story. "Sita" is also autobiographical in content. The 'three happy children in a darkened room' are none else but Abju, Aru and Toru, who used to gather in the evening by the side of fire and the mother used to narrate the pathetic tale of Sita to them, they were deeply moved. Among the Miscellaneous Poems, "Near Hastings," "The Tree of Life," the two sonnets, "Our Casuarina Tree" are distinctly autobiographical in detail and in execution. In the last-named poem, we have:

But not because of its magnificence
Dear is the Casuarina to my soul;
Beneath it we have played; though years may roll,
O sweet companions, loved with love intense,
For your sakes shall the tree be ever dear! (p. 174)

It is reminiscent of the poetess's girlhood and the 'sweet companions' with whom she then played. By the way, the glimpses of the poetess's personal life may be best had in her letters.

The subjects that attract Toru Dutt most were pathetic. There are scores of poems in the *Sheaf* to confirm it. "The Young Captive," "The Emigration of Pleasure," "The Lost

Path," "Romance of Nina," "Morning Serenade," "The Death of a Young Girl," "The Captive to the Swallows," and many others are full of pathos and tender feelings. The captives, the vanquished, and the sufferers easily caught her attention and moved her to write. Seldom does she speak about Love, and when she does so, it is invariably pure and sublime. Patriotic themes were no less dear to her. Her ballads are couched in patriotic instincts and native traditions. The stories of the past evoked a sympathetic response from her. Of all the themes, the French War against the Prussians touched her profoundly. Her two poems, "France 1870" and "On the Fly-Leaf of Erckmann-Chatrian's Novel Entitle 'Madame Therese,'" celebrate it in a grand manner. *Ancient Ballads* shows that for her themes Toru usually drew upon the *Ramayana*, the *Mahabharata*, the *Vishnu Purana*, and the folklore (as in case of "Jogadhya Uma"). Like Shakespeare, Toru shows little originality in inventing new themes for her poetry; her real originality lies in the way she executes them. That is also the considered opinion of Mr. Vaish when he remarks: "Toru was less original in themes but she was original in versifying them."[13] The delicacy and lightness of touch displayed in Toru's verse bear testimony to her faultless and refined poetic taste, and the music of her poetry is not the least negligible feature of her work. There is abundant simplicity and spontaneity in her verse.

If in the *Sheaf* Toru found vocation as well as her voice, in *Ancient Ballads* she attained technical virtues, which may do credit to any modern poet. In the latter, she managed the octosyllabic line with considerable dexterity; her rhymes are rarely far-fetched and the sense glides along without interruptions. In connection with her 'wooden' blank verse, it is to be noted that it yields its peculiar charm only to the lucky few like Christopher Marlowe, John Milton, and William Shakespeare. A few more years could have perfected the form; and is likely that she might have written a powerful sonnet sequence or poetic tragedy in the age of her maturity.[14]

Speaking of the technical character of *Ancient Ballads*, Sir Gosse suggests that in spite of much in it that is "rough and incholate," it shows that "Toru was advancing in her mastery of English verse."[15] There is, therefore, no need to plead for indulgence in the critical estimate of Toru's poetical works. Her poetical treasure is too valuable to sink into oblivion, and she has exhibited, within its short compass, many of the essential virtues, including the technical ones, of a genuine poet.

## NOTES

1. The textual quotations that follow in this article are from Dr. Jha's edition of *Ancient Ballads*, p. 40.
2. The textual quotations that follow in this article are from the second edition of *A Sheaf*.
3. Edmund Gosse, "Introductory Memoirs," *Ancient Ballads*, p. XXV.
4. *Ibid*., p. XXVII.
5. Anant, "Gifted Poetess," *The Times of India*, March 7, 1954.
6. EJ. Thompson, "Supplementary Review," *The Life and Letters of Toru Dutt*, pp. 342-43.
7. Shri Aurobindo, *Letters* (Third Series), p. 245.
8. A.B. Purani, *Evening Talks with Sri Aurobindo* (First Series, 1959), p. 282.
9. B.K. Talookdar, "The Poetry of Toru Dutt," *Journal of the University of Bombay*, IV, part 6, p. 77.
10. Toru Dutt, Notes, *A Sheaf*, p. 267.
11. Amarnatha Jha, *Introductory Memoir*, *Ancient Ballads*, p. 30.
12. K.R. Srinivasa Iyengar, *Indian Writing in English*, p. 72.
13. Y.N. Vaish, "Toru Dutt," *The Modern Review* (December 1966), p. 437.
14. See. Mr. Iyengar's *Indian Contribution to English Literature*, p. 20, for details.
15. Edumund Gosse, "Introductory Memoir," *Ancient Ballads*, p. XXIX.

# Chapter 2

# Religious Co-Existence: A Study in the Light of Sri Aurobindo

*N. Sharma*

India has traditionally offered a very congenial and hospitable environment to the emergence and existence of religions and even to the mutual co-existence of dissenting and contradictory religious faiths and practices. This tolerance and the inner urge to accommodate apparently hostile religious creeds has rather gone to such an extreme that it has been the cause of social, political and cultural undoing of the country. Historically, the Indian people have tried their best to eschew sectarian malevolence, religious bigotry and fanaticism. Given essentially to the pursuit of mental, intellectual and spiritual goals, the Indians thoroughly understood that it was the demand of good Reason that they lived in peace and cherished good-will towards every one irrespective of culture, custom and religion. Even Western thinkers have recognized this. Sir John Woodroffe remarks:

> Those (Indians) who...imagine, that reasoning and freedom of thought are a distinctive appendage of the West are very ignorant of the history of their own country. If one had to make the comparison, and one did make it over a period extending from say (to go no further) 2000 B.C., the statement must be reversed in favour of India. No country has honoured Reason more, or given it greater freedom than India.[1]

It is a sad quirk of destiny that in contemporary history, religious intolerance has inflicted the curse of partition on this peace loving and non-violent country and as regards sectarian violence and religious hostility, there seems to be no end to them. So much so that religious cordiality and co-existence are now confronting our intellectuals and policy makers as two of the most urgent problems. To understand this problem, it is necessary at this stage, to enquire into the conditions that led to the emergence of religion and the needs of mankind that it catered to and which brought about its development, sustenance and continuity.

Earliest forms of religion appeared as the primitive man's desire to establish contact with the awe-inspiring forces of Nature and to please them or to control them for his own benefit. Starting with such crude attempts the course of religion has went on to reach considerable refinement, development and systematization through millennial ages. Prof. James Frezer observes:

> ...We shall adhere more closely to the facts of history if we allow most of the higher savages at least to possess a rudimentary notion of certain supernatural beings who may fittingly be called gods, though not in the full sense in which we use the word. That rudimentary notion represents in all probability the germ out of which the civilized peoples have gradually evolved their own high conceptions of deity; and if we could have the whole course of religious development, we might find that the chain which links our idea of the God-head with that of the savage is one and unbroken.[2]

Whenever this chain gets shortened and the savage element in man overpowers his civilized self, religion becomes an edifice to barbarism. Voices of sanity have also been repeatedly heard against religious savagery exhorting humanity to adore fraternal love and communal harmony as comer stones of religion. Manu says:

विद्वद्भिः सेवितः सद्भिर्नित्यमद्वेषरागिभिः।
हृदयेनाभ्यनुज्ञातो यो धर्मस्तं निबोधात॥[3]

(Know *Dharma* to be that which is practised by the learned and the moral people who are free from hatred and which is accepted by their conscience). This emphasis of eschewal of hatred and being true to conscience is the true message of *Dharma*, Swami Vivekananda was more explicit when he spoke that:

> For such people who went to destroy their brothers because they seem to follow a different path towards God for them to talk of love is absurd...How can they preach of love who cannot bear another man to follow a different path from their own?...do not quarrel...the moment you quarrel you are not going Godward, you are going backward towards the brutes.[4]

According to Dr. S. Radhakrishnan:

> ...the ancient religious tradition of India...tries to build up a fellowship of believers not by subordinating individual qualities to the group mind but by bringing them into harmony with each other...religious fellowship is possible, not by imposition of any one way on the whole world but through an all inclusive recognition that we are all searchers for the truth, pilgrims on the road, that we all aim at the same ethical and spiritual standards.[5]

The advice in *Parasuram Kalpasutras* is more pointed and specific:

सर्वदर्शानानिन्दा। अगणनं कस्यापि।[6]

which means, 'no criticism of other philosophies; depreciate no one.'

The argument for love, respect and tolerance is more weightily advanced in *Devi Bhagwat* and *Swachhand Tantra*. Says the *Devi Bhagwat*:

सर्वम खल्विदमेवाहं नान्यदस्ति सनातनम।[7]

which means, "All this is verily Myself, eternal. There is no other." The *Swachhand Tantra* says:

नाशिवम विधते क्वचित।[8]

That is, "there is nothing that is not Shiva or divine."

Besides these there are any number of scriptural injunctions laying down love, harmony and peace and respect for life and all that lives as absolutely essential not only for a spiritual quest but even for ordinary civil and orderly life of happiness and security in this world.

All these exhortations have been both revered and despised by different members of society at the same time and man's need for religion continues to persist and religious interactions between different religious and even amongst followers of the same religion continue to alternate from sweet to sour. To understand the strange destiny of man's religious evolution, it is necessary to look into the causes that brought about the existence of religion, the purpose that it has served and the future that it can hope for itself. This will be helpful in examining the issues of religious co-existence and inter-religious strife.

We can be greatly helped in this work if we study the writings of Sri Aurobindo, one of the greatest saints and thinkers and writers of this century. He has thought deeply and written profusely. Though he has not written on religious co-existence as an issue in itself, yet his writings on the necessity, the origin, development, function and future of religion that are both sagacious and profuse can help in understanding inferentially his views on religious co-existence also. Spirituality and Yoga comprise his main field of work. But in his writings there are many pages on religion also and it is to these that we resort now.

According to Sri Aurobindo, in the very nature of things all evolution proceeds by a slow unfolding; for each new principle that evolves its powers has to make its way out of an involution in Inconscience and Ignorance. Nature affirms at first a vague urge and tendency which is a sign of the push of the occult, subliminal, submerged reality towards the surface. Then there are small, half-suppressed hints of the things that is to be, imperfect beginnings, crude elements, rudimentary appearances. Afterwards there are small or large formations. Then finally there is the decisive emergence which is the beginning of the possibility of its radical change. In all matters, this is always the process of Nature and to ignore it is to miss the intention in her works and get lost in the maze of her procedure. Religion too has been subject to this process and the seeds and possibilities of dissent and assent and conflict are obviously inherent in this process. Sri Aurobindo points out:

> It is evident that the first beginnings of religion must be crude and imperfect, its development hampered by admixtures,

> errors, concessions to the human mind and vital part which may often be of a very unspiritual character. Ignorant and injurious and even disastrous elements may creep in and lead to error and evil; the dogmatism of the human mind, its self-assertive narrowness, its intolerant and challenging egoism, its attachment to its limited truths and still greater attachment to its errors, or the violence...may very easily ivade the religious field and baulk religion of its higher spiritual aim;...under the name of religion much ignorance may hide, many errors and excessive wrong-building be permitted, many crimes even and offences against the spirit be committed.[9]

Besides these characteristics that are attached to religious growth as the very result of the processes of its development, the potential to invite defiance and revolt from others are also inherent in the claims and functioning of religion. This too is succinctly pointed out by Sri Aurobindo:

> Religion has opened itself to denial by its claim to determine the truth by divine authority, by inspiration, by a sacrosanct and infallible sovereignty given to it from on high; it has sought to impose itself on human thought, feeling, conduct, without discussion or question. This is an excessive and premature claim....[10]

This quality is inherent in all religious and is singly in itself bound to attract dissent, defiance or even violent revolt. But there is justification for this. Religion is essentially a matter of Faith. Faith is an important light and support on the tedious pathways of life. And Faith cannot be explained, analysed or proved before acceptance. This too has been realised by Sri Aurobindo and he very wisely comments:

> Faith is indispensable to man, for without it he could not proceed forward in his journey through the unknown; but it ought not to be imposed, it should come as a free perception or an imperative direction from the inner spirit... the premature claim has obscured the true work of the religious instinct in man....[11]

But inspite of these potentialities for unrest and conflict inherent in religion, man has clung to religion and continues to cling for the safe and easy escape it provides out of the difficulties of the unknown. This aspect of religious life has also been recognized by Sri Aurobindo. He says:

> This indeed is the way out usually indicated by religion; a divinely enjoined morality, a pursuit of piety, righteousness and virtue as laid down in a religious code of conduct, a law of God determined by some human inspiration, is put forward as a part of the means, the direction, by which we can tread the way that leads to the exit, the issue. But this exit leaves the problem where it was, it is only a way of escape for the personal being out of the unsolved perplexity of the cosmic existence.[12]

Whatever good purpose religion might have served in this aspect of its character, its possibilities to provoke disagreements in this field too are quite obvious. The doctrine and the faith that might have helped one person or a group might easily have failed or appeared unacceptable to another person or group evoking feelings of bitterness and being let down or of hatred even if imposed upon forcibly.

Sri Aurobindo has pointed out that Religion has been just one avenue discovered by man or provided by Nature to the solution of various puzzles and dilemmas of life. To regard it as the one and only help in its related field would be a mistake. Sri Aurobindo says:

> There are four main lines which Nature has followed in her attempt to open up the inner being,—religion occultism, spiritual thought and an inner spiritual realisation and experience: the first three are approaches, the last is the decisive avenue of entry. All these four powers have worked by a simultaneous action, more or less connected, sometimes in a variable collaboration, sometimes in dispute with each other, sometimes in a separate independence.... Religion has admitted an occult element in its ritual, ceremony, sacraments;.... But also religion has sometimes...pushed away the philosophic mind as a dry intellectual alien, leaned with all its weight on creed and dogma, pietistic emotion and fervour and moral conduct; it has reduced to a minimum or dispensed with spiritual realisation and experience.[13]

This infatuation with creed and dogma and banishment of spiritual realisation and God contact have afflicted all religious—even the greatest ones—at one time or the other and has been the cause of much oppression, violence and bitterness in their relations with other religions and even amongst its own members at different times.

Another cause of much religious intolerance and consequent barbarities is the multiplicity of religions and a large variety of religious creeds that have developed during the long course of human civilization. Claiming divine revelation as their source and authority, many of these religions have taken upon themselves the duty to 'enlighten' the non-believers as a divinely orgained task. The good lying underneath the multiplicity of religions gets ignored. This is very nicely pointed out by Sri Aurobindo:

> A unity behind diversity and discord is the secret of the variety of human religions and philosophies, for they all get at some image or some idle clue, touch some portion of the one Truth or envisage some one of its myriad aspects. Whether they see dimly the material world as the body of the Divine, or life as a great pulsation of the breath of Divine existence, or all things as thoughts of the cosmic Mind...the truth behind must ever be the same because all is the one Divine Infinite whom all are seeking. Because everything is that One, there must be this endless variety in the human approach to its possession; it was necessary that man should find God thus variously in order that he might come to know Him entirely.... All religions are seen as approaches to a single Truth....[14]

Ignoring this vital metaphysical truth, prophets and followers of all religious groups at one time or another got deluded with the belief that their creed alone was a valid religion and that they alone had the real knowledge of God. This one single delusion has been responsible for the worst possible and every continuing religious intolerance.

This cannot, however, be said that this variety of religions should not have been there. Its emergence was inherent in the very nature of the Reality that Religion proceeds to investigate. In this regard, Sri Aurobindo writes:

> All these variations were necessary; the evolutionary endeavour of Nature has experimented on all lines in order to find her true way and her whole way towards the supreme consciousness and the integral knowledge.[15]

It would, however, be a blunder to regard this religious multiplicity as only a source of unrest and ruin or to wish that it were better if it had not been. Sri Aurobindo writes in this regard:

> Nevertheless, the principle of this great and many-sided religious and spiritual evolution was sound...its great justifying result has been an unexampled multitudinous richness and a more than millennial persistence and impregnable durability, generality, universality, height, subtlety and many-sided wideness of spiritual attainment and seeking and endeavour. It is indeed only by such a catholicity and plasticity that the wider aim of the evolution can work itself out with any fullness.[16]

Sri Aurobindo recognizes the individual demands that followers can make on their Faith and the multifaceted character of religion to rise upto such demands. Sri Aurobindo comments:

> The individual demands from religion a door of opening into spiritual experience...a communion with God...there is also the wider purpose of Nature to prepare and further the spiritual evolution in man...religion serves her as a means for pointing his efforts and his ideal in that direction and providing each one who is ready with the possibility of taking a step upon the way towards it. This end she serves by the immense variety of the cults she has created, some final, standardised and definitive, others more plastic; various and many-sided.[17]

Another handicap from which religion has suffered and this too has contributed a lot towards mutual bickerings and lack of acceptance between religious groups and even between members of the same religion towards each other and also sometimes towards their religious institution itself, is the fossilisation and vanishing of the true and original spirit of Faith and spirituality with the passing away of their founding prophets. This aspect has also been commented upon by Sri Aurobindo. He writes:

> Another untoward result or peril of the diffusive movement and the consequent invasion has been the intellectual formalisation of spiritual knowledge into dogma and the materialisation of living practice into a dead mass of cult and ceremony and ritual, a mechanisation by which the spirit was bound to depart in course of time from the body of the religion.[18]

From the above minute observations of Sri Aurobindo on the purpose, origin, development, scope and potential of religion, we can easily reach the conclusion that the potential for intolerance and dissent is inherent in religion and if peace, amicability and mutual co-existence are to be created and preserved—as they must doubtless be for the broader security and prosperity of the people—then it can be achieved only if the religions rise to the demands of the changing intellectual and social milieu and if the people cultivate the qualities of patience, accommodation and social responsibility.

The qualities in religion that work against social cordiality are various and because different members of society are at different levels of mental growth, intellectual development and spiritual aspiration, the potential to attract dissent and defiance are built in all religious dispensations.

A rigid doctrinaire approach may not appeal to some members. But if the doctrine is changed, or compromised, the religion would lose its identity. There may be more than one religions in any one country. Their mutually exclusive identities breed distrust, jealousy, and oppression and violence. A religious group may fall into conflict with the law of the land like the *Bahais* in Iran and the *Ahmediyas* in Pakistan. Some enlightened members of a religion may question or challenge its principles or may even realise through experience that its doctrines do not lead to the promised results. In some cases, oversimplification of rigidities of a religion by a group of reformers or dissidents leading to the opening of a sort of a rival shop as happened in the case of *Brahminism* and *Buddhism* may lead to hostile contests and crusades. Excessive oversimplification may even lead to disillusionment amongst the members who get attracted to a religious body leading to desertion and bickerings. Thus discouraged by the strict and unpleasant demands of celibacy and moral purity many people thronged the new religious movements promising *Samadhi* through sex only to meet disappointment and to indulge in charges, counter-charges and rejection.

Man's need for religion as a system that can bring him spiritual realization, God contact, and light, guidance and security on the pathways of life is compelling. The solution lies not in rejection of religion but in refinement and evolutionary development of religious doctrines and individual and social character. Envisaging such a possibility, Sri Aurobindo writes:

> Religion itself has shown its power of survival and is undergoing on evolution the final sense of which is still obscure. In this new phase of the mind that we see beginning, however crudely and hesitatingly, there can be detected the possibility of a pressure towards some decisive turn and advance of the spiritual evolution in Nature. Religion, rich but with a certain obscurity in her first infra-rational stage, had tended under the overweight of the intellect to pass into a clear but bare rationed interspace; but it must in the end follow the upward curve of the human mind and rise more fully at its summits towards its time or greatest field in the sphere of a suprational consciousness and knowledge.[19]

Reviewing the course of religious evolution and intuitively anticipating its future, Sri Aurobindo says:

> Religion and its thought and ethics and occult mysticism in ancient times produced the priest and the mage, the man of piety, the just man, the man of wisdom, many high points of mental manhood; but it is only after spiritual experience through the heart and mind began that we see arise the saint, the prophet, the Rishi, the Yogi, the seer, the spiritual sage and the mystic, and it is the religions in which those types of spiritual manhood came into being that have endured, covered the globe and given mankind all its spiritual aspiration and culture.[20]

Reaching the stage of such spiritual aspiration as well as realization, mankind will have become ready to make the ideal of religious co-existence a reality. For, according to a *Narad Bhakti Sutra*, in such a society:

नास्ति तेषु जातिविद्या रूप कुल धन क्रियादि भेदः।[21]

which means that amongst the real devotees of God there can be no distinctions of community, learning, appearance, family, wealth, activity and the like. Religious co-existence will then be not a dream but real fact of existence.

## NOTES AND REFERENCES


1. Sir John Woodroffe, *The Garland of Letters* (Madras: Ganesh & Co., 1974) 6th ed., p. 295.
2. Sir James Frezer, *The Golden Bough* (London: Macmillan & Co., 1956), p. 93.
3. Bhagwan Manu, *Manusmriti* (II-1).
4. Swami Vivekananda, *The Complete Works* Vol. III, pp. 131-32.
5. S. Radhakrishnan, *The Recovery of Faith* 1904 ed., p. 185 (quoted by J.R. Kamath in "Secularism," The Kalyan Kalpatru Oct. 1993, G. Press, Gorakhpur, p. 331).
6. Parasuram Kalpasutras (1-14-15) quoted by M.P. Pandit in *Gems From The Tantras* (Madras: Ganesh & Co., 1970), p. 20.
7. Devi Bhagwat: quoted by M.P. Pandit in *Gems From The Tantras*, p. 29.
8. Swachhand Tantra: quoted by M.P. Pandit in *Gems From The Tantras*, p. 30.
9. Sri Aurobindo, *The Life Divine* (Pondicherry: Sri Aurobindo Ashram, 1990), p. 863.
10. *Idem.*
11. *Ibid.*, pp. 863-64.
12. *Ibid.*, p. 626.
13. *Ibid.*, p. 860.
14. *Ibid.*, pp. 699-700.
15. *Ibid.*, p. 861.
16. *Ibid.*, p. 873.
17. *Ibid.*, pp. 873-74.
18. *Ibid.*, p. 871.
19. *Ibid.*, p. 868.
20. *Ibid.*, p. 881.
21. *Narad Bhakti Sutra* No. 72.

# Chapter 3

## Sri Aurobindo's Poetry: Message of a Visionary

*Rashmi Gaur*

Sri Aurobindo is a multi-faceted personality. To the common man he is a mystic yogi. His reputation as a sociologist and a philosopher of history and culture is wide-spread and well-founded. He has been characterised as the prophet of Indian nationalism. His creative genius is equally exemplified in his poetry which has been greatly admired for its aesthetic and philosophical values. His poetry and prose writings represent a rare combination and integration of some of the best elements of philosophy and literary beauty. All his writings contain strong ingredients derived from philosophy and many of his themes spill over into the areas of cultural anthropology, psychology, history, sociology, politics, arts and religion. But these various strains are blended into a single composition in which all lose their separate identities and from the integral parts of a harmonious whole. Sri Aurobindo's work, particularly *The Life Divine, The Human Cycle* and *The Ideal of Human Unity* present a morally enhancing social philosophy supported by an attempt to grasp the totality of his philosophy and to interpret its development as it is gradually exhibited in his poetry.

Sri Aurobindo's first collection of poems *Songs to Myrtilla and Other Poems*, which was printed in 1895 at Baroda for private circulation only, contained several poems which were written by him between his eighteenth and twentieth year. These early poems reveal a skillful craftsmanship in verse, and significantly record his imagination and ideas, feelings and thoughts engendered by a purely European culture. At this time, his acquaintance with the Indian culture was rather sketchy. But these poems foreshadow the maturer Sri Aurobindo, as they are radiant with spiritual glow. In his poem *Estelle*, he writes—

> Why do thy lucid eyes survey,
> Estelle, their sisters in the milky way?
> The blue heavens cannot see
> Thy beauty nor the planets praise.
> Blindly they walk their old accustomed ways.
> Turn hither for felicity.
> My body's earth thy vernal power declares,
> My spirit is a heaven of a thousand stars,
> And all these lights are thine and open doors on thee.[1]

However, it is the later-dated poems of this collection that his resolution to return to his beloved country becomes significantly clear. During his stay in England, he was continuously conscious of his own country, "the oppressor's wrong, the proud man's contumely, the insolence of office and the pangs of subjection—and of things that needed to be done there before she could redeem herself in her own and in the eyes of the world?"[2] In his poem *Envoi*, which appears at the end of *Songs to Myrtilla*, Sri Aurobindo declares:

> For in Sicilian olive-groves no more
> Or seldom must my footprints now be seen,
> Nor tread Athenian lanes, nor yet explore
> Parnassus or they voiceful shores, O Hippocrene.
> Me from her lotus heaven Saraswati
> Has called to regions of eternal snow
> And Ganges pacing to the southern sea,

Ganges upon whose shores the followers of Eden blow.[3]

Sri Aurobindo came back to India in 1893, after spending fourteen years in England. It was the beginning of his Indian experiences which changed the course of his life. In a letter to one of his disciples, Sri Aurobindo refers to this transfiguring experience as follows:

> "...since I set foot on the Indian soil on the Apollo Bunder in Bombay, I began to have spiritual experiences, but these were not divorced from this world but had an inner and infinite bearing on it. Such as a feeling of the Infinite pervading material space and the Immanent inhabiting material objects and bodies. At the same time I found myself entering supraphysical worlds and planes with influences and an effect from them upon the material plane, so I could make no sharp divorce or irreconcilable opposition between what I have called the two ends of existence and all that lies between them."[4]

Sri Aurobindo spent about thirteen years in the Baroda State Service. It was during his stay at Baroda, that he learnt Bengali, Marathi and Gujarati. He also studied the Sanskrit literature in depth. He also contributed some articles to *Indu Prakash*, published from Bombay, on the contemporary Indian political situation. He also translated many literary pieces. His close contact with the Indian people and the Indian culture released in him a hidden spring of literary activity. Most of his writings during this period, prose as well as poetry, original as well as translated—are patriotic and nationalist. His translation of Dwijendralal Roy's *Mother India* was published in the *Modern Review*. His translation of Bankim's song *Bande Mataram* appeared in the *Karmayogin* in 1909. Although this anthem is difficult to translate into verse in another language "owing to its unique of sweetness, simple directness and high poetic force,"[5] his poetic rendering comes reasonably close to the original in its rhythmic power:

> Mother, I bow to thee!
> Rich with thy hurrying streams,
> Bright with thy orchard gleams,
> Cool with thy winds of delight,
> Dark fields waving, Mother of might,
> Mother free....
>
> Thou art wisdom, thou art law,
> Thou art heart, our soul, our breath,
> Thou the love divine, the awe
> In our hearts that conquers death....[6]

The strain of this poem is continued in *Baji Prabhou*, which is also is heroic poem. It was published in 1910 in the *Karmayogin*. It is a story of Maratha heroism, which is told with a breathlessness and power of language that perfectly match the sanguinary theme. The poem is rich in "tragedy and triumph, and it both ennobles and exalts the subject."[7]

> Make iron of your souls.
> Yet if Bhavani wills, strength and the sword
> Can stay our nation's fixture from 'erthrow....[8]

The poem has a sonorous vigour and precision of phrasing which suggests a vitality of movement appropriate to the occasion. With the help of the goddess Bhawani Baji saves the situation. His imperishable sacrifice represents the sovereign strength of purpose. The poem also suggestively personifies Sri Aurobindo's message that only when a person is able to sacrifice his life for a worthy cause, it becomes a true gateway to the soul's eternal freedom and immortality. *Baji Prabhou* and some other poems like *Urvasie*, *Love and Death*, *Chitrangada* and *Vidula* are notable not only for their literary beauty, but they are also significant for their purposeful theme and its equally powerful evocation. "How shall man conduct himself on what seems to be no better than the constant challenge of "life's scaffold?" The challenge taken for granted, how was manly man to meet it, master it and exceed it? Love like Pururavas' for Urvasie or Ruru's for Priyumvada was a marvellous and glorious experience, but even such love by itself was not enough! The individual might find his felicity, but only at the cost of the great good of the community, the country, or future humanity.[9] It is this capacity for self-abnegation, to sacrifice one's immediate interest and happiness for a noble cause, which Sri Aurobindo preached in his works and practised in his life. Sri Aurobindo once wrote, "The Yoga we practise is not for ourselves alone, but for the Divine, its aim is to work out the will of the Divine in the world, to effect a spiritual transformation and to bring down a divine nature and a divine life into the mental, vital and physical nature and life of humanity. Its object is not personal *Mukti*...but the liberation and transformation of the human being."[10] Sri Aurobindo wanted his countrymen to come out of their frivolity, cynicism and superficiality which had become their fate during the British slavery. He had also criticized those Indians who used to ape the European manners and scorned their own heritage.

Sri Aurobindo had to spend a whole year in prison, and this year brought to him an internal awakening, a new spiritual consciousness. He experienced Divine manifestation in everything. He could feel the intimations of an impenetrable mystery. He invokes the people to enter the deathless world of a mystic harmony, defying the hazards and difficulties of material world.

> With wind and the weather beating round me
> Up to the hill and the moorland I go.
> Who will come with me? Who will climb with me?
> Wade through the brook and tramp through the snow?
>
> Not in the petty circle of cities
> Cramped by your doors and your walls I dwell;
> Over me God is blue in the welkin,
> Against me the wind and the storm rebel.[11]

During this time a new knowledge pervaded in his conscience and "the human in him paced with the divine."[12] He spent some time in Chandernagore and finally came to Pondicherry. His first few years in Pondicherry were for him a period of silent yoga and he visualized glimpses of an ennobling transcendental metaphysics. He felt the divine presence of God in him. He has immortalized such experiences in his beautiful sonnets, such as,

> In a town of gods, housed in a little shrine,
> From the sculptured limbs and Godhead looked at me...
> A living Presence deathless and divine,
> A Form that harboured all infinity.
>
> The great World-Mother and her mighty will
> Inhabited the earth's abysmal sleep...
> Now veiled with mind she dwells and speaks no word,
> Voiceless, inscrutable, omniscient,
> Hiding until our soul has seen, has heard
> The secret of her strange embodiment....[13]

Sri Aurobindo felt that true religion, grounded on spirituality, would prove to be, not the opium, but the elixir of the people. It shall encourage a deeper brotherhood among people, a "yet unfound law of love," which alone can be the only sure foundation possible for a perfect social evaluation.[14] In *The Human Cycle* and *The Ideal of Human Unity* (1919) he examined the problem of collective man, in sociological terms, projecting a plausible and prophetic vision of future possibilities for the human race. He clearly states that the whole process of nature is based on a poise between, the individual and the aggregate, a mutuality of interdependence and a harmony of the whole. In the discussion of his ideal world-state in *The Ideal of Human Unity*, neither a dominant minority would exploit the vast majority, the dumb millions, nor a ruling majority oppress the minorities; but in the larger interests of integration, a cultural minority will have to give up the inessential elements in its separative existence. He also sees the social development as a movement from the subjective to the spiritual age-in which the human thought and action shall be transfigured by the infusion of the consciousness of oneness and harmony. The world-state shall be sustained by a religion of harmony and humanity. In his poetry too, we find the sense of awaiting the phoenix hour when this "too too sullied" earth that was in travail would give birth to a supramentalized blissful world:

> ...for the golden age
> In Kali comes, the iron lined with gold,
> The Yoga shall be given back to men,
> The sects shall cease, the grim debates die out
> And atheism perish from the Earth,
> Blasted with knowledge; love and brotherhood
> And wisdom repossess Sri Krishna's world.[15]

He strives for cosmopolitan liberalism. At no point in his life was Sri Aurobindo unaware of the spiritual reality behind the material actuality. Even his writings about the world—order are, thematically, dependent on his mystic or Yogic experiences. There is a constant development along these lines in his poetic graph. From the imaginative and sensuously evocative poetry of *Urvasie* and *Love-Death* to the palimpsest of the *Nine Poems*

Particularly—Ahana, to the yogin-singer of *The Rose of God* and the futurist baurd of *Savitri*, there is a constant and interrelated organic development. From the early poems which deal with romances, idyllic thoughts, innocence of childhood and poetry, he moves to the poems which symbolize his gradual transition into a metaphysical yogi and are a beautiful blend of joy in the natural world and introspection and interrogation on the other. Ahana's poesy is particularly a mingling of fact, myth and symbolism; hope, aspiration and ecstasy, presenting before us dazzling images and striking evocations—

> But I descend at last....
> Lo, I come and behind me knowledge descends and with thunder
> Filling the spaces Strength, the Angel, bears on his bosom Joy to the arms....[16]

Ahana is dawn, the advent of which causes a universal rejoicing. As she appears on the mountains of East, the Hunters of Joy great her first; behind them are the seekers after knowledge and the climbers in quest of Power also. The poem states that the human knowledge shall be completed only when it realizes Joy born of Love and the consequent dawning light:

> Vision delightful alone on the hills whom the silences cover.
> Closer yet lean to mortality human, stoop to the lover...
> Tread through the edges of dawn, over twilights grey, lidded margin;
> Heal earth's unease with they feet, heaven-born delicate virgin.[17]

Ahana embodies a dream *i.e.* of humanity; and a vision—which a Yogi sees from the heights of his creative writing—

> Deep in our being inhabits the voiceless invisible Teacher; Powers of his godhead we love; the Creator dwells in the creature. Out of his Void we arise to a mighty and shining existence....[18]

However, even in these poems, Sri Aurobindo does not want to lose himself in the Inevitable, his desire is to transform earth in Heaven's image. In this background, his *Collected Poems and Plays* which appeared in two volumes in 1942, prove to be a forerunner to *Savitri*, a divine comedy of spiritual action. With her Beatrice like powers Savitri redeems Satyavana, the besieged Troy of the triune Satyam-Sivam-Sundaram. It is sometimes treated as the spiritual biography of Sri Aurobindo and is definitely a culmination not only of his philosophy, but also of his poetry. *Savitri* is in twelve Books of Forty-nine Cantos. The archetypal theme of man's immense capacity to transform his terror and apprehension into a sublime saga of endurance and ultimate victory has been presented in sonorous rhythm in *Savitri*. The earlier narrative poems, *Urvasie* and *Love and Death*, with their pre-occupation with the problems of death and of human felicity, find their remote consummation in the legendary and symbolic tale of Satyavana, Savitri and Yama; the dramatic heroines, Andromeda, Rodogune, Aslang, the warrior queens Chitrangada and Penthesilea, are all included and exceeded in *Savitri*; the philosophy of *The Life Divine* and the ten limbs of Sri Aurobindo's Yoga find superb enactment in *Savitri*; the whole history of earth and man and society and human polity, the part failures, the present confusions, the future possibilities, are also dramatised on the multi-tier stage of *Savitri*, the evolution and architecture of the occult worlds—the worlds of light above, the regions of darkness below, the twilight realm between—are presented in *Savitri* as compellingly living realities and finally, whatever was of universal relevance in Sri Aurobindo's personal, political or spiritual life finds memorable recordation in *Savitri*.

The story of Savitri was already old in the time of Mahabharata, for it was recounted by Rishi Markandeya to Yudhisthira, during the years of his exile to console him. Sri Aurobindo was fascinated by it. Over the years—drafts are available from the dates of 1916 to the dates of 1930. The concept grew into him and it ultimately emerged on the poetic counterpart to his philosophical treatise, *The Life Divine*. The August, 1946 issue of *Sri Aurobindo Mandir Annual* carried the 1 Canto, *The Symbol Dawn* alongwith Sri Aurobindo's essay on *Mystic Poetry*—

> A gate of dreams ajar on Mystery's verge.
> One lucent corner windowing hidden things
> Forced the world's blind immensity to sight.[19]

Savitri symbolizes inner power and strength she does not flinch at the prospect of Satyavan's threatened death, nor even in the face of death or the sight of Yama the Lord of Death. By going within herself and forging the links with her secret self, she has prepared for the event. She neither indulges in self-pity, nor cries when the crisis is upon her—even when her heart was being sawed in two, not a single tear appeared in her eyes. It was Savitri's divine solitariness and strength, her propensity to incarnate in herself the will to triumph in a world surrendered to resignation and defeat, and her consciousness of mission and might to rectify the very engines of our incapacity and anguish—it was this radiant vision and experience of Savitri's personality and power that had attracted Sri Aurobindo towards the story, and this is the very spirit which he has reincarnated and sustained in his cosmic epic. Although at a cursory glance one may feel that the discussion of the occult and the incomprehensible and the sheer mass of it raise barriers between the poem and its readers.

Sri Aurobindo himself wrote in one of his letters, "*Savitri* is the record of seeing, of an experience which is not of the common kind and is often very far from what the general human mind sees and experiences.... There must be a new extension of consciousness and aesthetics to appreciate a new kind of mystic poetry.[20]

Thus we find that Aurobindo's poetry and other writings are basically an exposition and extension of his inner journey towards onehood with a cosmic soul. His poetry presents before us a vision and an experience that do not come in everybody's way and is sustained by an aesthetics that is geared to the quality of this vision and the nature of this experience. Much of his poetry proves to be rather unfamiliar and difficult to a common uninitiated reader owing to the subject-matter and the impregnated meanings. His poetry also has beautiful and sonorous passages, for example:

> But I have felt a touch as sweet as spring,
> And I have heard a music of delight
> Maddening the heart with the sweet honied stabs
> Of delicate intolerable joy.[21]

But his writings are not simply for the here and the now, they are also for the future. They present the quintessential essence of his mystic and spiritual experiences, and they gain in significance with the passage of time. His aesthetic yoga has converted his poetic verse into a mantra. His poetry therefore touches the whole of our being and not a part of it. It does not speak merely to our spirit or address our intellect or touch the sensuous part of our life—it positively and affirmatively makes a contact with the whole of our personality. He had maintained that the mantra represented the ideal towards which our poetry should move. This is the ideal our poetry should attain. Poetry is an incomplete mantra. *The mantra* differs from a *verse* in the fact that in it there is not only a realization of the ideal of beauty but something indescribably more which we can feel and intuit. His poetry throbs with an upsurge of the whole consciousness, culminating in a readiness to surrender our whole being to the illimitable vastaness that slowly opens out before our gaze. His poetry cannot be enjoyed and assimilated without understanding his philosophy in its totality.

His poetry teaches us introspection, to have faith in ourselves and in our capacity to transcend the immediate which limit our selfhood. Sri Aurobindo's poetry represents his philosophy of transformation and teaches us that supramental capabilities are within our reach and man can perfect his quality of life. The close relationship between thought and action, which Sri Aurobindo has advocated in his poetry makes him immensely relevant in our times.

## NOTES

*All the quotations of Sri Aurobindo's poetry are from the Sri Aurobindo Birth Centenary Library edition published in 1972.*

1. Sri Aurobindo, *SABCL*, Vol. 5, p. 9.
2. K.R. Srinivasa Iyengar, Sri Aurobindo: A biography and a history, Sri Aurobindo International Centre of Education, Pondicherry, 1972, p. 42.
3. Sri Aurobindo, *SABCL*, Vol. 5, p. 26.
4. Sri Aurobindo, *SABCL*, Vol. 22, p. 121.
5. Sri Aurobindo, *SABCL*, Vol. 8, p. 311.

6. *Ibid.*, p. 309.
7. Sri Aurobindo, *A Biography and a History*, p. 111.
8. Sri Aurobindo, *SABCL*, Vol. 6, p. 383.
9. Sri Aurobindo, *A Biography and a History*, p. 171.
10. Sri Aurobindo, *SABCL*, Vol. 16, p. 411.
11. Sri Aurobindo, *SABCL*, Vol. 5, p. 39.
12. Sri Aurobindo, *SABCL*, Vol. 28, p. 44.
13. Sri Aurobindo, *SABCL*, Vol. 5, p. 139.
14. Sri Aurobindo, *SABCL*, Vol. 15, p. 206.
15. Sri Aurobindo, *SABCL*, Vol. 5, p. 85.
16. *Ibid.*, pp. 535-36.
17. *Ibid.*, p. 523.
18. *Ibid.*, p. 528.
19. Sri Aurobindo, *SABCL*, Vol. 28, p. 103.
20. Sri Aurobindo, *SABCL*, Vol. 29, p. 794.
21. Sri Aurobindo, *SABCL*, Vol. 5, p. 71.

# Chapter 4

# Vedantic Thoughts in the Poetry of Krishna Srinivas

*S.C. Dwivedi*

That style is the man, is a very famous saying. When we think of the poetry of Krishna Srinivas, we must remember this dictum. Krishna Srinivas's contribution to English language cannot be forgotten. His language is vitally metaphorical. His poetry shows unnoticed relations between religions, thoughts, things, objects and names them afresh. Thoughts and ideas shine in his poetry as integral pictures. When we go through his poetical works we find that they creates afresh new associations. Krishna's following lines from Sankara would testify to my point:

> What we see fade away
> What we hear fade away
> What we smell fade away.
> What we touch fade away.
> Just reflectional realities:
> the orange in mirror
> is worth not a bite
> The snake feared to hiss
> is just a rope
> When felt and found. (Sankara: p. 184)

This is the most eloquent tone that I have heard in our times in English language. Krishna Srinivas's poetry compels us to keep in mind the right standards of excellence. This is why his tone and idiom of poetry are so different from other poets.

Other Indian and foreign poets are not so much obsessed with sublimity, high seriousness in life and right standards of life as Krishna Srinivas. It is certainly with a purpose of achieving right type of standards in language and life that he is writing epics after epics. His epics on Sankara, Ramanuja, Madhva, Mahavir, Vallar, Christ, Muhammad, Buddha, Five Elements etc. are full of his uncommon search for excellence. He has turned the philosophy, mythology and religion into excellent poetry. His epics point to the fact that great poetry is not common and abundant. Whereas most of the contemporary poets waste much of their time and energy in celebrating the trivia, Krishna Srinivas has always celebrated excellence, sublimity and divinity with enthusiasm. His poetry tells us that excellence dwells on high Himalayas. His hands are always active to catch excellence. The lines that I have quoted above present the beautiful pictures of the philosophical ideas of Sankar through the analogy of mirror and rope. What belongs to Sankar ultimately belongs to Krishna, and what belongs to Krishna ultimately belongs to Sankar. The present and the past begin to sing and dance together. The tradition and the contemporaneity begin to sing and dance together. What was disorganised before has been ordered and organised. The metaphorical language of Krishna Srinivas connects the past and the present and points to the future. Krishna Srinivas has developed a rhetorical art to achieve his goal as a poet. Let us look at the following examples:

> The sun never rises or sets:
> It perennially shines.
> Enveloped in Maya
> We creep through crevices of Night
> but Brahman wills:
> May I Become Many.... (Sankara: p. 185)

Brahman is described in the following lines:

> Brahman
> is Sat, Chit, Ananda....
> inseparable as sweetness from sugar:
> It is absolute Reality, Non-Dual.
> In Duality one smells another

One sees another
One hears another
One speaks to another
One thinks of another
One understands another. (Brahman: p. 188)

God is in fact one though he has been called by different names:

When in Communion
with bewitching Maya
He is hailed with thousand Names:

Saguna Brahman—
a penetrating Siva
a reverberating Rama,
a luscious Krishna,
a dark Kali,
a benevolent Buddha.
a forgiving God. (Brahman: pp. 189-90)

Krishna describes the true nature of Brahman as Nirguna:

But real Brahman
is Nirguna—
no colours,
no desires—
It is All the Everywhere
as nothing outside for it to get:
It is inner core
and kernel immaculate,
infinitesimally minute
and indefinitely mighty. (Brahman: p. 190)

Krishna Srinivas succeeds in changing language into universal absorber. He emerges as the master of diction on the basis of above quotations though thousands of such quotations can be collected by any reader of Krishna Srinivas. He goes to the shores of Sanskrit, Urdu, Persian, Tamil and several other languages in order to perfect his diction and language. He identifies himself with the subject which he chooses to write. When he writes on Sankar he absorbs the philosophy and poetry of Sankar so much that not only translated lines begin to dance and sing but they shine like rainbow in sky. As a modern poet he translates a lot. The original words in Sanskrit and lines in Sanskrit are presented as part of the original body of poetry. In his epic Sankar one notices that Sanskrit words like Maya, Tat TvamAsi, Brahman, Sat, Chit, Anand, Saguna Brahman, Neti-Neti, Jiva, Ome etc. have been frequently used by the poet. Sanskrit words create a matric atmosphere in the epic. When we read the poet we feel that we have been elevated from a mean and mundane world to the world of Brahman. Krishna Srinivas gives us the right standard of excellence. He goes to the Saints, prophets and Classical languages to find it out in our times. This sense of right standard of language seems to have lost with other contemporary poets. He fuses different religions, amalgamates them here and there with a view to integrating humanity which is on the thresh hold of disintegration and chaos. The purpose is not to retell the ancient philosophy but to see whether that philosophy can live again as he lives it again.

Krishna Srinivas is a valuable epic poet of our times. His style is epical. His rhetoric, language and wit are epical. Krishna Srinivas has written the epic for Modern India which has easily become the epic for the modern world because of its universality. Like Goethe, Whitman, Dante, Homer and Virgil he is universal. His epics have universal appeal. His epics on Sankar, Ramanuja, Madhva, Vallar, Buddha, Christ and Mohammad we find the expositions, interpretations, translations of various religious texts. He is hoisting the flag of Indian Renaissance through his epics. He has imbibed Sanskrit language, Literature and Philosophy in a much wider, deeper and passionate way than even T.S. Eliot. He has fused and integrated various religions, languages, civilizations and cultures in a unique and artistic way. In this quality alone his poetry is far superior to many contemporary poets who have not bothered about this problem at all. Krishna Srinivas goes to Hinduism, Islam, Christianity, Buddhism, Jainism and other religions to find the uniting threads for human unity and brotherhood. After all Truth is one and one only though the sages often describe it in different idioms. Like Sri Aurobindo he is a great orientalist who must be honoured because his poetry is so honourable, delightful and readable. He examines and analyses religions and the sayings of prophets and accepts only as much as it should be accepted for the benefit of humanity. The poetic personality of Krishna Srinivas has filtered the religious thoughts and what remains after filtering is so much useful for the health of humanity. In his epics we find the most literary and aesthetic analysis of the religions. His poetry will never become stale because it contains the quaintessence of all religions. I do not know of any other poet except Tulsidas who has laboured so much to master all the religions for creating excellent artistic beauty in poetic language. His epics are golden treasuries of religion and civilizations. It is not sufficient to know our neighbour we should also acquaint ourselves with the neighbour's religious and cultural mode of life. As an epical poet he takes into his consideration only the high and noble thoughts of the prophets. Thus the epics serve the double purpose—they discuss the high thoughts of the prophets and make them a part and parcel of our literary and cultural life. Krishna's epics are as indispensible as *The Ramayana* and *The Mahabharata* and we cannot think our modern world without Krishna Srinivas and his everlasting epics. The religion enters into our lives, and our lives enter into religions. Man becomes God and God becomes Man. Nothing is untouchable in Krishna Srinivas's world. The high thoughts, the inspiring sentences, and the artistic beauty of his epics begin to charm us in a new way. Krishna catches us by our fingers. We begin to think, talk, walk, dance and sing with him. We begin to see the world and the universe through his eyes. And once we enter into his world we develop a fancy for his world. His world is so lovely and charming that no one will like to come out of its magical domes.

Krishna Srinivas's mastery of Hinduism, Islam, Christian, Buddhism, Jainism and other religions of the world is astonishing. His epics present not only the secrets of Vedic Hymns but they unlock the secrets of other religions and civilizations in whose contact the poet has lived and breathed for the last eight decades. He has made the most profitable study of the noble thoughts of Sankara, Ramanuja, Madhva, Mahavir, Vallar, Christ, Muhammad, etc. From the study of the various saints, prophets and religions flow and perennial ocean of his poetry. Others have derived their poetry from one religion or so but no one has drunk the nectar of Sarva Dharma Sambhava (Universal respect for all the religions of the world) like Krishna Srinivas. In this quality alone he is a heavy weight champion poet. The world's survival is endangered because of the communal fires and dogmatic attitude of the followers of religions. Krishna at least tells us to distinguish between the right path and the wrong path. He has certainly chosen the right path and the poets of entire world rightly show their unstinted and unreserved praise for him. The whole world is bowing its head before him for contribution to world culture. The world is heading towards multinationalism and multiculturalism. It is also heading towards the necessity of world government for the sake of world peace. Krishna's emergence on the poetic firmament is therefore revolutionary and of immense significance. He is the best poet of integration in our times and humanity can never forget his poetry for this quality.

Sankar's influence on India and the whole world is very large indeed. Krishna writes on Sankar, the great philosopher and the saint to raise the moral standards of our times. One should not forget that Krishna is always concerned with the high seriousness, the noble and the sublime in human life. To think of Sankar is to think of great and noble ideas. Krishna cannot live without them. He propagates the immortal philosophy of Advait (non-duality) to the whole world. God is one and one only and hence the ills of Hindu Politics, Islamic Politics, Christian Politics can be corrected if we approach Sankar as Krishna approaches him. Never was anything more wanted than non-duality in our country and other countries. Krishna is a poet of the modern consciousness. Whatever is modern in ancient saints is conveyed in modern poetic idiom. When we read his epic on Sankar we are virtually swayed by its high thoughts and the epic voice of the poet. We start trusting him as the hero of non-duality of our times. All boundaries begin to fall down. We find the expansion of everything in Krishna. Our hearts, minds, souls, thoughts, expand unusually. Krishna writes, "Space in earthen pot is same as limitless space. And our human bodies and cosmos begin to dance together because it has been rightly said 'Yathaiva Pinde, Tathaiva Brahmande." The poet has swayed in the epic and there is no wonder then that others are equally swayed by it. Krishna has enriched national literature and in this process he has also enriched international literature.

## EVEREST

*Everest* must be read and reread for the fusion of various elements. This is how the poem beings:

Aflame I felt
Bearing broken Sun on back
Down the vast abyss:
Into the dark, dark, dark
Inconceivably dark
Breathless inane
And crashed on a swirl.
Gytating round and round
A mammoth miraged bound
Rooted on everest crest:
I gaze on blazing infinity
And polared non-entity
The spiralling vast
And vortexing deep
Mammoth galaxies
Weave magic zodiacs
On looms of trinity time—
Present echoing ravished beyond.
Fifty millenniums ago
From rage of atoms rose
Cephalized metazoa—
Rolled up and enveloped
And god burnt to bone
Rose over fossiled earth. (*Everest*: p. 15)

Krishna develops a theory of history in the above lines. His personal history and the history and geographical birth of everest join hands with each other. The images of vast abyss, darkness, everest, magic zodiacs, fossilized earth and image of the poet gazing on blazing non-entity, the image of the past and the present fuse into a unified whole. The poet comes to regard everest as a natural beauty which has a history of fifty millenniums. As a religious poet Krishna needs a systematic study of human and geographical history. The systematic study of history fills him a purposive sense which is the need of our civilization. As a poet he closely watches and interprets the history of everest which is closely linked with the history of mankind. Thus the personal history, the history of everest and the history of mankind are fused together. *Everest* is a geographical and historical event just as the epic of the poet is also a great event. The past event and the present event are interconnected. After the beautiful description of everest the poet writes about Man in these words:

> Are you not that fury
> That spins reality
> Round the kernel flame?
> He frets and fumes
> To find himself,
> And universes
> Join the search—
> I searching Me
> And Me searching Thee
> And I and Me
> Mirrored in He—
> I and Me no different He. (*Man*: p. 17)

In *Everest* the poet shows the perfection of rhythm and diction. The poem is flawless in every respect. It is full of the harmonies of heart, mind and soul of the poet. After enjoying the beautiful harmony and music of the poem one feels totally dissatisfied if one reads the poet's collected in various anthologies of our times especially those which are prescribed in our universities. *Everest* is surely the finest example of epical poem where the poet creates an enchanting world of eloquence, harmony and genius. This poem will be read for ages as the poet sings of our culture, civilization, time and eternity. Krishna Srinivas is a mighty-mouthed poet who prefers epical style to ordinary style.

He is a skilled poet who prefers to sing of eternity or Time rather than celebrating ordinariness or trivia. The musical expressions and the philosophical ideas of the poem move our hearts as nothing has moved them earlier. The adaptation of the sound to sense, and the movement of lines is matchless. The references to Ganga, Kaveri, Yamuna, Upanishads, Buddha, Bhagwad Geeta, Gandhi and Nehru simply demonstrate the vast learning of the poet. Lord Krishna's famous commandment is given in original as well as translation. The poet shows his study of history and various civilizations and the allusive technique of the poem puts together the fusion of all that is known, thought, imagined or planned on earth. The poet watches the cycles of civilization. He puts several religions and several civilizations together as part of a great pattern of World Civilization and World Culture. In poem after poem we find an urgency to unite and find out harmony in our world. The disunited world will do great harm to our unity. Equality, liberty, fraternity, universal brotherhood and love are possible only after Krishna Srinivas type of fusion. The poet wants to save humanity from the great global loss. The two world wars and the holocaust of future wars tell us to prepare ourselves for peace. One country, one religion, one race cannot build great human culture. Hence, the need for multi-culturalism. *Everest* is the noblest specimen of multi-culturalism. The various thinkers, religions, signs, symbols, ideas point only to the prophetic genius of the poet. In *Everest* we find Spiritus Mundi. We find the religious and the cultural mind of the world. The poem shows the possibility of the arrival of the futureman of the earth. The futureman definitely will be multi-cultural and multi-lingual and multi-national. The crux of the various religions has been presented here as various signs and symbols which the citizens of the world must understand for quick national and international understanding. The poem shows underground connections and seeds of comparative religion, philosophy, culture and anthropology. The last lines of the poem draw our attention:

> And that day will dawn
> When gods churn again
> An everest morn. (*Everest*: p. 26)

*Everest* is a wonderful epic. It is a serious poem embodying sublime thoughts to establish world peace and world order. The poet does not attempt to satirise or indulge in pleasantries or fun anywhere in the poem. Krishna Srinivas is an epical poet of great purposes. The distinguishing characteristic of Krishna lies in the sublimity of thoughts. It is a pity that sublimity of thoughts has been banished from our public and private lives. The poets of the *Ten Twentieth Century Indian Poets* edited by R. Parthasarathy do not possess sublimity and magnanimity of thought like the poems of Krishna Srinivas. Like mass media, politics and our contemporary civilization our university courses are also celebrating trivia we cannot have a bold peace proposal. Som Benegal, a great critic on Krishna Srinivas, rightly concludes in his scholarly essay "A Bold Peace Approach" (*The Hindustan Times*, Friday, August 2, 1966, p. II) "I will not go into tiresome cliches but assert that despite notable lapses, the tradition and heritage of India, through the ages, inspired by its philosophy and its leaders—Buddha, Mahavira, Ashoka, Akbar, Nanak, Kabir, Vivekanand, Gandhi, to name but a few—have celebrated the arts of peace and tranquility.

I hold that deep down the Indian psyche harbours an abhorrence for violence and destruction and certainly mass destruction. India must turn its face away from any participation in any activity which entails horror or even encourages it without presuming any high moral ground. Krishna's *Everest* must be read in the light of Som Benegal's above remarks about India's role in present times. Like other epics of Krishna this epic presents a bold and passionate peace approach to life and other issues. This epic is totally immersed in the tradition and heritage of India and Krishna sings of them most eloquently. His poetry is inspired by the wisdom of Mohammad, Christ, Dante, Shakespeare, Vyasa, Bardrayana, Vedic chants and Upanishadic Mantras. *Everest* is like a cup which is full of the Som Rasa of wisdom derived from tradition and heritage of India and the world. The use of the word manna is full of Keats's impact on Krishna. The lines of this epic contain greatness of sentiments wherein Krishna triumphs over almost all the poets collected in *Ten Twentieth Century Poets* edited by R. Parthasarathy. None of them has that greatness of sentiments and emotions, that sublimity and high seriousness of thoughts, that epical and grand style which Krishna Srinivas's poetry always shows in abundance. Krishna is next only to Homer, Virgil, Dante, Kalidas, Tulsidas, Shakespeare, Surdas, Kabirdas, and Spenser. Whereas other contemporary poets have devaluated their art because of their love for trivia, Krishna Srinivas leaves them far behind because of his natural love for sublimity, divinity, moral ideas, high seriousness and greatness of sentiments.

His poetry is always inspired by the tradition and heritage of India. His imagery and symbolism are derived from the writings and speeches of the great saints of India. Buddha, Mahavir, Ashoka, Akbar, Nanak, Kabir, Vivekanand, Vedas, Upanishads etc. give him the essential language, idiom and content to celebrate the art of peace and tranquility. His poetry sings of peace and tranquility in abundance. Whereas Bombay poets are producing poetry of body and celebrating trivia in the cliches and jargons of advertisement and vulgarity, Krishna fills our hearts and minds with the best wisdom of the tradition and heritage of India and the World. Thus he is the only living poet who sings of the Indian psyche which detests isolation, loneliness, violence, destruction and mass destruction. In so far as the poetry of *Ten Twentieth Century Indian Poets* edited by R. Parthasarathy fails in depicting the Indian psyche truly and as faithfully as Krishna does, they are certainly inferior to his poetry. The poetry of V.K. Gokak is full of the celebrations of arts and tranquility. It is a pity that both Krishna Srinivas and V.K. Gokak are out of the *Ten Twentieth Century Indian Poets* ed. by R. Parthasarathy. The poets included in this volume are poets of tenth order only so far as the celebration of the art of peace and tranquility is concerned.

This volume cannot prepare our students to understand the Indian psyche in a better and meaningful way as we always do after reading Krishna Srinivas nor does it develop an abhorrence for violence and destruction. The world is standing today at the brink of nuclear catastrophe. And our best poets are writing for pleasantry and fun. They are not conscious of the horrors of a nuclear holocaust. When Rome is burning, our Neroes are happily fiddling. But Krishna like Vivekanand, Ramkrishna

Paramhnsa, V.K. Gokak, Sri Aurobindo is an exception. His personality is as great and large as that of Milton. His poetry wages a war on terrorism, violence, trivia, nuclear catastrophe and holocaust and therefore it must be read and heard with great care. To ignore Krishna Srinivas is to ignore a bold peace approach in our times. To ignore Krishna Srinivas is the high moral ground and platform upon which the grand Taj Mahal of World Peace and World Order is going to be built in future years. Krishna Srinivas is the best poetic voice of peace and tranquility and the more we love him, respect him and read him the more we prepare ourselves for World Peace. The poet's aim is song. But his is full of manna dews of peace.

## Five Elements

Krishna Srinivas is an eternal traveller. He is travelling in time and space. Each and every travel of the poet is unique. He has given the best outstanding poetry of our times. His cosmic consciousness and beautiful poetry have won readers and lovers which are drawn from all the six continents. Tin-Wen-Chung praises *Five Elements* in these words, "The sweep of his memorable epic *Five Elements*—Water, Wind, Fire, Earth and Void—is from time to eternity. It reaches the universal level." In his learned Introduction Tin-Wen-Chung further writes about this epic, "With the consumate art of a Poet-musician, Krishna travels from the atomic dust, past the blood soaked history of man to the awesome perilous present. He energizes his spiritual resources for the future generations. He is a man with all the foibles and frailties, yet he has tested his strength and tested his virtues. He has walked the face of earth and visited all nations. He has shared their achievements and experienced their agonies. In his passion for reality, he fuses an audacity of verbal coinage with an elemental energy of utterance." Reading Krishna Srinivas's work does not induce fear, horror and terror in our bones. Whenever I read *Five Elements* I am swayed by the force of the poetic lines. Krishna's mysticism reminds me of Tulsidas. He writes:

> Kshiti, jal, pavak, gagan, samira
> Panch rachit, adham sarira.

Tulsidas the greatest Hindi poet says that our mundane body is verily made of earth, water, fire, firmament (void) and wind. Tulsidas is certainly the greatest poet of the world. His *Ramcharitmanas* and other poetical works are superior to the works of even Homer, Virgil, Shakespeare, Dante, Spenser, and all other ancient and modern and contemporary poets. Since his works are in Hindi language, therefore, the West or even the South India does not know much about him. But his poetry fulfills Sri Aurobindo's demands from a poet to make his words and lines mantric. In mantric power Tulsidas is certainly superior to Sri Aurobindo, Krishna Srinivas, V.K. Gokak and almost all the ancient and modern and contemporary poets. But Krishna Srinivas is second only to Tulsidas. Therefore his poetry is certainly far superior to other moderners and contemporary poets. Others go to poetry for pleasantry, fun and celebration of trivia. Not only the poets but our governments, mass media, films, T.V. serials, dailies, weeklies, monthlies, quarterlies, yearlies and souvenirs are full of trivia. But Krishna Srinivas always goes to poetry for its mantric power. His epics are the proofs of the articulation of his mantric power. The fascination of Krishna's *Five Elements* goes on increasing. Like Keats's image of Beauty Krishna's epics are a joy forever. Their eternal, charm, beauty and mantric power will never decrease. Their loveliness will always increase as the pressures of terrorism, violence, horror and nuclear wars are mounting upon the humanity. They will never pass in nothingness for their mantric power is as fresh as the power of the *Five Elements*. Krishna writes:

In passion I am born
In passion I live
In passion I perish:
So too, you My Kaveri.
Eerie whispers waters chant
Water, water, everywhere,
ringing solace everywhere.
At Kaveri ghats.
sages and saints chant their beads
and lisp a million Om:
grow million fires.
char million desires. (Water: p. 49)

At another place Krishna writes:

> This is full
> That is full
> From full, Full fulfill full. (Water: p. 48)

When Full, from fulfill leaves, full, full, fully, Full remains. In the final sense Krishna Srinivas's poetry achieves the power of the mantra to register and master experience. This is the best poetry in the best order. Krishna repeats words and sometimes sentences to depict and master experiences. He parodies Sanskrit Mantras in order to gain mantric power. He takes recourse to a lot of translation from Sanskrit, Tamil Arabic and other languages. But he is not a mere translator. In this quality he is Shakespearian. Whatever is borrowed is totally absorbed and made as his own. The translations and borrowings and derivations are necessary in Krishna's style to achieve poetic articulation and master experience. Krishna creates and perfects English Language for the expression of spiritual and moral thought. As a stylist he is rich in eloquence and loud speeches. He does not whisper mantras in our ears. Like a Modern Rishi he shouts them from the top of the Everest. He shouts them and utters them in his full-throated voice.

He is capable of doing it because as Tin-Wen-Chung rightly observes that he knows his strength and weaknesses. No one knows this thing as Krishna knows it. He is endowed with the noble gift of proclamation and prophesy. He has acquired and mastered epical style. His connections with Tulsidas, Homer, Virgil, Dante, Shakespeare, Keats, Coleridge and many other ancient and modern poets is deliberate and conscious. But his voice is inimitable. It is unlike the voice of his contemporaries like Nissim, Ezekiel, R. Parthasarathy, P.K. Joy, Syed Ammeruddin, I.K. Sharma, O.P. Bhatnagar, Richard Eberhart, Suresh Chandra Dwivedi, Osman Turkey, Montri Umavijani, Virginia Rodas, Joy B. Cripps, Rosemary C. Wilkinson, Tin-Wen-Chung and many others. Krishna Srinivas is very popular among the world poets. I wrote my epical poem *The Mouth of Truth* under his magical influence. His influence is there on many poets of Madras and other places. What I want to say is that despite his friendship with world poets despite his allusive and scholarly approach to poetry his voice is singular. This is why there is only one Krishna Srinivas in the whole world and his singular voice will be heard in the temples of literature for a very long period of time.

Tin-Wen-Chung describes the poetical qualities of Krishna in long detail in his Introduction to *Five Elements*. They are many-cosmic consciousness, memorability, epical style, mysticism like Tagore, the imagery of Eliot, profoundity, essence of Hinduism, perfection of art of poetry, musical quality, the capacity to energize his spiritual resources for coming generations, the ability to know his strength and weaknesses. Tin-Wen-Chung goes on telling us qualities after qualities of Krishna Srinivas as a poet. According to him Krishna's felt experiences are immense. I agree with Tin-Wen-Chung because most of the female poetry and contemporary poetry demonstrates poverty of felt experiences of life. Poets included in *Ten Twentieth Century Indian Poets* suffer from larger experiences of life. Their obsessions with marginal life and trivia make their output meaninglessness galore. Out of meaninglessness comes only meaninglessness. Thus the blind men lead the blind men. The result is meaninglessness galore, disunity galore, useless galore and chaos galore. Like T.S. Eliot, Krishna Srinivas is valuable to us and his epic is as revolutionary as Eliot's poem *The Waste Land* or Tulsidas's *Ramcharitmanas*. Krishna Srinivas at least looks at ideals and moral ideas of life like Tulsidas and Eliot and like them understands the mantric power of poetry. Such poetry is not only powerful, valuable but also rare because it constantly guides like a lighthouse to the humanity which is wandering aimlessly like ships which have lost their ways in a dark night.

Krishna Srinivas is like a tireless traveller. He does not know when to stop. He sings like the inferential narrator in Forst's famous poem, "Stopping By Woods on a Snowy Evening:"

> The Woods are lovely dark and deep
> But I have promises to keep.
> And miles to go before I sleep.
> And miles to go before I sleep.

Krishna is the follower of Vedic proclamation Chariveti, Charaivet. He will always go forward in his poetic mission. Tin-Wen-Chung rightly says:

"Krishna Srinivas is a poet with a mission. His mission is peace through poetry, and he is the torch bearer." As a pioneer he says that: "In the delirium in which the world is caught up the poet has a vital part to play. New frontiers, newer horizons, and newest vistas of space grow so cataclysmic, that the poet has to raise his mind into the white radiance of super realities, visioning and revisioning the patterns futurity. He must cut across centuries and best the scientist in the race of discovering the roots of delight that weave and unweave life."

I am simply amazed at the critical faculty of Krishna Srinivas. No one has pointed out the role of the poet so clearly as Krishna Srinivas. On the basis of this passage alone Krishna Srinivas has emerged as the critic of literature. It is the most scholarly and intelligent approach to poetry and to poets. I do not know of any other poets who can integrate so much, unite so much and think so much. Only Tulsidas is capable of doing it. This is why millions and millions of people read his epic *Ramcharitmanas* everyday. It is the most quoted poem in the world. *Ramcharitmanas* is the epic of our democracy. Our democracy cannot function with Tulsidas and his book *Ramcharitmanas*. The humanity cannot survive from the terrors of wars without the books of Krishna Srinivas. As I have told earlier Krishna Srinivas is second only to Tulsidas. But as I have told earlier the poets of the *Ten Twentieth Century Indian Poets* and other contemporary poetry anthologies come nowhere Tulsidas. They are tenth grade poets if we have Tulsidas, Kalidas, Shakespeare, Homer, Virgil, Kabirdas, Surdas in our minds.

Krishna Srinivas at least comes nearer to the epical tradition of India. I do not mean to say that his poetry has achieved the same mantric power as Tulsidas's poetry has achieved but of this much I am quite sure that Krishna Srinivas's poetry invites comparison with Tulsidas. There are some lines which are comparable. The *Ten Twentieth Century Indian Poets* are far removed from the poetry of Tulsidas. We cannot think of comparing them with Tulsidas as we cannot compare nectar and poison. The religious tendencies dominate in Eliot, Tulsidas and Krishna Srinivas. Good and bad are parts of life and Krishna Srinivas succeeds fairly in showing them whereas the interpretations in the above-mentioned so called *Ten Twentieth Century Indian Poets* the concern for good is consciousness its absence. In Krishna Srinivas the historian, the literary critic and the metaphysician are working together for the same purposes, but in these so-called poets (they are rather versifiers) the entertainer, the verbal juggler, the lover of fun and pleasantries are at work. Both Eliot and Krishna Srinivas are storehouses of literary and religious influences and are comparable to Tulsidas whose power of personality and power of impersonality, whose sense of tradition and whose sense of individuality is far superior even to the ancients.

Tulsidas sings of the glorious deeds of Lord Rama whose grace is unlimited. Eliot's *The Waste Land* is read and reread because it is an epic of our times. Krishna Srinivas writes in epical style only because he is a literary and cultural giant who cannot write in any other style rather than epical style. He knows that all political, social orders will certainly collapse. He knows that power has the tendency to corrupt. He knows that absolute power ultimately ends in absolute corruption. He is the best poet of our era of corruption. Man has forgotten god and has become worshipper of Mammon only. The contemporary poets are interpreting only the utterances of Mammon but they have forgotten the pious act of interpretations of the utterances of both God and Mammon. In Krishna's epics we get the beautiful reinterpretation of the sayings of both God and Mammon. He is conscious of the terrifying history of mankind. He knows that not only our democracy but the whole mankind is in peril. He is writing to save mankind with all his force. We are witnessing the downfall of secular machineries in our times. The result is that Krishna Srinivas has emerged as the outstanding poet, critic, editor, social worker, prophet and friend, philosopher and guide of the world poets. No other ancient and modern poet has influenced the contemporary family of poets in such a big way as Krishna Srinivas.

He is the Secretary General of the United Nations of Poets. I am proud of his epical books because they tell me about the significance of the divine grace. After having read Tulsidas, I prefer to read Krishna Srinivas because in him at last I found the last hope for mankind. Whenever mankind will be in a mood to and will be prepared to develop world peace, world order, world culture and follow the virtues of humility, charity, purity, morality, sublimity and divinity it will turn the pages of Tulsidas, Surdas, Eliot, Sankar, Ramanuja, Vallar, Saint Poets and Krishna Srinivas. There is no other way to develop the principles of humility, charity and purity. The only way to learn the art of non-difference, tolerance, non-violence is to appreciate the poetry of Krishna Srinivas in our times. Krishna's epics are the signposts of his creative activity where he teaches us to develop self-control, Sarva Dharma Samabha (Equal respect to all religions because they are nothing but the descriptions of the Divine Grace, control of language, balance and all the virtues which Arjuna learns from Krishna in *Bhagwad Geeta*. The art of civilization is the art of balance, control and non-difference. Krishna teaches non-difference in our times in modern English language. His poetry has been liked throughout the world. Krishna Srinivas has consciously trained his mind with the study of European literary-religious tradition besides his own and also analyses, interprets and reinterprets the political, literary religious tradition in it. Like Tulsidas and Eliot he must be read with respect and must become a permanent part and parcel of our Indian and World Culture. Like Tulsidas he begins as a poet but ends as a cultural hero.

These two trends, literary and religious, coexist in Krishna. He fuses them together artistically. The qualities of his poetry like wit, idiomatic sentences, quotations, allusive technique, his love for translations, borrowings, derivations in order to modernise himself and make himself epical dignified irony, objective correlative, metaphorical use of language are simply praiseworthy. Even one thousand Doctorates and Doctoral theses are not sufficient to discover the total meaning of his books. They contain ocean of meaning. He goes to Vigril, Dante, Vyas, Badareyana, Shankar, Ramanuja, Vallar, Christ, Buddha, Mahavir and other prophets because he himself is a great poet and prophet like them. Like Eliot Krishna's religious poems are full of his questioning, probing and suffering. His poetry is full of pious serenity. But as Eliot is conscious of the Waste Land,

Tulsidas is conscious of the Kaliyug, Krishna is conscious of his awesome perilous present. Read Tin-Wen-Chung's Introduction to *Five Elements*.

In *Five Elements* Krishna shows a rare verbal genius, a gifted intelligence, a sound sense of culture, history, philosophy and aesthetics made readable and bearable by his wit. It is certainly his masterpiece and touches classical heights. Krishna Srinivas successfully manages in one fine stroke to establish himself as India's finest poet. Nissim Ezekiel, Shiva K. Kumar, Arun Kolatkar, Mamta Kalia, Kamala Das, N.V. Subbaraman, Sheila Gujral, I.H. Rizvi, I.K. Sharma, R.K. Singh, Suresh Chandra Dwivedi, A.N. Dwivedi, K. Jagannathan, D.H. Kabadi, Mahesweta Chaturvedi, P.K. Joy, Syed Ameeruddin, Bhaskar Roy Barman, Kumar Hassan, Hazara Singh, Simanchal Patnaik, O.P. Bhatnagar, K.N. Daruwalla, A.K. Ramanujan, and a host of other poets have written good poetry and enriched the treasure-house of Indian English Poetry. Krishna Srinivas has published many Indian poets in his *Poet* and *World Poetry Anthologies*. He has always liked to promote poets who are struggling for poetic expression. Krishna Srinivas finally emerges as a mountain whereas others are only mole-hills. My purpose is not to compare and contrast Krishna Srinivas with other Indian or foreign poets. But as a critic it is my humble business to distinguish grade A from grade B. None of them has taken the profession of poetry so seriously as Krishna Srinivas. None of them has produced as many epical poems as Krishna Srinivas. None of them has edited so many *World Poetry Anthologies* as Krishna Srinivas.

Krishna has become an agent of Indian and World Culture just like them. The type of culture that the people included in *Ten Twentieth Indian Century Poets* demonstrate and the type of India that they depict is simply understandable. They show scant respect for Indian and World Culture. Thus their poetry is far removed from the great tradition of Poetry that is the tradition of Valmiki, Vyas, Kalidas and Tulsidas. The genius of Daruwala, Pritish Nandy, Saleem Peeradina, Gieve Patel, Gauri Despande, Kamala Das, I.K. Sharma, O.P. Bhatnagar, Nissim Ezekiel, R. Parthasarathy is not epical. India's poetic genius is epical. It is a happy coincidence that Krishna Srinivas's poetic style and genius are epical. Krishna conceives and makes his epics in accordance with the design of the epics of both East and the West. He is an experimentalist so far as language and his epical style are concerned. But his genius is dictatorial. The theme of his epics govern the style and language and tone of his epics. His epics satisfy the rules of an epic in an admirable degree but the powerful poet moulds the design as per the strong wave of his poetic emotions. His epics are like Eliot's *The Waste Land* without its difficulty and obscurity. Whereas Eliot fails to communicate adequately, Krishna Srinivas communicates aptly. He employs his poetic tools like an adept and skillful poet. The language he writes is entirely his own. It is Tamil in spirit, English in body and Sanskritized in temperament.

He has Sanskritized his English like Vivekanand, Raja Rao, and Sri Aurobindo. He is great in line, art, freedom, wisdom, kindness, exceedingly rich in intelligence, full of poetic sensitivity, rich in imagination and wit, last but not the least he is a great and beautiful poetic god. He is so indispensable to India and the world. He is like life-breath to our trouble-ridden world. His epics are a superb performance all grace and dazzle. How he writes, how he influences, how he travels, how he recites his poems will be asked even after hundreds of years hence. His epics break the surface, like the great white whale. They are gigantic like the whale. His poetry gives us solace, relief, as we must get them for our survival. His poetry contains solace for humanity in abundance. Others are verbal jugglers at their best. But poetry is more than verbal jugglery. And if it is true that poetry is more than verbal jugglery it certainly warns us from the poets of *Ten Twentieth Century Indian Poets* whose strength is only cliquish character, caucus, and cheapness and vulgarity. The more you read the poets included in this volume the more you cry for oxygen. This book has less of oxygen and more of carbon-dioxide. This is why the more you read it the more depressed you become.

You can understand neither India or Indian Culture, or World Culture. In Krishna's epics we get a truly fine, dazzling and excellent poetry in all its breadth, depth and profundity. But in the poets of *Ten Twentieth Century Indian Poets* what you get is cheapness, ordinariness, vulgarity and verbal jugglery. The result of this type of poetry is a natural hatred for all type of poetry. Others are creeping and crawling lying down in the depths of a valley Krishna is standing like a Commander on the top of the mountain. Krishna suggests so much that your imagination becomes active when you start reading him. Others demonstrate mediocrity at their best. Krishna Srinivas is a master poet who explains in tantalising detail the mundane and the divine shades and colours of human life. As a poet he is a supreme force, all grace and dazzled. It opposes mediocrity, banality and triteness of all sorts. Krishna is an awesomely accomplished poet like Tulsidas, Valmiki and Kalidas. The mediocre poets do not show universal appeal like Krishna Srinivas. His epics embrace the whole space and should be read as having noble words denoting noble emotions. The poets included in *Ten Twentieth Century Indian Poets* are full of baser emotions. Such mediocre poets write for entertainment, pleasantry and fun and underestimate the great role of the poet and poetry. They are like a cup full of superfluous ideas, emotions and thoughts.

Krishna Srinivas is like a cup full of noble thoughts, noble ideas and noble emotions. Besides this he constantly shows a sublime style like the epical poets of the past. His language is metaphorical, he utilizes lines and ideas of other languages, and always speaks from a very high pitch. He uses all the methods for raising the tone and worth of his language. His metaphors and idioms and phrases are aptly said and used and he employs a great many foreign words also to achieve an epical style. Besides his epics contain peculiar allegory of the moral. In so far as the moralising of his epics is concerned it is equal to the epics of Milton, Tulsidas, Homer, Virgil and Dante. Moral purpose is the essential part of his genius as superfluousness, cheapness, vulgarity, triteness, pleasantry and fun is the purpose of *Ten Twentieth Century Indian Poets*. Krishna's epics and poems constantly show the ways of Brahman (God) to man. Therefore they are as valuable as Milton's *Paradise Lost* and *Paradise Regained*. The choice is between epical genius of Krishna Srinivas and non-epical genius of mediocre poets.

Krishna's poetry has a universal appeal. They do not belong to any one nation or time. Krishna's works have relevance not only for the Hindu World, but they have been liked in the Christian and the Mohammedan World too. As it shows the combat of good and evil it is universal and it belongs to all people. It will be found interesting to all mankind because it forms the sure basis of religions and all philosophies.

## Maya

*Maya* is a socio-philosophic poem which must be read and reread by the poetry lovers all over the world. *Maya*, in fact, reveals the mystery of all existence. Those who denounce Maya must be ignorant because Maya is not and should not be seen as distinct from Brahman. Though Maya is a Vidya but we should keep this fact in mind that both Maya and Vidya are properties of Brahman. Whenever there is failure to see the world as creation of Brahman, there arises Moha, Shoka and Dukh. The self and the entire World are nothing but Absolute Brahman.

In Krishna's epic we are told the story in beautiful verses. It is an interesting narrative poem and it deals with the archetypal relationship between man and woman, daughter and mother. Like all other epical poems of Krishna this poem is also epical in style and tone. This is how it beings:

> From the Unreal lead me to Real:
> From languor lead me to Light.
> From death lead me to Eternity. (*Maya*: p. 148)

The poet tells here the story of a woman named Maya who is 19 years old. She is the daughter of Geetha who works in an office. One is reminded here of the typist lady in Eliot's poem *The Waste Land*. Though Geetha showers all her love, affection and kindness on Maya, the teenaged girl is unable to understand her mother's crystal clear and good, too good love for her. The poet described their house as temple. One day the girl is informed by her maid-servant that her mother's character has not been...and upto the mark. She tells Maya about her mother's illicit relationship with her office boss. I am reminded here of Tulsidas's Manthara who brings about untold sufferings to Dasharath and his entire family. Rama's exile is caused by Manthara's crookedness. Here it is done by the maid-servant. Herein lies the true success of Krishna. When you read his modern epic you are reminded here of the other epics of the past and the present. One is also reminded here of Satan's corrupting influence of Eve in Eden in the Biblical story. Krishna is undoubtedly a first rate mythological poet. Here he discovers the modern myth of corruption. *Bhagwad Geeta* rightly proclaims "Strishudushtasuvarshneya jayate varnasankarah." The purity of human race has been emphasized upon in *The Bhagwad Geeta*. When the women become corrupt they produce corrupt children and then the whole civilization becomes corrupt. The corrupt ministers, bureaucrats and businessmen have all come from the wombs of their mothers.

The purity of human race surely depends upon the purity of mothers. *Maya* is a beautiful narrative poem where poet Krishna has emerged as an experimentalist. This poem is an answer to all the critics who have ignored their experimental poetry. The poem deals with the man-woman, mother-daughter paradoxical relationship. *Maya* must be read by all those who look at man and woman relationship as creative endeavour and cooperative action. It is in their creativity, cooperative attitude as confidence and purity that future of world community depends. The whole poem has been written in a philosophical mood, vein, tone and language. The title of the poem is significant. It has been derived from the Upanishadic. But Krishna Srinivas has filled more meaning into the Upanishads doctrine of illusion. The poem is innovative. It is not repetitive. This repetition results in a dead language. But the poet's purpose is not to give repetitions of the old texts. The language of the epic is metaphorical. The language of *Maya* is vitally metaphorical. It has connections with the old and modern epics. The poet concentrates on the characters of Maya and Geetha. The problem of our century is generation gap. The relationship of the mother and the daughter manifests itself clearly. And the prevailing eroticism is in the offices puts a question mark on the characters of males and females in our times. The poet utilizes mythology, fables, morality and philosophy according to his requirements as an epical poet and twists and turns them to his higher literary purposes. Whenever the poet goes to the old texts and mythologies, he comes back with new jewels in his hands.

## Tamil Vedas

Krishna Srinivas is a poet of Tamil sensibility. It is quite in the fitness of things that he should have written on Tamil Vedas. Four thousand lyrics in Tamil Vedas are externally popular. The Tamils all over the world sing them as a part of prayer. They are the soul of Vaishnavism which has gone a long way in bringing about reformation and renaissance on earth. Krishna's ambition has always been to write on such themes which were not attempted on earth either in prose or poetry. What was achieved by Twelve dedicated saints of Vaishnavism, has been superbly achieved by Krishna Srinivas here. In the words of Dr. Syed Ameeruddin, "Since all the four Vedas are sung in Sanskrit, these Apostles, called Alwars, have transported into Tamil all the messages of Vedas. Even today, in all the countries where Tamils live, these immortal lyrics of Alwars are sung with great devotion every morning. Especially in East, descendants of Tamils who migrated into these countries millenniums ago sing with gusto those soul-stirring verses."

Krishna's all epics on philosophy combine delight and wisdom. He chooses to write on saints, philosophers and their philosophies. His books of poems combine prophesy, mysticism, philosophy, vision, dream and preaching. There is not a single line in Krishna that can be called trite, superfluous, mundane, ordinary or unprofitable from the point of view of World Peace and World Culture. Thus his style is sublime and epical. Krishna is always simple, unaffected, and honest in his poetical aims and practices. He is a Sadhaka and his entire corpus is a long sadhana. He will not use a long word where a short word will do. Simplicity is the main characteristic of his poetry and therefore I am quite sure that his poetry will be read by future generations. His poetry is thus free from the blemishes of Sri Aurobindo or Milton. Krishna Srinivas is a pundit but he never becomes pedantic. That is his great merit. He is always high serious but never unreadable.

He is always sublime but his sublimity is aimed to bring about the Kingdom of heaven on earth. His epics open up new possibilities of speech. He develops a cosmopolitan language and a cosmopolitan religion for the benefit of humanity. There is no other way than this to understand the relevance of his poetry. His epics are experiments in language and for this sake alone he does a lot of translations from the masterpieces of the past. But so does Eliot, Pound, Agyya, Yeats have done in our times. Hence we should welcome Krishna Srinivas as we welcome them. He develops a new idiom for our times. His lines are successful and effective as the lines in an epic should be. Krishna Srinivas is surprisingly successful. His poetic Hall is the Hall of a monarch. The monarch is without a sword. Though he is fighting for peace. His lines are majestic because they have come out from the mouth of a Monarch of Peace.

Krishna Srinivas is the greatest epical poet of our times. Those who have not produced epical poems are certainly far behind him. The influence of his epics is very large upon the minds of lovers of poetry all over the world. His style is sublime and epical and contains wisdom of philosophers, prophets, philosophers and saints. He joins the company of the best poets of the world—Valmiki, Vyas, Kalidas, Tulsidas, Shakespeare, Virgil, Dante. His poetry is certainly superior to the poets collected in *Ten Twentieth Century Indian Poets* edited by R. Parthasarathy. They do not show sublimity, high seriousness, religious tolerance, kindness, humanity of Krishna Srinivas. Krishna Srinivas's poetry demonstrates these qualities in abundance. His corpus is free from the compulsions of profit and loss. Hosts of the contemporary poets are the poets of trivia whereas Krishna Srinivas has given us the moral force and vigour through his poetry. He has followed the Vedic dictum *Charaivet, Charaiveti*. Hence all originality has come to him in the process of writing. The originality and the vision of his poetry are embedded in the processes of his writing. He has not got them as windfall.

He is a poet of World Civilization and World Culture and is addressing his poetry to the futuremen. I am quite sure that he will be more popular hundred years hence. It is a pity that in both South India and North India people like Krishna has supplied poetry which has a mantric effect. It has the capacity to purify the hearts and minds of humanity. Thousands of poets are writing poetry today under the healthy influence of Krishna Srinivas. He has emerged as the friend, philosopher and guide of numberless poets of hundreds of nations. Dr. Syed Ameerudin rightly says that Krishna's Divine Blaze illumines the most universal theme—KNOW THYSELF. It is to discover one's archetypal being through a complexity of imagery and thought, uniting life and pursuit. His imagination transcends the permutation of paradoxes used to uncover the mysteries of existence.

As a man and a poet and a citizen Krishna loves India. But this love for his country compels him to love all the religions and cultures of the world. One who loves his mother must also love all the mothers. One who loves his own religion must also love and respect all other religions of the world. Krishna has developed this love for the entire universe consciously and laboriously. His labours have not gone in vain. Read his corpus and you will experience what I have experienced myself. His poetic pieces and activity are aimed at the good, the noble, the beautiful and they cannot be confined to one individual or race. Hence his attempts to write epics on Tamil Vedas, Mahavir, Buddha, Christ, Mohammad. His poetry is not for one particular race or nation; it is for the entire world. His religion transcends all limits. His corpus rather shows their interrelatedness. It is in mutual interdependence and interrelatedness that his poetry has tremendous value for ourselves. He derives his values from religious masterpieces. The secular Govts. are unable to derive good from the religious masterpieces. What Govt. cannot do, the poet like Krishna has done successfully. His corpus is not a prison-house of one ideology, nation of culture. It is as vast as the blue sky. I am reminded here of Goldsmith's famous lines while reading *Maya*:

> When lovely woman stoops to folly
> And finds too late that men betray
> What charm can soothe her melancholy
> What art can wash her guilt away,

The only art her guilt to cover
To hide her shame from every eye.

To give repentance to her lover
And wring her bosoom is to die.

In the words of Dr. R.K. Singh, "Here Krishna demonstrates the belief in the reality of God as well as the reality of the world. He presents the ethics of the Upanishads that do not ask to renounce life, do not taboo desires as such. A healthy joy in the life of the world pervades the old atmosphere. There is no call to renounce the world, rather the Upanishads ask us to pierce behind the veil, to realise the presence of God in the world of nature and society to look upon the whole world as born of God as the self of man is. Through Maya, Krishna gives the message of liberality, restraint and trustfulness."

The poem is important because it points at the importance of regulation and sexual behaviour. In the words of Dr. Syed Ameeruddin, "The institution of marriage has been created not only to streamline the way of flesh and 'the hunger of ravishment' but also to blow off 'the last particles of broken dust' paving way to serene calm and thrusting man and woman into 'a dual heaven, everlasting Eden, perennial paradise'."

Man and woman should lead the life of purity as husbands and wives and should learn that their identity with the Divine is potential. They should rise above the clash of limbs and the kisses of lips. Eating, drinking, sleeping and copulation is common to both animals and human beings. Only the strict adherence to the path of religion differentiates mankind from the world of animals. *Maya* emphasizes the importance of the divine character of husband and wife—tat tvam asi—that art thou. Man-woman relationship is important for this realization to see divinity in their inward parts and hearts to find the spirit of Truth and to realise the Kingdom of heaven upon this earth. The true light that lighten their limbs, lips and hips comes straight from God. They must wage a war "to quench the Fires that picnic in their bones." It is archetypal poem and its parallels can be found in other poems.

Krishna has extended the boundaries of older myths by inventing a myth of our times. Man-woman relationship in ministries, bureaucracies, temples, churches and other holy and secular purposes must establish and find the concept of the divine. Then and then only they can find peace, harmony, social justice on earth. Man has still to find the kingdom of heaven in his heart. He has yet to discover the spirit of Brahman in each and everything. The outer experiences, the kissing of lips, the clash and enjoyment of limbs alone are not sufficient. Man's true nature is divine. All apparent animality is for something. Today or tomorrow both man and woman will have to concentrate on the inward reality. Their relationship gives a golden opportunity for inward penetration, inward understanding. Only the knowledge of the Self can make them illumined. The bond of the body must be destroyed before it is destroyed by Death itself. After the death the bones burn like wood and the hair like grass. Hence man and woman as husband and wife must transcend the barrier of the body. All finiteness has to be transcended to experience the light of Brahman. The poet's discovery Maya in our Modern World is praiseworthy. But this Maya is different from the *Maya* of the Upanishads. It is full of the poet's ability to invent new situations, new characters, to find an appropriate idiom.

## REFERENCE

All the quotations of Krishna Srinivas are from his *Complete Political Works* (Volumes I to IV) published from Poets Press India, 118, Madras.

# Chapter 5

# To the Divine Beloved Visionary

*Shubha Tiwari*

Love of God is common to many religions, but it is most prominently seen in three schools of thought—Medieval Christianity, Madhura Bhakti cult and Sufi-mysticism. From time immemorial religion and poetry are inter-related. In the present context, religion is taken as something which evolves in the minds of the believers, that particular thing which provides man with an understanding and helps him name the unknown. In the struggle of the individual to reach the far beyond, the ineffable takes the form of several religions depending upon the geophysical conditions. But one thing marks every religion—that is the insatiable thirst to reach the beyond. In fact, religion moves from the ordinary to the extraordinary. This is evident in all the three above-mentioned cults. Doctrinally, religion may be just a set of rules, narrow and persecuting. But in practice, it is adjusted to the natural needs of the spiritual seekers and sanctifies human emotions. Love is a universal feeling without which human life cannot be imagined. Love, which is understood as a base passion, if it is diverted from its mundane level of being selfish, ego-oriented emotion, it becomes a devoted, all absorbing love of God. This concept extends the horizons of religion and enriches literature. For instance, Christianity thinks that God is the Supreme Creator, the Father. Strictly speaking, it cannot be conceived that Christian devotees have any other figure before them, but that of God the Father. But numerous saint-poets from St. John of the Cross belonging to different climes and times have written superb poetry imagining God as the Lover. On the other hand, the American Puritans have adored the jealous and angry God of the Old Testament. But the poets from the time of Edward Taylor have sought an exception writing in the metaphysical trend. Later, Emily Dickinson, though brought up in a staunch Puritan family, has written numerous love poems addressed to man and God, occasionally becoming the bride of God as a Catholic nun or indulging in a gay abandon of erotic imagery and sensuous language, competing with the Indian poets of Madhura Shakti. Mixing the sacred and the profane and approaching the Super-sensuous through the senses is sanctified by great mystic poets. According to Blake everything that lives is holy and if the doors of perception are clean everything would appear to man as infinite. In Hinduism also human emotions are sanctified inspite of the Hindus, insistence on the Attributeless Absolute and their description of Brahman as not this, not that (*neti-neti*). Religious sects like that of Ramanuja and Chaintanya have evolved accepting love as a medium of approach towards God. When compared to Christianity and Hinduism, Islam is of a different code of conduct. It condemns idol worship in its approach to God, conceived of as an abstraction rather than as an individual or a feeling. But many Sufi-mystics have revelled in the idea of imagining God as a Beloved and utilised human forms as stepping stones to the love of Divinity:

> In the fair and ugly forms of worldly we see the effulgence of God manifest in them. Our hearts are turned to God and eyes towards beloveds.[1]

Emerging from the three above-mentioned backgrounds, a number of poets have written poetry enriching perceptive vision with conceptual clarity. When, the transcendent and the evanescent feeling are caught in apt diction, when the abstract ideas receive concrete imagery and the ineffable experience gets expression in an emotional outpouring of superb then the age-old Indian saying one who is not a seer (saint) cannot be a poet (Nanrsih Kavirityakulum)[2] gets confirmed. God, conceived of as the Lover or the Beloved, is the common ground of comparison of the poets in this study. However, a sort of contrast is also involved. Religion is not a set of philosophical concepts, but a boundary marker to the life of people that sets a way of living. It defines social roles to the people in a particular community and in its ultimate form emerges as a language of symbols. Thus, the same poets, who write poetry with similar love and devotion to God culminating in a celestial marriage, talk of their experience through a particular culture milieu and address themselves to the world in general through their respective cultural up-bringings. The feelings are universal but the modes of expression are individualistically bound by religion and culture. This is the evolution of the universal from the particular or the *vice-versa*.

Saints, poets and mystics have looked at love as a reaffirmation of life and instead of forming a new religion they have evolved a principle of Universal Love. According to Plato, our love of beautiful things on earth is due to the search of our soul for the Absolute Beauty. All visible things are types in which are mirrored the beauty of eternal archetypes. In the *Symposium*, Plato says that man has to use the beauties of the earth as steps along which to mount towards the notion of the Absolute Beauty. Love is the lamp guiding the feet and the light illuminating the path of the human seekers, who, but for their strong feelings and passions to reach the Divine, would grope in the dark. The ardent searchers, infused with love, perceive the reality, present and permeating in all of us. At this stage, intellect and logic fail and instinctive conceptions of passion are sanctified and harmonized in divine love and illumined intellect conceives of a spiritual personality, imbued with love. An instinctive sense of spirituality endows divinity to the ordinary senses as Tagore says, "No, I will never shut the doors of my senses. These delights of sight and bearing and touch will bear thy light."[3] For Tagore, deliverance is not in renunciation and he would rather fill the cup of his life to the brim. The senses are numerous lamps to be sacredly placed at the altar of the Lord's temple. In such instances the poet integrates emotion with intellect, which enable him to have a sort of creative insight springing from an unconscious part of the psyche. Mystic poets have a tendency to subsume their emotions, usually worldly, into aspects of Divine

Love. For instance, Andal refers to directing the natural desires towards God (in the form of Krishna):

> Oh Lord, in the still small hours before the dawn
> We have come to your presence
> We will be bondsmaids for yourself alone;
> Be pleased to redirect this way our other desires;
> Hail to Thee.[4]

The dual aspects of love, belonging to the world and God are not controversial, contrasting aspects, but complementary to each other in the opinion of the poets. A union of opposites is achieved by Tagore in a poem in his *Gitanjali.* Starting with an apparently childish desire, the poet touches upon a universal phenomenon. It may be said that through the feeling of innocent, unblemished joy and selfish absorption in the seemingly petty things of life, the microcosm in the human being aspires to grasp the macrocosm in the universe. Tagore as a child was unprepared for the coming of God into his heart and did not keep it in readiness for that momentous event; but many fleeting moment[5] of his life are stamped by His signature and are mingled with ordinary events. The poet recognises the supreme importance of those moments when there is a co-ordination of rhythm in the sound of the steps he had heard as a child is as the steps "I heard in my playroom are the same that are echoing from star to star."[6] If ordinary emotions are rendered holy by the poets, the reverse takes place in an Upanishadic utterance. The entire universe is conceived of as of an apparently dual nature, united in the union of the male and the female. He divided himself into a Twain and this Twain was like the female and the male in close embrace.[7] While the whole universe in its special aspects is described thus the same terminology is used by Tagore to show the temporal and permanent aspects of time. God kisses the finite in love and man the infinite.[8]

This universality of love has been accepted in Indian thought and Indian thought in its turn seems to have influenced the whole world. Stratified maintains that "Indian mystical thought passed over into Africa and Western Europe" and blossomed forth in Plotinus and passed into Christian thought through the monk mystic the theosophical pantheist, the so-called Dionysus the

Areopagite.[9] But here the point of discussion is not to establish identity of origin, but to indicate affinity of content and style by showing that love towards God permeates different literatures as a dye. We see Platonic words in St. Paul when he says "I live not but Christ lives in me."[10] In the same vein, St. John of the Cross writes "Each lives in the other, and each is the other, and the two are made out in a transformation of love."[11] The same identification between the poet and God receives a more dramatic expression in Kabir's lines: "The day is clear to me above all other days, for today the Beloved is a guest in my house."[12] In a typically Indian way Kabir washes "His feet as a host should do to a guest."[13] Then comes the final moment of surrender and identification. "I lay before Him as an offering my body, my mind, and all that I have."[14] The same feelings of love and host's obligation are revealed in a poem of Emily Dickinson; but while Kabir's presentation is picturesque and extended, Emily Dickinsons's is suggestive, crisp and cryptic in her poem "The Soul that hath a Guest/Dost seldom go abroad." In her typical way, she refers to God as "Diviner Crowd at Home" "The Emperor of Men" who is visiting upon her and courtesy forbids her to "go abroad."[15] Similarly Trahene refers in his poetry to "Centers in eternity" opening upon "innumerable infinite"[16] and about the inner, hidden, spiritual world:

> To those pure things we find
> In his mind Who made the
> World (My spirit) There is
> A Spiritual World standing.[17]

Here the point of identification between the self and the spirit is brought home in a typical manner of the metaphysical poets. The immediate shock received by the phrase "enclosed in skin" is absorbed when it is realised that it is used for a sacred purpose in this poetic paradox. The merger of man and God into One Being is referred to by the Sufi-mystic Jami in his own way. Here it is conceived of as an entrance into the city of love where there is no room for two, but only one:

> All that is not One must ever
> Suffer with the wound of Absence
> And Whoever in Love's City

Enters, finds room for One
And but in Oneness Union.[18]

It is an accepted fact that no logic or reason can take one to the stage of union, but emotion alone counts. Omar Khaiyam has his own inimitable way of poetizing this idea through the image of vining and womanising:

You know, my Friends, how bravely in my House
For a new Marriage I did make Carouse;
Divorced old barren Reason from my bed
And took the Daughter of the Vine to Spouse.[19]

The merger of the poet, Omar Khaiyam with his beloved is something which cannot be realised by opening the door with a key, nor can it be seen through veils; but it is done as the poet says "Some little talk a while of Me and Thee/ There was—and Then no more of Thee and Me."[20]

It has been the experience of many mystics that the rapture and ecstasy of union in love do not last long. In a mystic's life there is always an experience of separation resulting in a feeling of dejection and desolation. Many reasons are attributed to it and what St. John of the Cross says seems to be accepted in general. He writes "As to actual union,...there is not and cannot in this life, any abiding union in the faculties of soul, but only that which is passing."[21]

St. Augustine also describes the restlessness involved in the urge of reunion "Thou hast made us for thyself, O God, and our hearts are restless till they rest in thee."[22] It is a human limitation that the ecstasy does not last long and the disciples grope in gloom feeling desolate and dissatisfied with the incomplete union. But the poets have enriched this plight with passionate outpouring of emotional content in such a way that there are beautiful poems, describing the pangs of separation and waiting in love called *Viraha* and *Pratiksha* in Sanskrit. In Madhura bhakti, every disciple, irrespective of sex becomes a maiden stricken with the pangs of love. Thus the heroine in *Alone with the spouse divine* complains that when she is in a concentrated trance, lost in devotion mediating on the sublime image and putting everything else to naught, her lover played tricks of histrionics on her and disappeared.[23] She implores to the "embodiment of Love" not to go away leaving her a "miserable plight."[24] Here in these poems, the poets do not take resort to poetic paradoxes or metaphors as the other poets so far discussed do. Here it is a careful culling together of details to suit the occasion and successfully bring before the reader's eyes a love-stricken woman, lost in her own paradise, which is too slippery for her to enter into. For instance, the heroine pitifully deplores that she has not committed any mistake except standing in awe, as hairs bristled over all my body. She is just trying to install the image of the Lord in her heart and has done no other falsehood:

> except allowing the image
> of none other than all knowledge
> and container of cosmic whole
> buoy up in half-closed limpid eyes.[25]

Here along with depicting the devotion of the heroine, the poets have shown consummate craftsmanship in painting the picture, stroke after stroke, as it if were with paint and brush. While the feelings are explicit in these poems, Kabir presents before us the feelings of separation through the picture of a bashful bride, who conceals her feelings "My body and mind are grieved for want of Thee./ O my Beloved come to my house/ When people say I am Thy bride, I am ashamed."[26] The poet is restless and "dying for sight of Him"[27] and "As water is to the thirsty so is the lover to the bride"[28] similar sentiment is expressed by Emily Dickinson in her poem "I dreaded the first Robin, so." In this poem the objects of nature, which come in spring do not appeal to the poet in that mood. She complains that:

> They're here though, not a creature failed—
> No blossom stayed away
> In gentle deference to me
> The Queen of Calvary.[29]

"The Queen of Calvary" suggests the drift from the ordinary to the extraordinary. Calvary denotes Christ's crucifixion and the poet's (Queen of Calvary's) endless suffering for a noble purpose. The same kind of pathos and sympathy are invoked by Mirabai in her pitiful state of separation and endless waiting in the poem "I shall not survive without the company of my Lord Hari. Thus forsaken by Him, the spirit shall leave my mental frame."[30] Mirabai compares her condition to that of fish without water or wood eaten away by worms, that is slow approach of death through sorrow. In one of Kabir's poems he combines the feeling of separation and death in a dramatic fashion. He explicitly states the pangs of separation in the first lines of the poem:

> Dear friend, I am eager to meet my Beloved
> My youth has flowered, and the pain of separation
> from Him troubles my breast.[31]

But by the end of the poem a twist of thought takes place and the poet says that he has an unutterable message[32] and proudly announces "I have got for my gift the Deathless one."[33]

The above-mentioned poem of Kabir leads us to another related theme in search of the Divine Beloved. The human fetters do not bother the mystic poets, blessed with God's love. For example, Tagore Says:

> O youth! Must you remain imprisoned in the
> cage of Happiness,
> You are pilgrim of the pathless shores
> Your Wings are restless and untiring
> And your flight
> Soaring in search of your unknown nest, steals,
> from the tempest its thunder.[34]

In the next stanza this impassioned, timeless and endless journey to an unknown destiny leads to the realization that death is a marriage to eternity:

> In her cup
> Death always keeps for you her nectar,
> And your proud beloved waits for you
> Lift it and see her high loveliness.[35]

In presenting a similar theme in his poem "The Fear of Death" unlike Tagore, Aurobindo does not refer to youthful strength and adventure, but goes to the point straight by saying that death is sweet and is busy with each intake of our breath. Death "is but changing of our robes to wait/ In wedding garments at Eternal's gate."[36] Tagore and Aurobindo refer to death and marriage as synonymous, but their language is imbued with serious feeling. On the other hand, Omar Khaiyam says the same thing in a different manner through a detailed description of the moon, the sweet heart and the leaves:

> But see! The rising Moon of Heaven again—
> Look for us, Sweet-heart, through the quivering plane,
> how oft hereafter rising will she look
> Among the leaves—for one of us in vain[37]

Once the human limitations are crossed, the mystic poets speak of an all pervading divine consciousness in which the human will is surrendered and subsumed to be conquered by a Divine Will. For St. Theresa this sort of ecstasy is betrothal leading up to the "spiritual marriage in which the soul always remains in its centre with God."[38] An absolute self-surrender is shown by poets as to be seen in a *Kannada vacana by Siddarana*:

> There is nothing like "I" and "mine;"
> Whatever I do, is thy sportlers; my delights
> are Thine;
> I do not act all; I exist only through
> and in Thee.[39]

In the above poem written by a Shaivite poet, emotion is kept at an abeyance. But to the disciples of Chaitanya like Chandidas love is no longer a feeling but a spontaneous abandon. In Chandidas's "City of love" love reins supreme as it is said "I would make my residence in the city of love/ I shall build there a hut with love."[40] In her dedication to love, the heroine of the poem has love for her bed, pillow, playmate and love is her religion; she will bathe in the lake of love and "wear the collyrium of love." The poet reaches the pinnacle of his poetic achievement, when he chooses, according to his cultural upbringing, the sacred ornament of a married woman, a nose-ring, which dallies in the eyes of the heroine in consonance with her feelings of love:

> I shall make a nose-ring of love
> which will wave to and fro, by the corner of the eye
> says Chandidas, I too will wear the collyrium of love.[41]

The same celestial happiness in love is displayed in a poem in *Alone with the spouse divine*. The part played by the nose-ring in Chandidas's poem is done by "the solemn thread sanctified with turmeric" here as in South India the yellow thread is a symbol of marriage and sacred to a married woman: "the solemn thread sanctified with turmeric is linked with continuous conjugal bliss."[42] The whole poem brings out a happy mood of absolute satisfaction of desire. In a similar celestial marriage, Emily Dickinson celebrates the merger of the individual life into the divine trinity through the sacrament of marriage:

> Given in marriage unto Thee
> Oh Celestial Most—
> Bride of the Father and the Son
> Bride of the Holy Ghost.[43]

In exemplifying a similar union with God, Mirabai takes the example of "sohaga" dust and gold: "Fearlessly my heart is given to the Divine Beloved/ Like the fine Sohaga dust mixed to gold, so I joined my Girdhar."[44] It is interesting to note that the two poets use symbols of marriage, pertaining to their respective cultures. Mirabai imparts the atmosphere of marriage to her poem through the Sohaga dust (signifying the sacred mark of vermilion powder worn by a married woman) and gold, while Emily Dickinson does it with the ring, the symbol of marriage (the exchange of rings signifying the bond of marriage):

> Other Betrothal shall dissolve
> Wedlock of will, decay,
> only the keeper of this Ring
> Conquest Mortality.[45]

In Christian orthodoxy, as it is professed by medieval scholars like St. Thomas Aquinas reality is conceived of as an ordered hierarchy of existence, whose being is from Himself. He is conceived of as an embodiment of perfection, the pure being, the pure act and He is in no sense corporeal. All other existences are imperfect and the individuals, in their limited status owe their existence only to Him, who is the True Being. But this concept of God has changed down the ages and many mystics and poets consider themselves parts and parcels of His Being. There is a mutual attraction between the individual and the Divine Being. Along with the phases of loving, union, separation, dejection, marriage, ecstasy and surrender there is another phase, where God comes down in search of human soul as He does in Francis Thomson's "The Hound of Heaven." Jalal-ud-din Rumi gives apt expression to the idea that human love is but a reciprocation to what God feels for the individual:

> No lover ever seeks union with Him
> But the lover's love makes his body lean
> When the love of God arises in the heart,
> Without doubt God also feels love for Thee.[46]

In a similar vein Tagore says that God is incomplete without the poet's love:

> Thus it is that thy joy in me so full.
> Thus it is that thou hast come down to me.
> O thou lord of all heavens,
> Where would be thy love if I were not?
>
> Thou hast taken me as thy partner of all this wealth
> And for this thy love loses itself in the
> love of thy lover, and there art thou seen
> in the perfect union of the two.[47]

Emily Dickinson also conceives of God, the lover coming in search of her for loving union:

> know his eye
> Where'er I ply
> Is pushing close behind....
>
> Nor any port
> Nor any flight.
> But he doth there preside
> What Omnipresence lies in wait
> For her to be a Bride.[48]

St. John of the Cross describes an ineffable union of love and here too God comes down for the sake of the disciple:

All things I then forgot
My cheek on Him who for my coming came
All ceased, and I was not,
Leaving my cares and shame
Among the lilies and forgetting them.[49]

The soul's journey towards its ultimate source is always described as the flight of the alone to the alone. But mystic poets have found out their own ways of dramatizing this inward journey. The progress and growth in love has its ecstasies, exasperations, pitfalls, pains and pleasures. But love imbued with such a lofty purpose as leading the pathway to the Divine Beloved does not stop short of attaining its highest goal. Love perfects and evolves the human soul in such a way that the most perfect of the perfect, the Divinity Incarnate in his love goes more than half-way to reach His Beloved. At this stage of perfect union, the intimacy and splendor experienced are revealed in Jalal-ud-din Rumi's lines:

With Thy sweet Soul, this soul of mine
Hath mixed as water doth with wine.
Thy love has pierced me through and through
Its thrill with Bone and Nerve entwine
I rest a flute laid on Thy lips; a lute on
thy breast recline
Breathe deep in me that I sigh
Yet strike my strings and tears shall shine.[50]

This is a synthetic vision of God common to all and special to each as one Christian mystic says. In Ruysbroeck's words, each love is melted and merged in the unity. Love is throughout the absolute and sole lord for all these mystics. They are soaked in love and look at it in Johanine language as the Form of God. Every thing said by mystic poets leads to prove the Upanishadic aphorism "*Rasovasah*" (the infinite is love itself).

## NOTES

1. Quoted by Mir Valiuddin, *Love of God: The Sufi Approach* (Hyderabad: Motilal Banarsidass, 1960), 150.

2. V. Raghavan and Nagendra, eds., *An Introduction to Indian Poets* (Bombay: Macmillan, 1970), 23-24.
3. Rabindranath Tagore, *Gitanjali* (London: Macmillan, 1967), 68.
4. K. Santhanam, ed., *An Anthology of Indian Literature* (Bombay: Bharatiya Vidya Bhavan, 1969), 582.
5. Rabindranath Tagore, *Gitanjali* (London: Macmillan, 1967), 35.
6. *Ibid.*
7. Brihadaranyaka Upanishad, quoted in *Triveni* No. III, VXXIX, Jan. 1959), 189.
8. Rabindranath Tagore, *Stray Birds* (London: Macmillan, 1951), 78.
9. Quoted by S. Radhakrishnan, *Eastern Religion and Western Thought* (New Delhi: Oxford University Press, 1989), 215.
10. Radhakrishnan, 223.
11. *Ibid.*
12. Kabir, *One Hundred Poems of Kabir,* trans. Tagore and Underhill (London: Macmillan, 1945), 94.
13. *Ibid.*, 94.
14. *Ibid.*, 95.
15. Thomas H. Johnson, ed., *The Poems of Emily Dickinson II* (Harvard: Belknal, 1970), 521.
16. Quoted by Rufus M. Jones, *Spiritual Reformers in the 16th and 17th Centuries* (Boston: Beam Hill, 1914), 328.
17. Jones, 329.
18. Jami, quoted by Evelyn Underhill, *Mysticism* (1911, rpt. London: Methuen, 1957), 79.
19. Omar Khaiyam, Tr. Fitzgerald, quoted in *Rubaiyat* (Bombay: A Narayanadas, 1932), 98.
20. Fitzgerald, 60.
21. Quoted by Charles A. Bennett, *A Philosophical Study of Mysticism: An Essay* (New Haven: Yale University Press, 1923), 37.
22. F.C. Happoid, *Mysticism: A Study of an Anthology* (Middlesex: Pelican, 1963), 40.
23. Ekanta Seva in Telugu by Sri Venkata Parvateeshwara Kavulu, *Alone with the spouse divine.*
    N. Rajani Kanta Rao (Tirupathi: Tirumala Tirupati Devastanam, 1980), 11.
24. *Ibid.*, 12.
25. *Ibid.*, 39.
26. Kabir, *One Hundred Psalms of Kabir*, trans. Tagore and Underhill (London: Macmillan, 1945), 41.

27. *Ibid.*
28. *Ibid.*
29. Thomas H. Johnson, ed., *The Poems of Emily Dickinson I* (Harvard: Belknap, 1960), 278.
30. Mirabai, *Bhakta Mira,* trans. Bankey Behari (Bombay: Bhartiya Vidya Bhavan, 1961), 102.
31. Kabir, *One Hundred Poems of Kabir,* trans. Tagore and Underhill (London: Macmillan, 1945), 57.
32. *Ibid.*
33. *Ibid.*
34. Rabindranath Tagore, *A Fight of Swans: Poems from Balaka* Trans. Aurobindo Bose (London: Hunnay, 1955), 76.
35. *Ibid.*
36. Aurobindo, *Complete Poetical Works: Collected Poems Sri Aurobindo Birth Centenary* Edn. V (Pondicherry: Aurobindo Ashram, 1975), 562.
37. Omar Khaiyam, Tr. Fitzgerald, Quoted in *Rubaiyat* (Bombay: A Narayanadas, 1932), 182.
38. Quoted by S. Radhakrishnan, *Eastern Religion and Western Thought* (New Delhi: Oxford University Press, 1989), 79.
39. Siddarana, quoted in *Triveni No.* III, VXXIX (Jan. 1959), 189.
40. Chandidas, quoted by Gora Sastry in Preface to *Alone with the Spouse Divine* (Tirupati: Tirumula Tirupati Devastanam, 1980), XII.
41. *Ibid.*
42. *Ibid.*
43. Thomas H. Johnson, ed., *The Poems of Emily Dickenson II* (Harvard: Belknap, 1970), 618.
44. Mirabai, *Bhakta Mira,* trans. Bankey Behari (Bombay: Bhartiya Vidya Bhavan, 1961), 106.
45. Thomas H. Johnson, ed., *The Poems of Emily Dickenson II* (Harvard: Belknap, 1970), 618.
46. Jalal-ud-din Rumi, quoted by Evelyn Underhill, *Mysticism* (1911 rpt. London: Methuen, 1957), 133.
47. Rabindranath Tagore, *Gitanjali* (London: Macmillan, 1967), 51-52.
48. Thomas H. Johnson, ed., *The Poems of Emily Dickinson III* (Harvard: Belknap, 1970), 1033.
49. F.C. Happoid, *Mysticism: A Study of an Anthology* (Middlesex: Pelican, 1963), 66.
50. Jalal-ud-din Rumi, quoted by Srinivesachari, *Mystics and Mysticism* (Madras: Sri Krishna Library, 1951), 149-50.

# Chapter 6

# Perspectives on Kamala Das's Poetry: Confessionalism and Scientific Positivism

*S.D. Sharma*

Long back I wrote a conference paper entitled "Kamala Das's Poetry: An Amatory Hiatus," which subsequently appeared in my book named *Thematic Dichotomy of Writing in Indian English, Indology and Culture.*[1] One of the inferences that I drew in the paper was the Darwinian interpretation[2] of love, which Kamala Das rarely terms as spiritual wonder. In support of my argument, I had chiefly cited some poems such as Ghanshyam, The Swamp, A Man is a Season, An Introduction, Jaisurya, The Fancy-dress Show etc.[3] The paper ended with the conclusion, In a bitter tone, like Hardy, she (Kamala Das) sardonically hints at the rotten love in this nonchalant, stinking world:

> God is in heaven and all
> Is right with this stinking world.
>
> ("The Fancy-dress Show," lines 15-16)[4]

In continuation of the same treatment, let me first deal with the confessionalism in Kamala Das's poetry. Her poetic collections—*Summer in Calcutta* (1965), *The Descendants* (1967) and *The Old Playhouse and Other Stories* (1973) contain a wide range of themes, yet they are largely confessional in tone and tenor. Generally, "the literal Self"[5] becomes the nucleus, the central point of treatment in all the confessional poets, if at all, the label of confessional poets is perfectly appropriate to be applied to a group of post-World War II poets in America, England and other Commonwealth Countries including India and if this label may uncontroversially be applied to them simply because they talk of themselves and try to render their literal self to be universalised for a larger section of humanity. For the time being, let us not enter into any controversy as to the appropriateness or otherwise of the label of confessional poets as such. However, for carrying my point of confessionalism through, I would like to take help of this label.

So Kamala Das frankly and frequently confesses in her poetry. Her confessions are tall, far-reaching and meaningful. Frequently, they do verge on the point of revolution in the poetic world. But a million dollar question is—what does she confess? What is the subject of her great confession? Is the so-called confession genuine or fake? Is her confession so voluminous so as to make a specific *ISM*? Is confessionalism associated, in any way, with aesthetic experience, creativity, sublimity etc.?

Yes, Kamala Das confesses a number of things exclusively related to her own self—self as a woman with her strong feminine sensibilities, self as a person with powerful proclivities and antipathies, caprices and whimwhams. She does not feel shy of exhibiting her frailties and virtues as a woman; her superior self as a mother and her inevitable exploitation as a wife; her delicate and precarious position as a daughter and grand-daughter; her weaknesses as an enlightened companion to an enlightened husband and so on and so forth. She feels happy by confessing/ by peeling off [her] layers/ by reaching closer to the soul/ and to the bone's/ supreme indifference. She openly asserts, I must let my mind striptease/ I must extrude/ autobiography (*The Descendants*, pp. 32-33). She boldly confesses the futility and meaninglessness of physical love and in a repenting and remorseful tone, she confesses, As the convict studies/ His prison's geography/ I study the trappings/ Of your body my dear [lover/husband] love/ For I must some day find/ As escape from its snare (*The Old Playhouse and Other Poems*, p. 29).

So Kamala Das performs anatomy on her own self, on her own female psyche. Her own self emerges so powerfully in her poetry that even the moribund system, lying concealed under the veneer of social sanctity, is totally punctured by her virulent attacks. The carnal exploits, a woman is subjected to so inhumanely, is fully and exclusively exposed. Her own traumatic experiences in love and in sex are candidly confessional and absolutely forthright. But poetry provides her the strongest outlet to give vent to her pent-up feelings; for, poetry for her is very personal and private. It is like prayers. I don't want to share it with the public. I write a lot in my private diary and only a fraction of it has been published.[6] In a highly confessional tone, she does not even hide her own body-changes, joys and failures in love and sex and her own attitude towards her own husband/lover. In a poignant, articulated tone, she writes, I was child, and later they/ Told me I Grew, I became tall, my limbs/ Swelled and one or two places sprouted hair. When/ I asked for love, not knowing what else to ask/ For, he drew a youth of sixteen into the/ Bedroom and closed the door. He did not beat me/ But my sad woman-body felt so beaten/ The weight of my breasts and womb crushed me/ (An Introduction, *Summer in Calcutta*, p. 60). Kamala Das openly revolts against the traditionally accepted, strange, queer womanhood concepts in the Indian society, which is so awkwardly full of abominable shams and cants. Rigid trammels of tyranny, she does not like at all. In a bitter, piercing, cathartic tone, Kamala Das ridicules traditional imposters, show of masculine strength and also man's lust,... you were pleased/ with my body's response, its weather, its usual shallow/ Convulsions. You dribbled spittle into my mouth. You poured/ Yourself into every nook and cranny, you embalmed/ My poor lust with your bitter sweet/ Juices (*The Old Playhouse*, p. 1).

Kamala Das's Poetry is replete with a powerful force of catharsis and protest. This is so because of her intensely confessional trait and ultra-subjective treatment. Like all confessional poets, who give literary form a new sense of personality, attaching value to the image of man presented by clinical psychology,[7] Kamala Das raises her confessional traits to the level of a specific universal appeal. The struggle of one self ultimately becomes the struggle of the whole humanity and herein lies her *forte*: for, the best confessional poetry is that which rises above subject-matter to achieve some sort of victory over pain and defeat, poems which are glosses on the triumphs of life.[8] Because of absolute confessions made by a group of poets in their poetry, particularly in America, such poets as Robert Rowell, Theodore Roethke, Anne Sexton, Sylvia Plath and John Berryman, have raised themselves to a level known as confessional poets and Kamala Das's place is certainly secure in the ranks of these poets. Even suicide is a subject they are ready to confess. In a poem named Dream Songs, John Berryman appears to ponder over and mastermind his suicide, "It all centred in the end on the suicide/ in which I am an expert, deep and wide" (p. 153). In the same vein, another confessional poet named Sylvia Plath writes in her famous poem entitled Lady Lazarus, Dying/ is an art, like everything else/ I do it exceptionally well (*Ariel*, p. 17). Often these poets had parleys on their paranoia, disappointments, psychological break-downs and even looming suicide. One such parley has come to light between Anne Sexton and Sylvia Plath, as authenticated by Barbara Kelves, "We talked death with burned-up intensity, both of us drawn to it like moths to an electric bulb, sucking it. She told the story of her first suicide in sweet and loving detail and her description in *The Bell Jar* is just the same story."[9]

So far an effort has been made by me to prove that Kamala Das's Poetry is full of the elements of confessionalism, if at all, confessionalism is any label appropriate to be applied to the type of poetry/replete with confessional overtones. Nevertheless, Kamala Das's poetry has cathartic effect: for, the more poignant her confessional tone is, the more is her cathartic import. While dealing with the cathartic effect in his *Poetics*, Aristotle regards the most perfect tragic pleasure as possible only through the purgation of the feelings of pity and fear. In fact, Catharsis is a process of learning, and, therefore, pleasurable.[10] In summation, catharsis means a variety of tragic pleasure,[11] mostly intellectual, what O.B. Hardison and G.E. Else term as clarification theory.[12] Cathartic effect is closely related to the intensity of poetic sensibilities. The more the intense the poetic sensibilities are, the more powerful will be the poetic sublimity: for, "Our sweetest songs," in the Shelleyean tone, "are those that tell of saddest thoughts." A perfect poetic sublimity consists of five elements—grandeur of thought, capacity for strong emotion, appropriate use of figures, nobility of diction and, finally, harmonious composition.[13] In Section VII of the treatise, Longinus states, "There are five principal sources of elevated language. Beneath these five varieties, there lies, as though it were a common foundation, the gift of discourse, which is indispensable. First and most important is the power forming great conceptions.... Secondly there is vehement and inspired passion. These two components of the sublime are the most part innate. Those which remain are partly the product of art.... Next there is noble diction, which in turn comprises choice of words, and use of metaphors, and elaboration of language. The fifth cause of elevation—one which is the fitting conclusion of all that has proceeded it—is dignified and elevated composition.[14] Out of these five sources, two namely—*High Thinking* and *High Feeling* depend on nature.

The rest three are entirely subservient to technical skill.[15] Kamala Das achieves poetic sublimity largely because of cathartic effect and partly due to achieving success in different constituents of sublimity.

Cathartic effect ends in providing *rasa*, which Vyas Muni considers to be the soul, the essence of poetry, "वाग्वैदरध्यप्रधाने रस एवामजीवितम्" (*Dasrupak*, 5, 85).[16] It has been said in the *Upanishads* that *rasa* is Brahma Himself.[17] The *Tytriyoonishada* says, "रसोवेस: रसहनोवायं लब्ध्वाडडनन्दी भवति।"[18] *Rasa* is said to be the soul of Indian poetics and it has gradually come to be accepted as the soul of Indian aesthetics and aesthetic experience. For old pedagogues like Bharata and Bhamana, and also for celebrated men of learning like Acharya Dhananjaya, *rasa* is closely connected to the poetic vision. Significantly, Acharya Dhananjaya says, "रभ्यं जुगुप्सितमुदारम-थापि नीचन्। उग्रप्रसादि गहनं विकृतिं च वस्तु। यद् वाप्यवस्तु कवि भावक भावनीवं। तन्नास्ति यन्न रस भावनुपैति लोके।"[19] Kamala Das's aesthetic experience, whether sublime or not, is the soul of her poetry and, as such, her poetry is, if we accept that there is a very strong cathartic import hidden dormant in her confessional, autobiographical poetry, full of creativity and an awakened perception of poetic truth. "Some call poetic truth a kind of *Yoga* or meditation, grooming or cultivation, spiritual evolution or creative process."[20] However, the fact remains that aesthetic experience or sublimity is synonymous to creativity. "Anything created in consonance with the inner perception is definitely great."[21]

In my papers named "Creativity in Literature: Basic Concepts and Promoting Factors" and "Promotion of Creativity: Some Empirical Suggestions with Special Reference to Local Requirements" published in *Perspectives on Creativity*,[22] I have talked of sublimity versus creativity in detail and have proved the fact that the more the chiselled and intense the poetic vision is, the more will be the cathartic import. Viewed from the standpoint, Kamala Das's poetry has a very strong element of catharsis. In my papers, cited above and also in Chapter X[23] entitled "Aesthetics: Sublimity and Creativity" of my book named *Longinus's on the Sublime* (cited in Notes and References), I have tried to establish the fact that aesthetic experience, sublimity and creativity are but the different nomenclatures or names of the same creative process of an artist, writer or a poet. In some, the aesthetic experience is more powerful than the sublime perceptions. In others, the sublime perceptions are keener and more powerful than the aesthetic experiences. In fact, it is a rarity to find all these three elements in perfect equilibrium and, if per chance, these elements are traceable in plenty, the artist or the poet must be blessed with the pure divine poetic urge. In Kamala Das, these elements are certainly there, but to ask as to what is their level at this stage, is too preposterous a proposition to answer. However, I find the level of sublimity in her poetry much lower than the level of aesthetic experience, and, hence to place her in the rank of highly celebrated woman poets is, I think, not appropriate at the moment. Let us find some more inherent plus point in her poetry and let us then re-assess and re-evaluate her place and make a true appraisal of her poetry.

With these general parameters, let us look closely at her tragic aesthetic experiences in her recalcitrances; for it is not possible here to deal with them in detail. Pathetically, Kamala

Das humours male ego rather ironically with this piece of advice to other women, "Turn your home into merry/ dog-house/ marriage is meant to be all this/ anyway/ being arranged in/ most humorous heaven" (Composition, *The Descendants*, p. 33). The most intense experience is one when women are taught to believe that adoration of the child in womb is an important event in her life and that all other activities are meaningless:

The child gives meaning and fulfilment to the mother:

> Love is not important, that makes the blood
> Carouse, nor the man who brands you with his
> Lust, but is shed as slough at end of each
> Embrace, only that matters which forms as
> Toadstool under lightning and rain, the soft
> Stur in womb, the foetus growing:
>
> (*The Descendants*, p. 27)

Even death, she admits, is no fear to her:

> Each night when darkness turns
> Me blind, I think of death,
> Understanding it to
> Be like night-fall, just a
> Temporary phase which
> Strings no loss.
>
> (*Summer in Calcutta*, p. 61)

In a poem named "The Suicide", Kamala Das embraces death, "O sea, I am fed up/ I want to be simple/ I want to be loved/ And/ If love is not to be had/ I want to be dead/" (*The Descendants*, p. 20). In the same vein, she further says, "I feel my age and my/ Uselessness/ All I want now/ Is to take a long walk/ Into the sea/ And lie there, resting/ Completely uninvolved" (*The Descendants*, p. 34). Elsewhere, too, she longs for:

> Morning tree, on your brown bony branch, one day,
> I shall see a sudden flower, and know at once
> That my death is just a flower, a red, red
> Morning flower, and then from behind the cold
> Window-pane, I shall smile my last morning's smile.
>
> (*Summer in Calcutta*, p. 45)

These are some representative extracts from Kamala Das's poetry, which do cast a cursory reflection on her poetic experiences, and, again, which, too, are aesthetic processes to prepare the real heaven of her poetic vision in the long run. Whether the tragic aesthetic experience is highly sublime or powerfully creative—is a question to be analysed and answered separately. Nonetheless, we are here concerned with another closely connected issue—probably very pertinent to our hitherto treated subject—and that is—how to interpret her tragic aesthetic experience apart from its force of creativity and sublimity—the much discussed theme by now by other experts of Kamala Das's poetry. I don't know if anybody has embarked upon to interpret Kamala Das's confessional or autobiographical traits closely related to tragic aesthetic experience; and then aesthetic experience closely linked with sublimity and creativity. The point to be proved now is—is there any definite direction in which Kamala Das's poetry move? Or, are we to interpret her poetry in any other way than the present one? To me, Kamala Das's poetry is highly scientific and every theme of her poetry may be first interpreted in accordance with the Darwinian philosophy of evolution and then also according to the postulates of spiritual evolution.

Let us come to the first point—*viz.*, Kamala Das's acceptance of Darwinism. One of the basic postulates of Darwinism or the philosophy of evolution as propounded by Charles Darwin is the physical evolution of man. This has now been taken as accepted by all; for, science has proved it. We now believe that man has been evolved through thousands of years and his present physical status has been achieved through physical changes and consequent evolution. Earlier we used to believe the Biblical version of the creation of man by God is seven days. This Biblical version, or religious view got a shattering blow by the Darwinian interpretation of the creation of man. As such, this nudged the whole Christianity; and well-entrenched citadel of Papal authority jerkingly crumbled. With the collapse of religious superiority, science triumphed to make inroads into other domains of life. Even man's physique, love, sex, hunger etc. were interpreted in accordance with the Darwinian postulates.

Viewed from the Darwinian Philosophy of evolution, Kamala Das's poetic experience is highly scientific.

Kamala Das's acceptance of Darwinism naturally leads to another important aspect. Struggle for existence or survival of the fittest is another postulate of the Darwinian philosophy of evolution. Related to it is the existential vision of Kamala Das lying strewn in her poems. Her concept of the survival of the fittest is another postulate of the Darwinian philosophy of evolution. Related to it is the existential vision of Kamala Das lying strewn in her poems. Her concept of the survival theory and that of existentialism should be analysed and considered side by side: for, the interrelatedness of the one to another is inextricably mixed. Often both appear to be one and the same aspect. For example, in Composition, she talks of survival by force. In "The Suicide", she talks of freedom of soul after the body is decomposed. In Death Brings No Loss, she treats death Just a/ temporary phase which/ brings no loss. In Ghanshyam, Kamala Das talks not only of physical evolution but also of spiritual evolution:

> Ghanshyam,
> You have like a koel built your nest in the
> arbour of my heart
> My life until now a sleeping jungle is at
> last stir with music
> You lead me long a route I have
> never known before
> But at each turn when I near you
> Like a spectral flame you vanish.
>
> (*Summer in Calcutta*, p. 37)

Kamala Das's poems on Radha-Krishna myth namely Ghanshyam, Radha, *The Maggots*, Radha-Krishna etc., are specifically representative of her faith in spiritual evolution of man. She has candidly admitted:

> I have always thought of Krishna
> as my mate. When I was a child I used to
> regard him as my only friend, when
> I became an adult I thought of him

> as my lover. It was only my imagining
> that he was with me that I could lie beneath
> my husband to give pleasure. Often I have
> thought of Radha as the luckiest of all women,
> for did she not have his incomparably
> beautiful body in her arms, we do not
> have him physically to love us; we have
> to worship a bodiless one.[24]

In another poem named "Radha," Kamala Das talks of spiritual love and evolution by means of surrender. Radha, in this poem, represents the spirit of surrender, the very first step towards spiritual evolution, and which George Meredith and George Eliot so fondly talk of in their novels:

> The long waiting
> Had me their bond so chaste, and all the doubting
> And the reasoning
> So that in his first true embrace, she
> was girl
> And virgin crying
> Everything in me
> Is melting, even the hardness at the core
> O Krishna, I am melting, melting
> Nothing remains but
> You.

(*Tonight This Savage Rite*, p. 23)

For the consummation of spiritual love, Kamala Das mingles her complete self with the self of Krishna, she says:

> I was entirely without lust. I hoped
> that some day as I lay with a man,
> some-where beneath the bone,
> at a deadened spot, a contact would be
> made, and that after words each movement
> of my life became meaningful. I looked
> for the beauteous Krishna in every man.
> Every Hindu girl is in reality wedded to
> Lord Krishna.[25]

In fact, to prove the point of spiritual evolution in Kamala Das's poetry as well as to authenticate Darwinian interpretation thereof, I have given no detailed treatment of either Darwinism or spiritual evolution: for, the size of the present chapter/paper does not admit of such a detailed treatment. This subject is fit to be dealt with separately. The discriminated reader is advised to consult my another book named *Darwinism and Victorian Fiction* to have a fuller view and comprehension of this theme.[26] However, somewhere I have talked of Kamala Das's scientific approach to and also of the impact of Darwinism[27] on her, particularly in case of death:

> Death is moisture
> Life is water, semen and blood,
> Death is drought
> Death is the hot sauna leading to cool rest-rooms
> Death is the last, lost sob of the relative
> Beside the red-walled morgue.
>
> ("Ghanshyam," lines 10-15)[28]

While dealing with Anita Desai's short-stories, I have dwelt upon the same theme of "Spiritual Struggle" in her stories and novels, despite the fact that Anita no where mentions her acceptance of scientific influence on her.[29] This has been dealt with in a recent publication in 1991, the beginning of which is as under:

> Nanda Kaul in *Fire on The Mountain*
> conducts herself in a way that reminds
> one of the possibility of spiritual evolution
> of man, of the likely extinction of bestiality
> in man, and, of course, of the emerging
> potential that may deter him from
> indulging in whatever is subversive
> of the divine scheme of things.[30]

The same hopeful inference has been drawn by me from Anita Desai's novels in a paper appeared in 1991 in *The Quest*:[31]

> Weltschmerz provides her [Anita Desai]
> cosmic vision a tinge of deterministic
> pessimism as in most of her earlier

> novels as *Cry, The Peacock* and *Voices in The City*, Yet her sombre vision does remain unimpaired by a deep sense of helplessness as in Hardy's case. Most of her psychological propinquities are more with George Eliot's than with Jane Austen's, Emile Bronte's and Maria Edgeworth's.[32]

In case of Kamala Das's Poetry, I infer the same conclusions on the basis of the hitherto available evidence as well as on the strength of her representative poems. Weltschmerz also provides her cosmic vision a tinge of deterministic pessimism, yet she is verily endowed with a sombre vision—a vision seeing man as essentially good and capable of rising to unimaginable heights of divine deeds. The same hopeful inferences I have drawn from Tennyson,[33] Aurobindo,[34] Shelley and Peacock,[35] Eunice De Souza,[36] Gauri Deshpande,[37] and D.H. Lawrence.[38]

Thus synoptically, the above treatment has many stages—first, Kamala Das's confessionalism has been authenticated with all possible adumbrations of this label. Secondly, confessional poetry of Kamala Das has been inferred to be associated with cathartic effects and intense woman sensibilities. The third step of treatment is that cathartic import of Kamala Das's poetry has powerfully led to the element of creativity and aesthetic experience. Aesthetic experience, then, has been concluded to be associated with the element of sublimity and also an effort has been made to assign a specific place, a decided echelon to her as a woman poet of great merit. The next stage and perhaps the most significant one of treatment is, then, the stage of connecting sublimity and aesthetic experience to scientific *isms*, particularly to that of Darwinism, though Kamala Das never mentions having directly influenced by Darwin himself. The last stage is the inference of revelation of the element of spiritual evolution and existentialism in Kamala Das's poetry. I think, the approach, in summation, is new and needs patient understanding on the part of an indulgent reader.

But the above stages of treatment of Kamala Das's poetry will not convince the indulgent reader, unless some representative poetic extracts highlighting conflict between bestiality and spirituality from her poetry are authentically analysed and interpreted. Absolutely, she wants to cling to higher levels of purity which her mother and grandmother so enthusiastically clung to. But the animal spirit in her forcefully disturbs her and she, therefore, finds her deviating from the established path of virtue. She forgets her high birth, her esteemed parentage, nobility and royal blood, once she is overpowered by the satanic feelings. In the continuous struggle between the good and the bad, it is largely the good which finally yields. Notwithstanding all good intentions, the poetess is sadly misled by the powerful evil and her object surrender to evil makes her repent subsequently. Like Thomas Hardy, she feels pessimistic about the basic designs of the providence, but the essentially spiritual Indian cultural ethos makes her feel optimistic about man's inborn, immense potential to grow and consequently to exist, to survive in a meaningful, gainful way. Kamala Das's faith in man's ultimate triumph is as absolutely apparent as in George Meredith's in the doctrine of spiritual evolution and as is George Eliot's in the *Law of Nemesis*. This faith of Kamala Das often seems to waver whenever naked materialism powerfully sways her. Nevertheless, her faith is largely sustained and vitally nourished by the doctrine of divine birth of man, despite his pithecoid origin. But by this interpretation of Kamala Das's poetry, this is not to suggest that her approach to and understanding of Indian cultural ethos is perfectly the Tagorean and the Aurobindoian. The fact to be noted is that Kamala Das scarcely ever rises to the *ne plus ultra* of the cosmic divine view of R.N. Tagore owing to the powerful impact of science on her view of life. In the lines that follow, probably a nostalgic reminiscence reverberates throughout, a dashing conflict between the body and the soul comes apparently to the fore:

> O mother's mother's mother
> I have plucked your soul
> Like a pip from a fruit

And have flung it into your pyre
Call me callous
Call me selfish
But do not blame my blood
So thin, so clear, so fine
The oldest blood in the world
That remembers as it flows
All the gems and all the gold
And all the perfumes and the oils
And the stately
Elephant ride.

(*The Old Playhouse*, p. 19)

Or, note the following lines also:

When I
Sleep, the outside
World crumbles, all contacts
Broken, so, in that longer sleep
Only
The World
Shall die, and I
*REMAIN*, just *BEING*
*ALSO BEING A REMAINING.*

(*The Descendants*, p. 9)

In fact, it is another issue if Kamala Das has ever admitted having been powerfully influenced by a number of scientific theories of the modern times as such. However, it is through a careful and discriminating perusal of her poetry that a systematic idea or this impact can be made. Looking at Kamala Das's sense of helplessness in the face of stark realities of life, one is easily reminded of the Victorian xanthoma, loneliness and squalour that powerfully swayed such creative minds as that of Thomas Hardy. This sense of helplessness also reminds the Audenian gloom, the Spenderian disillusionment of the modern milieu. Somewhere in *The Waste Land*, T.S. Eliot rightly says, "I think we are in rat's alley/ where the dead men lost their bones" ("A Game of Chess," lines 115-16); and, of men and women as "a handful of dust;" or "a mound of bones;" or "a procession of shadows;" and of great cities as "barren rocks:"

> A heap of broken images,
> Where the sun beats,
> And the dead trees give no shelter,
> the cricket no relief,
> I will show you fear in a handful of dust.
>
> ("The Burial of the Dead," lines 22-30)

or,

> The road winding above
> among the mountains
> which are mountains
> or rock without water
> There is not even silence
> in the mountains
> But dry sterile thunder
> without rain
> There is not even solitude
> in the mountains
> But red sullen faces
> sneer and snarl
> from doors of muderacked houses.
>
> ("What the Thunder Said," lines 333-45)

Stephen Spender, too, like Kamala Das, talks of men as "withered flowers" as Hardy talks of them as "frosted leaves." In one of his poems, Stephen Spender, like Kamala Das, is greatly perturbed due to inhuman changes spawned by scientific revolution:

> Living now becomes withered like flowers
> In the baring burned city which has no use
> for us but as lives and death to fill
> with fury the guns blazing back on the powers
> That scorch our 'small pot' of blasted hours:
> Death we cannot refuse
> Where everything stops but the wishes that kill.
>
> ("In Memoriam," lines 333-40)

Kamala Das, likewise, being powerfully swayed by the onward march of science, woefully laments the replacement of green fields by the smokeless chimneys, the conversion of feeling hearts into rotten hearts and the transmogrification of happy villages by the disturbed, assaulted cities—the infested centres of imposters. This is all because of the growing impact of scientific knowledge—a plea Thomas Hardy himself puts forth so emphatically in *The Dynasts* as "the plethoric growth of knowledge simultaneously with the stunting of wisdom;"[39] and of which Auden, too, says:

> Smoke rises from factory in field
> Memory of fire: on all sides heard
> Vanishing music of isolated lark:
> From village square voice in hymn
> Men's voices.

(*Poem*, XVI)

Kamala Das, like T.S. Eliot, Stephen Spencer, Auden, Thomas Hardy, George Meredith and other modern agnostics powerfully feel the scientific impact *ad nauseum* even to the extent of feeling highly pessimistic. Kamala Das is well aware of the fact, like George Meredith, that the only redeeming feature for the survival of mankind is spiritual evolution. When all else collapses, spiritual struggle will provide mankind the essential wherewithal to survive. A civilization, whose interior is rotten, and which is *in toto* "undulatory, with iron and coal everywhere;" with "stinking slums as perennial hotbeds of fever and ague;" of which Charles Kingsley wrote much earlier as "Luddite mobs, meal mobs, farm riots, riots everywhere,"[40] can only survive if mankind as a whole takes recourse to spiritual evolution as enunciated by George Meredith, R.N. Tagore and Aurobindo. A close study of Kamala Das's poetry will reveal, rather strangely, almost the same approach for human survival.

Chronologically speaking, genesis of evolutionary theories dates back to Homer, whose *Iliad* and *Odyssey* have sufficient traces of sceptical gloom—a chief ingredient of evolutionism. Besides Homer, Empedocles, Aristotle and Lucretius are other ancient celebrities amongst the Greek and Roman philosophers in whose works the seminal idea of evolution can perspicuously be traced. Synoptically speaking, Empedocles conceived of a divine world in fetters of certain external forces: whereas Lucretius, with great fervour, preaches the science of Epicurean materialism, which would inevitably free humanity from a supernatural dread. The Pantheistic Averroism, the Scholastic Nominalism, and the Libertine Individualism are the three distinct channels of the evolutionary principles. It was further strengthened by Machiavelli, Pomponazzi, Rabelais and Giordano Bruno. During the seventeenth century, Bacon extended its frontiers with Hobbes, Looke, Rousseau and the Cambridge platonists. During the eighteenth century, Newton and his followers testified to its potency, and in the age preceding Darwin's, Buffon, Erasmus Darwin and Lamarck gave it a fairly concrete expression. As we approach the date of the publication of *The Origin of Species* (1859), adherence to the doctrine not only by the naturalists, but also by poets such as Goethe and novelists like George Meredith and Thomas Hardy, became comparatively frequent; and before the joint announcement of Darwin and Wallace, Herbert Spencer had been supporting and applying it vigorously in the field of psychology. Now, Kamala Das's reactions to the evolutionism are more or less psychological: for, they are not cent per cent as purely scientific as those of Thomas Hardy and Samuel Butler. Rather, they are nearer to the Meredithian, the Eliotian and the Thackerayean concepts. In fact, Kamala Das does accept the physical evolution of man, but she also treats Darwinism as incapable of fully explaining man's arcane process of growth and evolution.

One of the principal tenets of evolutionism is the physical evolution of man. The fittest of all naturally survives and the weakest decays. In other words, the principle of the survival of the fittest operates steadily in the process of evolution. Evolutionism, Darwinism, Mendalism, genetic theory and other modern scientific *isms* have explained man in terms of air, water, fire, earth, sky, etc., and have banished God from world, leading to a wholesale collapse of religion and ethics from man's life, divesting man, in summation, of the divine origin. Herbert Spencer and Freud applied emerging scientific *isms* on sociological and psychological evolution of man. Kamala Das's approach in his poetry is linked with psychological interplay of emotions and passions, which is more or less identical to the Cloughian attitude to human existence vis-a-vis science:

And as of old from Sinai top
God said that God is one,
By Science strict so speaks He now
To tell us, There is None.
Earth goes by chemical forces; Heaven's
A Mechanique Celeste.
And heart and mind of human kind
A watch-work as the rest.

("The New Sinai," p. 24)

Kamala Das feels helpless and despondent the moment she watches Science proclaiming, *veni, vidi, vice* which simply means—*I came, I saw, I conquered.* The Platonic concept of *anima mundi* does not seem to convince Kamala Das. She, therefore, seems to believe *the animula vagula* concept which is so enormously popular during the modern milieu. If Kamala Das's poetry is interpreted in the light of this concept, the readers will certainly receive fresh appraisal of her poetry. Take, for example, the following lines:

What is this drink but
The April sun, squeezed
Like an orange in
My glass? I sip the
Fire, I drink and drink
Again, I am drunk,
Yes, but on the gold
Of suns.

(*Summer in Calcutta*, p. 24)

Or, the following lines:

But, I shall some day return, losing
Nearly all, hurt by wind, sun and rain,
Too hurt by fierce happiness to want
A further jaunt or a further spell
Of freedom.

(*The Old Playhouse*, p. 48)

Or, the following lines:

> Love is Narcissus at
> the winter's edge,
> haunted
> By its own lonely face,
> and yet it must seek at last
> And end, a pure, total freedom,
> it must will the mirrors
> To shatter and the kind night
> to erase the water.
>
> (*The Old Playhouse*, pp. 1-2)

The above lines can certainly offer fresh interpretation and consequently a different appraisal of Kamala Das's poetry, if the indulgent reader follows the course suggested in the foregoing pages. This is merely a hypothesis, a new approach to appraise, to understand Kamala Das's poetry. Let us wait for the outcome, response and reaction thereof.

## NOTES AND REFERENCES

1. S.D. Sharma, "Kamala Das's Poetry: An Amatory Hiatus," *Thematic Dichotomy of Writing in Indian English, Indology and Culture* (New Delhi: PBD Publication, 1985), pp. 35-38.
2. *Ibid.*, p. 36.
3. *Ibid.*, pp. 35-38.
4. *Ibid.*, p. 38.
5. M.L. Rosenthal, *The New Poets: American and British Poetry since World War II* (London: Oxford University Press, 1967), p. 30.
6. Kamala Das, *My Story* (New Delhi: Sterling, 1976), p. 58.
7. D.J. Palmer, "Editorial," *Critical Quarterly*, Vol. 7, No. 1, Spring 1965, pp. 4-5.
8. M.L. Rosenthal, *The New Poets*, p. 35.
9. Barbara Kelves, "The Art of Poetry: Anne Sexton," *Anne Sexton: The Artist and Her Critics* (ed.) J.D. McClatchy (Bloomington: Indiana University Press, 1978), p. 12.
10. (Quoted) S.D. Sharma, *Aristotle's Poetics* (Delhi: 88 Publication, 1984), p. 158.

11. *Ibid.*, p. 159.
12. *Ibid.*, p. 162.
13. S.D. Sharma, *Longinus's On the Sublime* (Delhi: PBD Publication, 1985), p. 43.
14. (Quoted), *Ibid.*, p. 43.
15. *Ibid.*
16. (Quoted), *Ibid.*, p. 153.
17. *Ibid.*
18. (Quoted), *Ibid.*
19. *Ibid.*
20. S.S. Radha, *Yoga for the West* (Canada, USA: Timeless Books, 1978), p. 277.
21. A. Koestler, *The Act of Creation* (London: OUP, 1970), p. 689.
22. S.D. Sharma, *Perspectives on Creativity. Proceedings of the National Symposium* (ed.) (Pantnagar: Faculty of New Education, 1989), pp. 85-103 and 193-209.
23. S.D. Sharma, "Aesthetics: Sublimity and Creativity," *Longinus's On the Sublime* (Delhi: PBD Publication, 1985), pp. 149-88.
24. Kamala Das, *My Story,* p. 105.
25. *Ibid.*, p. 150.
26. S.D. Sharma, *Darwinism and Victorian Fiction* (Delhi: Shri Publishing House).
27. S.D. Sharma, "The Treatment of Death in Modern Indo-Anglian Poetry (1960-80)," *Love and Death in Indian Poetry in English* (ed.) S.N.A. Rizvi (Delhi: Doaba House, 1989), pp. 159-60.
28. *Ibid.*, p. 160.
29. S.D. Sharma, "Anita Desai," *Studies in Contemporary Indian English Short Story* (ed.) A.N. Dwivedi (Delhi: B.R. Publishing Corporation, 1991), pp. 25-43.
30. *Ibid.*, p. 25.
31. S.D. Sharma, "Where Shall We Go This Summer? A Crisis of Conscience and Values," *The Quest,* Vol. V, No. 2, December, 1991, pp. 1-9.
32. *Ibid.*, p. 7.
33. S.D. Sharma, "Tennyson's *In Memoriam:* A Repository of Evolutionism," *Agra University Journal of Research* (Letters), Vol. XXIV, Pt. II, July, 1975, pp. 47-54.

34. S.D. Sharma, "Aurobindo's *Savitri*: A Spiritual Pabulum," *BSSS*, Sect. II, Vol. X, No. 3-3-4, January, 1974, pp. 1-5.
35. S.D. Sharma, "Shelley and Peacock: A Radical Propinquity," *Pantnagar Journal of Research*, 3(2), July 1978, pp. 262-65.
36. S.D. Sharma, "Eunice De Souza's Satire," *Journal of Indian Writing in English (JIWE)*, Nos. 1 & 2, Vol. 10, January-July 1981, pp. 17-21.
37. S.D. Sharma, "Gauri Deshpande's Poetry," *Treveni (Journal of Indian Renaissance)*, Vol. 51, No. 2, July-September 1982, pp. 50-53.
38. S.D. Sharma, "D.H. Lawrence's Existential Vision," *Essays on D.H. Lawrence* (ed.) T.R. Sharma (Meerut: S.B. House, 1987), pp. 153-61.
39. Thomas Hardy, *The Dynasts* (London: OUP, 1956), Preface, p. iii.
40. Charles Kingsley, *Preface to Alton Looke* (London: OUP, 1980), p. 11.

# Chapter 7

# The Last Fifty Years of Indian Poetry in English: An Appraisal

*A.N. Dwivedi*

The last fifty years of Indian Poetry in English have witnessed an unprecedented growth in this *genre*. They have not only produced a rich harvest but also an immense variety and complexity. The noted critic, William Walsh, rightly remarks that the 'highest achievement' of Indian English writing is in fiction, in the work of Mulk Raj Anand, R.K. Narayan and Raja Rao, but the future, the promise, lies in poetry, in the work of Nissim Ezekiel, A.K. Ramanujan and R. Parthasarathy.[1] These three poets have been picked up by Walsh at random, and there are many more who deserve to join their rank, and of such poets Kamala Das, K.N. Daruwalla, Jayanta Mahapatra, Shiv K. Kumar, Pritish Nandy, Keshav Malik, Dom Moraes, R.R. Menon and a few others must be mentioned. Here it has to be recorded that the last fifty years of Indian Poetry in English mark a break with the past, or with the Romantic tradition, and coincide with the dawn of Independence in India. They are definitely the dividing-line between the colonial and post-colonial periods of Indian history.

Much of Indian Poetry in English written before Independence belonged to the Romantic tradition and showed a tendency towards idealism and escapism. Since it very inception in 1828 with the publication of *The Fakir of Jungheera and Other Poems* by Henry Derozio, this tendency became paramount. Derozio's work describes the strange vicissitudes of the Brahmin widow Nuleeni's unfortunate life and is full of Byronic echoes. Similarly, Kasiprasad Ghose's *The Shah or Ministrel* (1830) is, according to Prof. T.O.D. Dunn, "agreeably imitative and everywhere pleasing,"[2] betraying as it does the influence of Sir Walter Scott. The first great poet of India, Toru Dutt, is often compared to Keats, while Sarojini Naidu, the Nightingale of India, bears correspondences to Shelley (whom A.C. Swinburne called 'the perfect singing god').

Manmohan Ghose composed some scintillating verses on Love and Death, and his younger brother Sri Aurobindo, the Milton of India, produced poems of soaring and visionary nature, full of spiritual overtones and symbolism. Rabindranath Tagore's poetry abounds in moral and mystical strains, and this Nobel Laureate through his *Gitanjali* (1912) took the literary world by storm by irradiating the age-old wisdom of the Peast. With Tagore and Sri Aurobindo ended the age of what M.K. Naik calls "the major Indian-English romantics."[3] The minor romantics who followed Sri Aurobindo, like K.D. Sethna and N.K. Gupta, and the academicians like B.N. Seal, G.K. Chettur, Armando Menezes, and V.N. Bhushan wrote a derivative and inconsequential verse.

The post-Independence scenario is radically different from the pre-Independence one. Politics now ceased to be 'an idealistic pursuit,' and the poet assumed greater responsibility and self-confidence in his new role as a critic of the present, the past and himself, shaking off his dreams and visions. Historically, two poets are of great significance—Nissim Ezekiel (1924-2001) and P. Lal (1930- ). *Ezekiel's A Time to Change* signals dissociation from the past poetic practice as well as a change in personal life from a philosopher to a poet. Ezekiel not only wrote a number of poetical volumes but inspired a host of upcoming and talented poets like Monika Varma, Gieve Patel and Eunice de Souza and others by writing Introductions and Forewords to their works. As for P. Lal, a poet of a sort no doubt, he spearheaded a movement against the older school of poets and divided Indian English poetry into two categories Aurobindonian and non-Aurobindonian. Initially, P. Lal and his collaborator K.

Raghavendra Rao dismissed the Aurobindonians with a snigger, but later P. Lal condescended to issue the following statement:

> Sri Aurobindo happens to be our Milton, and Toru Dutt, Sarojini Naidu, Manmohan Ghose and Harindranath Chattopadhyaya our Romantic singing birds. They provide sufficient provocation to experiment afresh, set new standards, preserve what is vital in the tradition and give a definition to the needs of the present.[4]

This statement seems to have stemmed from the subsequent realization on the part of P. Lal that there are some other ways of writing poetry than mere modernistic way, than mere Yeats-Pound-Eliot technique.

It was in 1959 that P. Lal and K. Raghavendra Rao, while introducing their anthology titled *Modern Indo-Anglian Poetry*, laid down certain direction for 'new' poetry of the Sixties and thereafter. These directions are contained in the Kavita Manifesto, and may be briefly recounted here point-wise:

(1) We affirm our faith in a vital language as sufficient to write poetry in.

(2) We think that poetry must deal in concrete terms with concrete experience.

(3) Poetry must be free from propaganda.

(4) We recognise the value of discipline, but commend the effort to experiment.

(5) We condemn all forms of imitation and suggest five whip-strokes as punishment.

(6) We claim that the phase of Indo-Anglian romanticism ended with Sarojini Naidu.

(7) We realise the full-time nature of the poet's vocation if he is to do a good job.

(8) We emphasise the need for the private voice especially because we live in an age that tends so easily to demonstrations of mass approval and hysteria.[5]

Expressing his reactions to these autocratic directions, Pritish Nandy observes that new Kavita Manifesto is "an interesting document, hortatory, too-smart-by-half, aggressive, and full of illogic."[6] The Manifesto is like a trend-setter, but largely rhetorical and partly unrealistic. As a trend-setter, the Kavita Manifesto is a welcome development, but the point is that mere descriptions of 'dos' and 'don'ts' do not count much for a practitioner in poetry.

An inevitable outcome of this Manifesto is the shying away of modern Indian-English poets from the conventional form and diction and their speaking in a self-searching and self-assuring voice. After a long discourse with Eternity and God, they turned to themselves to seek answers to the problems of humanity at large. It is not suggested that lyricists and sonneteers were totally exiled from the kingdom of the Muse, but that even they became reflective and introspective in their approach to her. Take, for example, Kamala Das with all her lyricism and spontaneity and urgency of purpose. Even she becomes reflective and thoughtful in her utterances about herself:

> It is I who laugh, it is I who make love
> And then, feel, shame, it is I who lie dying
> With a rattle in my throat. I am sinner,
> I am saint. I am the beloved and the
> Betrayed.[7]

This utterance reminds us of man's 'middle state,' neither too high nor too low, as Alexander Pope writes in his *Essay on Man* (Epistle 11).[8] Kamala Das does not paint herself as all saint, all sinless; she rather presents herself as posted between evil and good. This is a realistic portraiture indeed. And all this she says in no traditional metre or language. Obviously, there is a good deal of self-searching in this passage. Another good example of the use of unconventional form and diction is A.K. Ramanujan's poem "Still Another View of Grace," wherein he writes thus:

> Bred Brahmin among singers of shivering hymns
> I shudder to the bone at hungers that roam the street
> beyond the constable's beat.

and again:

> Commandments crumbled
> in my father's past. Her tumbled hair suddenly known
> as silk in my angry hand, I shook a little
> and took her, behind the laws of my land.[9]

This poem makes use of glowing words and phrases, and yet is shorn of all superfluities and ostentations. Ramanujan inserts internal rhymes, instead of poetic metres, in it. Taken as a whole, the poem recalls to our minds what T.S. Eliot said about good and great poetry in his *Four Quartets* (1943):

> Where every word is at home,
> Taking its place to support the others,
> The word neither diffident, nor ostentatious.
> The complete consort dancing together.[10]

This is what is expected of 'new' Indian English poetry, but unfortunately much of it does not meet the expectation.

One of the raging problems before the Indian English writers, especially poets, is the employment of a foreign tongue for the expression of an essentially native talent. This problem, coupled with the handling of English rhyme and rhythm, has racked many a thinking mind right from the beginning of Indian Poetry in English. This problem was discussed at some length in a symposium arranged by the Writers Workshop, the proceedings of which were published in the second number of *Miscellany* (1960). In that discussion, P. Lal maintained that "only in English can real Indian poetry be written; any other poetry is likely to be Bengali-slanted or Gujarati-biased, and so on," and that "Only Indian writing in English can hope to attain the 'Indian' flavour." Anita Desai spoke of 'a marvellous elasticity and expressiveness' in the English language. Deb Kumar Das, a poet himself, observed that, of the three languages (Sanskrit, Hindi and English), English alone was 'a living language,' which could be shaped by creative minds. Pradip Sen commended the capability of English to express 'Indian imagery and tradition.' Perhaps the need of the hour is to make a bold and fruitful use of the English language in our creative ventures in both prose and poetry. Our Constitution recognizes English as one of our languages, and Sahitya Akademi awards are being given to outstanding works in English. In fiction, the 'Big Three'—Mulk Raj Anand, R.K. Narayan, and Raja Rao—, Manohar Malgonkar, Bhabani Bhattacharya, Anita Desai, Arun Joshi and a few others have received this award, and in poetry a few lucky ones have benefited by it,—like Nissim Ezekiel, K.N. Daruwalla, Jayanta Mahapatra, Kamala Das, and Shiv K. Kumar.

Outside India, too, some of our creative writers have established their supremacy in English, and we may mention Vikram Seth, V.S. Naipaul (who is of Indian stock), Salman Rushdie, Arundhati Roy, Jhumpa Lahiri, Dom Moraes, Arun Kolatkar, and Jayanta Mahapatra. These illustrious sons and daughters of India have done us proud of their literary achievements. As regards the use of language by them, Raja Rao has aptly pointed out that it must carry the indigenous tone and colour and that it must not imitate the Westerners as their models. Let us see what Raja Rao has to say on this issue:

> One has to convey in a language that is not one's own the spirit that is one's own. One has to convey the various shades and omissions of a certain thought-movement that looks maltreated in an alien language. I use the word 'alien' yet English is not really an alien language to us. It is the language of our intellectual make-up—like Sanskrit or Persian was before—but not of our emotional make-up. We are all instinctively bilingual. We cannot write like the English. We should not. We cannot write only as Indians. We have grown to look at the large world as part of us. Our method of expression therefore has to be a dialect which will some day prove to be as distinctive and colourful as the Irish or the American.[11]

So Raja Rao clearly mentions here that though English is not our mother-tongue, we have learnt it so efficiently that we can make it a vehicle of our creative expression. The most emphatic answer to the question of the use of language comes from one of our celebrated poets, Kamala Das, who pens down the following lines:

> I am Indian, very brown, born in
> Malabar, I speak three languages, write in
> Two, dream in one. Don't write in English, they said,
> English is not your mother-tongue, Why not leave
> Me alone, critics, friends, visiting cousins,
> Every one of you? The language I speak
> Becomes mine, its distortions, its queernesses
> All mine, mine alone. It is half English, half

Indian, funny perhaps, but it is honest,
It is as human, as I am human, don't
You see? It voices my joys, my longings, my
Hopes, and it is useful to me as cawing
Is to crows or roaring to the lions, it
Is human speech, the speech of the mind.[12]

This is certainly a strong defence of Indian Poetry in English. And we need not feel brow-beaten about it. Gone are the days when Indian variety of English was looked down upon and when it was greeted with such contemptuous appellations as 'Babu English,' 'Pidgin English,' and 'Chee-Chee English.'

Now, we should have a bird's eye-view of the main trends and voices in Indian English poetry during the post-Independence era. No doubt, much of Indian English poetry produced during this period lacks authenticity and individuality, but some genuine poetry has also been published and a few names stand out in the matter. As stated earlier, P. Lal and Nissim Ezekiel blow the bugle of revolt against the conventional mode of writing. While P. Lal, mostly a poet of beauty and love, remains indigenous and autochthonous in his works, Nissim Ezekiel belonging to a Bene-Israel family, which migrated to India long ago, seems to be acutely conscious of his estrangement and alienation. After doing some fine pieces of poetry, P. Lal turned to 'translations' or better still 'transcreations' of Indian classics and epics, but Ezekiel remained committed to poetry unto the very last. Ezekiel is a poet of the city of Bombay and also wrote charming poems on Indian life and situations. His 'Indian Poems in Indian English' are really lively and topical. William Walsh rightly states that Ezekiel's poetry is "intellectually complex, mobile in phrasing, fastidious in diction, and austere in acceptance."[13]

Like Ezekiel, Dom Moraes also suffers from a sense of alienation from his roots. Being a Goan Christian by birth, he became a British citizen and published a number of poetical works. He was heavily influenced by the work of three modern poets, Eliot, Auden and Spender.[14] He began writing poetry when he was only twelve and made his mark in it with *A Beginning* (1957). Many if his poems have "a confessional cast and a subjective approach."[15] There is a reflective strain in them as well as "as a self-destroying exile's nostalgia and melancholy."[16]

Poets like A.K. Ramanujan, R. Parthasarathy and Arun Kolatkar are preoccupied with 'the problem of roots' and their search for self and society is really intense and staggering. Of these poets, Ramanujan conjures up early familial memories and childhood impressions and associations with a wonderful success. He is determined to 'seek and find/ My particular hell in my Hindu mind.' Some of his poems in *Second Sight* (1986) and *The Black Hen* (1995) deal with the Hindu myths and legends, the Hindu gods and goddesses. As for Parthasarathy, he is also obsessed with his Tamil heritage. In a repentant mood he says in his poetic autobiography, *Rough Passage* (1977), as follows:

> My tongue in English chains,
> I return, after a generation, to you
> I am at the end
> Of my Dravidic tether,
> Hunger for you unassuaged.
> I falter, stumble.[17]

After this book, Parthasarathy has published no poetry. And Arun Kolatkar, who won the Commonwealth Poetry Prize for his *Jejuri* (1976), discloses powerfully "the surrealistic similarities between an ossified Hindu religious tradition and an equally rigid scientific civilization represented by the railway station" and shows "the superiority of a value system older than both these."[18] There is a remarkable network of images and symbols in this poetical volume.

A distinct group of Parsi poets has made notable contributions to contemporary Indian English poetry; the group comprises K.N. Daruwalla, Gieve Patel and Adil Jussawalla. Of these poets, Daruwalla is a prolific writer who avoids sentimentality and morbidity in his works. He is a refreshing poet, not stale and sterile like many city-bred writers, and writes about the landscape of North India. The poems like "Ghaghra in Space," "Death of a Bird," "In the Tarai," "Haranag," and "The People" are enough to corroborate the statement. Daruwalla demonstrates in his poetry "depth of feeling, economy of language and originality of insight," according to Nissim Ezekiel.[19] One can't resist the temptation of mentioning his remarkable evocation of the river Ganga at Varanasi with all its *ghats* in *Crossing of Rivers* (1977, O.U.P.). The other poet, Gieve Patel, is a medical student and has written much on the anatomy of human body. His poetical work, *How Do You Withstand, Body* (1976), is of this type. His poem, "Naryal Purnima," provides him an occasion to "diagnose his own attitudes in the hope of knowing himself better as a human being."[20] Patel sympathises with the poor and the oppressed—those who have been denied the right to live. The third Parsi Poet, Adil Jussawalla, looks at the prevailing Indian scene with compassion on his return from the West after a long gap. He is also bothered about his identity for a while, but later when he settles down in Bombay he becomes calm and composed. His poems like "Approaching Santa Cruz" and "Sea Breeze, Bombay" seem to suggest it tacitly.

There is another group of poets called 'academicians,' and Shiv K. Kumar, Jayanta Mahapatra, A.K. Mehrotra, O.P. Bhatnagar, A.N. Dwivedi, Niranjan Mohanty, Saleem Peeradina, Syed Amanuddin, Syed Ameeruddin, and many others belong to this group. They come from the world of teaching and carry their learning through their works. Irony and wit are the hallmarks of their poetry. Thus, Shiv K. Kumar writes in his poem "Broken Columns" as follows:

> I carry my bride home—
> a fungal seed to breed hydras.
> The first sunrise leaves at my door
> a dead cockroach
> in the milk-bottle,
> news of the porcupine's resurrection
> and a defaced horoscope.[21]

Jayanta Mahapatra is well-known as a poet of Oriya landscape and seascape as well as for his startling imagery and catching diction. A.K. Mehrotra is primarily an experimentalist in 'surrealism' (a French movement of the 1920s) who makes his poetry out of "incongruity, choice and free association."[22] Both Mahapatra and Mehrotra are addicted to the drug of imagery. O.P. Bhatnagar's ironic vision comes out vividly in his poetry, and A.N. Dwivedi is a social realist having a keen eye on the social and political developments around him. In their innovative application of language and rhythm, Dwivedi and Syed Amanuddin come close to each other. This is how Syed writes in one of his poems:

> love me for what I am
> I love you what you are
> lets create a culture of younme.[23]

This extract reminds us of the poetic practice of E.E. Cummings, a famous American poet. Saleem Peeradina and Niranjan Mohanty employ the modern idioms, but Syed Ameeruddin glows in the 'maudlin mud' and sentimentality.

There are two poets (maybe, many more) belonging to the realm of journalism—Keshav Malik and Rakshat Puri. Malik was erstwhile the editor of *Thought*, a defunct literary magazine published weekly from Delhi, and of *Indian Literature*, a bimonthly published by the Sahitya Akademi of New Delhi. He has produced several volumes of poetry to date, beginning with *The Lake Surface* (1959). His fine artistic taste and mellow experience clearly surface in them. He takes a tolerant view of the human world and seems to be inspired from within. David Daiches judiciously remarked about three decades ago that Malik's poetry "represents a notable achievement" in English.[24] The other journalist poet, Rakshat Puri, has published at least three volumes of poetry, including *Nineteen Poems* (1972). Many of his poems are expressions of an agonized sensibility in the fear-ridden nuclear age.

Some highly individualistic voices and talents have yet not been mentioned in this hurried survey. Pritish Nandy, Rabindranath Menon, Dilip Chitre, Sharat Chandra, K.D. Katrak, and Vikram Seth are some of them. Pritish Nandy is a very fine poet indeed. According to a practising poet, Gauri Deshpande, Nandy is "innovative and profuse"[25] in his poetry. After Rabindranath Tagore, he is one great poet who has produced prose poems packed with passion, pulse and power (to use a Whitmanian expression). One such poem is "Wild Horses Rage in Your Tresses," where he writes thus:

Wild horses rage in your tresses on this savage
night of desire when primal fire breaks
through your loins
descend the dark mountain of sorrow tonight
let a black rain of stars bathe your
limbs in blood
wild virgin of death teach me the fury of the night
teach me to bleed and not feel pain teach me
to suffer the anguish of words.[26]

The poem is undoubtedly sweepy and sensuous, violent and impetuous. As for Menon, who hails from bureaucracy, he has published about a dozen volumes of poetry—almost all from Writers Workshop, barring *Sounds of Silence* (1993)—to this day. His poems appear regularly in different magazines and periodicals, particularly in *New Swatantra Times* (Hyderabad) and *The Quest* (Ranchi). Dilip Chitre, like Arun Kolatkar, is a bilingual poet. He writes in Marathi too. He privately published two hundred copies of *Ambulance Ride* in 1972, and his *Travelling in a Cage* appeared in 1980. His poems are mostly autobiographical and cast in a variety of moods. Chitre shows "his obsessions with sex, madness and death," as Bruce King puts it.[27] G.S. Sharat Chandra is like A.K. Ramanujan in showing his sense of insecurity in the United States, except when he is with his family members. Sharat's *Bharat Natyam Dancer* describes an artist—a heavy-footed dancer—who is acclaimed as a fine one by the applauding audience. His poem "Abdul and Fatima" is a moving tale of a wayside coconut seller and his daughter. K.D. Katrak, who runs an advertising agency in Bombay, has produced two volumes of poetry titled *A Journal of the Way and Diversions by the Wayside* (both published in 1969 from Writers Workshop). Elizabeth Reuben thinks that Katrak's works do not have "overwhelming floods of emotion, and no self-conscious Indianness."[28] In the matter of Indianness, he is contrasted to many other Indian English poets—Ezekiel, Ramanujan, Daruwalla, Mahapatra, V.K. Gokak, K.R. Srinivasa Iyengar, Krishna Srinivas, K.V.S. Murti, A.N. Dwivedi, etc. Harish Raizada characterizes Katrak's poetry as "poetry for itself" and opines that it "conveys no ethical 'message.'"[29] And

Vikram Seth, who has lived long in London, is a reputed poet torn asunder between the twin pulls of India and the West. His poetical volumes include *The Humble Administrator's Garden* (1985), which earned the Commonwealth Poetry Prize for Asia, and *The Golden Gate* (1986), a long novel in verse. Many of his poems are concerned with 'the nature of art.' Seth seems to delight in exile and is in contrast to the attitude of Sharat Chandra or Ramanujan in this respect. Commenting on his poetry, Bruce King says that it has "a highly self-conscious traditional poetic from and prosody."[30]

Well, it will be unfair to the fairer sex not to turn our attention to. Some women writers have woven their magic yarn in verses too. Kamala Das, Gauri Deshpande and Monika Varma are of good stature; Lila Ray and Margaret Chatterjee are also of the same rank and status. Very briefly I shall discuss them here. Kamala Das, whose personal life has been full of fluctuations, is very popular poetess, though she has published barely three volumes of English poetry. *Summer in Calcutta* (1965), *The Descendants* (1967), and *The Old Playhouse and Other Poems* (1973). She is largely a celebrant of the body, of its hungers and lusts, and writes like a Confessional poet without any inhibitions. So is also Gauri Deshpande with her three volumes. Deshpande employs the themes of love and human relationships in her poetry. Most of her poems create the effect of embarrassment in love, not of its intensity. She is at her best in short poems like "The Female of the Species" where her female feelings come out vividly:

> Sometimes you want to talk
> About love and despair
> And the ungratefulness of children.
> A man is no use whatever then.[31]

But such poems are not too many there. The third poetess, Monika Varma, has been profuse yet controlled in the articulation of her emotions. Her first volume, *Dragonflies Draw Flame* (1963), carried a thoughtful Preface by Nissim Ezekiel. She has also done a few works of translation, like Jayadeva's *Gita Govinda* (1968). As a poet, she remains sober and decent throughout; she, in fact, serves as an antidote to Kamala Das and Gauri

Deshpande. She tries to lift womankind above mere "sighs and thighs,"[32] as she puts it. She counsels the young ones thus:

> Hold your lamentations,
> in secret their Ariadne waits.[33]

In the poem "The Essence of Living," she asserts that "the essence of living is beauty" and "the flavour of love is living."[34] For Lila Ray and Margaret Chatterjee, English is the mother-tongue. Lila is an American and Margaret is a British by birth, and both have produced some good poetry, and both have tried to identify themselves with India. Speaking of Margaret, Basil Vitsaxis writes she has come to occupy, "an established place as a great poetess."[35]

Besides these poetesses, a number of other women writers have also yielded a fine harvest of poetry. A few names coming readily to my mind are: Ira De, Tapati Mookerji, Tilottama Rajan, Vimala Rao, Malti Rao, Sunita Namjoshi, Gauri Pant, Roshen Alkazi, Mamta Kalia, Eunice de Souza, Melanie Silgardo, Meena Alexander, Lakshmi Kannan, and Sunita Jain. Time and space do not permit me to furnish information about them now and here.

Similar is the case with some male poets too. Of such poets, we may mention Pranab Bandyopadhyay, S.C. Saha, C.S. Singh, Ravi Nandan Sinha, R.C. Shukla, I.H. Rizwi, D.C. Chambial, I.K. Sharma, R.K. Singh, B.K. Dubey, Suresh Kohli, Mahanand Sharma, and a few others. Many male and female poets mentioned cursorily here demonstrate their poetic talent and aptitude, not necessarily the fulfillment that befalls with maturity of mind and commitment to art.

This much about achievement of Indian English Poetry of today. Now some of its weakness. Perhaps one of its drawbacks is the "paucity of diction."[36] Barring a few major poets, there are many who are prone to repetitiveness of phraseology, vocabulary and construction. Also, Indian English poets have not experimented with form in a big way. The 'prose poems' of Pritish Nandy and Kamala Das and A.K. Ramanujan are the only exceptions. Ezekiel and Katrak and Dwivedi have used rhymed verses, but many have resorted to *vers libré*, thinking that they become 'modern' thereby. A third weakness of Indian English poetry of our day is that it lacks light-hearted verse. A few exceptions are there—like Ezekiel, S. Santhi, Eunice de Souza, and Ramanujan. A fourth weakness is its pro-city character, reminding us of the practice of Augustan poets like Pope. K.N. Daruwalla and Jayanta Mahapatra are again exceptions in this matter. A fifth charge against this brand of poetry is that it miserably lacks "social consciousness,"[37] except in the writings of Ezekiel, Mahapatra, Gieve Patel, Saleem Peeradina and Dwivedi.

Some scholars have suggested that much of Indian English poetry being written presently is 'trash' and 'rubbish,' and there is a grain of truth about what they say. B.K. Das in one of his papers remarked: "One chief danger to Indian English Poetry is the addition of a cart-load of bad poetry to thin body of genuine and good poetry."[38] Many protesters are roaming around. M.K. Naik also thinks that "the new Indian English poet has not so far produced a single work which can be hailed as acknowledged masterpiece."[39]

These weakness, as pointed out by various scholars, must not blind us to some genuine Indian English Poetry of our times. We need to develop a healthy and positive attitude towards it. While reading an anthology titled *Nine Indian Women Poets* (Delhi: O.U.P., 1997), I came to realize the diversity and complexity of this brand of poetry. Then I was suddenly reminded of the inspiring statement of A.K. Ramanujan made in the course of an interview in Delhi. The interviewer asked him about the fate of some three hundred Indian poets writing in English today. Ramanujan's instant reply was: "There are nearly one thousand poets in America; so 'three hundred' is not a staggering figure." He then hastened to add: "I wish good luck to all of them." This is the sort of attitude needed towards contemporary Indian English poets and their poetry. We must not approach them with pre-conceived notions and inhibitive attitudes. We should promote the cause of Indian English poetry and render it more authentic, individualistic and innovative. Frankly speaking, we must not carry 'a bale of biles' against it but 'a bag of blessings' for it. Then only it will be able to flourish in the right direction.

## NOTES

1. William Walsh, "Introduction," *Reading in Commonwealth Literature* (Oxford: At the Claredon Press, 1973), xviii.
2. T.O.D. Dunn, *The Bengali Writers of English Verse* (London & Bombay: Longmans, Green & Co., 1918), 5.
3. M.K. Naik, "The Achievement of Indian English Poetry," *Dimensions of Indian English Literature* (New Delhi: Sterling Publishers, 1984), 9.
4. Cited from K.R. Srinivasa Iyengar, *Indian Writing in English* (Bombay: Asia Publishing House, 1973), 653.
5. Pritish Nandy, "Introduction," *Indian Poetry in English Today* (New Delhi: Sterling Publishers, 1973), 12-13.
6. *Ibid.*, 13.
7. Kamala Das, "An Introduction," *Indian Poetry in English: An Anthology,* ed. A.N. Dwivedi (New Delhi: Arnold-Heinemann, 1980), 125.
8. Cited from Pope, *Fifteen Poets* (London: Oxford University Press, 1965 ELBS ed.), 186.
9. A.K. Ramanujan, "Still Another View of Grace," *Indian Poetry in English,* ed. A.N. Dwivedi, 118.
10. T.S. Eliot, "Little Gidding," *Four Quartets* (London: Faber & Faber, 1943), 11. 217-223.
11. Raja Rao, "Foreword," *Kanthapura,* ed. C.D. Narasimhaiah (Madras: Oxford University Press, 1974), v-vi.
12. Kamala Das, "An Introduction," *Indian Poetry in English,* ed. A.N. Dwivedi, 124.
13. William Walsh, *Commonwealth Literature* (London: Oxford University Press, 1970), 65.
14. P. Lal, "Dom Moraes: Stray Notes on His Poetry," *Critical Essays on Indian Writing in English,* ed. M.K. Naik, S.K. Desai & G.S. Amur (Dharwar: Karnatak University, 1972), 139.
15. A.N. Dwivedi, *Indo-Anglian Poetry* (Allahabad: Kitab Mahal, 1979), 253.
16. P. Lal, *loc. cit.,* 142.
17. R. Parthasarathy, from *Rough Passage, Ten Twentieth-Century Indian Poets* (Delhi: Oxford University Press, 1979), 80.
18. M.K. Naik, *loc. cit.*, 11.
19. Nissim Ezekiel, "K.N. Daruwalla," *Contemporary Indian Poetry in English,* ed. Saleem Peeradina (Madras & Delhi: The Macmillan Company of India, 1972), 67.

20. R. Parthasarathy, "Gieve Patel," *Ten Twentieth-Century Indian Poets* (Delhi: Oxford University Press, 1979), 85.
21. Shiv K. Kumar, *Woodpeckers* (London: Sidgwick & Jackson, 1979), 14-15.
22. Bruce King, *Modern Indian Poetry in English* (Delhi: Oxford University Press, 1987), 187.
23. Syed Amanuddin, *The Age of Female Eunuchs* (Sumter: Poetry Eastwest, 1974), 34.
24. Cited from A.N. Dwivedi, *Indo-Anglian Poetry*, 257.
25. Gauri Deshpande, *An Anthology of Indo-English Poetry* (Delhi: Orient Paperbacks, n.d.), 14.
26. Cited from A.N. Dwivedi, *Indo-Anglian Poetry*, 261.
27. Bruce King, *Modern Indian Poetry in English*, 171.
28. Elizabeth Reuben, "K.D. Katrak," *Contemporary Indian Poetry in English,* ed. Saleem Peeradina (Delhi: Orient Paperbacks, n.d.), 59.
29. Harish Raizada, '"Poetry for itself: The Poetry of K.D. Katrak," *Studies in Contemporary Indo-English Verse: A Collection of Critical Essays on Male Poets,* ed. A.N. Dwivedi (Bareilly: Prakash Book Depot, 1984), 129.
30. Bruce King, *op. cit.*, 229.
31. Gauri Deshpande, "The Female of the Species," *Contemporary Indian Poetry in English,* ed. Saleem Peeradina (Delhi: Orient Paperbacks, n.d.), 89.
32. Monika Varma, "Gauri Deshpande," *Facing Four* (Calcutta: Writers Workshop, 1973), 24.
33. Monika Varma, "The Young Ones," *Green Leaves and Gold* (Calcutta: Writers Workshop, 1970), 11.
34. Monika Varma, "The Essence of Living," *Gita Govinda and Other Poems* (Calcutta: Writers Workshop, 1968), 15.
35. Basil Vitsaxis, "Some Contemporary Indian Women Poets," *Commonwealth Quarterly*, 3, No. 9 (December 1978), 36.
36. Gauri Deshpande, "Foreword," *An Anthology of Indo-English Poetry* (Delhi: Orient Paperbacks, n.d.), 8.
37. *Ibid.*, 13.
38. B.K. Das, "Some Indian English Poets of the Seventies," *Indian Literature,* XXV, No. 3 (May-June 1982), 108.
39. M.K. Naik, *loc. cit.*, 12.

SECTION – B

# INDIAN ENGLISH FICTION

# Chapter 8

# Humanistic Trends in Contemporary Indo-English Fiction

*J.P. Tripathi*

Ever since creation man is regarded as the supreme being on the planet, next only to God, the paragon of animals, a strange piece of work in Shakespeare's view. His interest in the universe is considered paramount although discoveries of modern science have brought about a great change. Some people consider him divine and his suffering and primordial fall from heaven have aroused protest and rebellion. Most of literature written in the world so far sings of man's joys and sorrows, rise and fall in the world. Voices are raised against segregation and differentiation of any type. Of late interests of woman and her welfare have drawn international attention and a feminist chore is audible world wide. Rebellion against tradition, established practices of society, scheme of God's controlling the universe, anything which baffles human efforts is a typical note of modern writing. Humanism or the supreme interest of man is the central motive behind all such writings particularly contemporary Indo-English fiction.

Among 'the Big Three' novelists of Indo-English fiction, in Mulk Raj Anand humanism acquires a socialistic and realistic concern, in R.K. Narayan it has social and artistic colour, in Raja Rao it acquires metaphysical and philosophic garb. In Bhabani Bhattacharya it retains social and realistic colour and in Arun Joshi it takes an existential form. In Kamala Markandaya social concerns acquire a Hardian note. In Anita Desai humanism centres round the revelation of human psyche and sufferings particularly of women caused by psychic and emotional disharmony. In Shashi Deshpande humanism acquires cultural and also spiritual overtones. In Arundhati Roy there is a clear note of feminist preoccupation with psychological and romantic notions of repression and fulfillment of the ego and the result. Many rebellious tendencies against social and religious practices and institutions are notable.

In this paper we shall confine ourselves to the works published in nineteen-eighties and onwards. However, cursory references to certain works before the eighties will also be made. In Raja Rao's first novel *Kanthapura* the central concern is the alleviation of the sufferings of the Indian masses by driving away the British rulers from India and giving the people the right to rule themselves and thus get rid of their suffering.[1] In *The Serpent and the Rope* the core issue is the psychic wound received by Ramaswamy from the separation of his French wife and beloved Madeleine and his determination to go to his Guru for the healing of his wound for survival in life.[2] In *The Cat and Shakespeare* the general issue is suffering caused by the World War and the rampant corruption and nepotism in the Indian polity.[3] In *Comrade Kirrilov* the central issue is Padmanabha's dream (humanistic turned into socialistic) of removing suffering of the world through a communist paradise.[4] In *The Chessmaster and His Moves* the predicament of man and his destiny as a chesspiece in the hands of the divine player is the central issue—this is humanism rising into spiritualism and devotion. Sufferings can be assuaged by resignation.[5] In *The Serpent and the Rope*, Ramaswamy's heart was lacerated by separation from Madeleine and Savitri. The burning pain of his heart was unrelieved. Hope of comfort coming from the Guru was only a distant dream and so the humanistic appeal of the novel was great. At the close of *The Chessmaster and His Moves* Sivaram Sastri, separated from Suzanne and Jaya talks of the burning[6] fire in Rama's heart at the separation from Sita in Bhavabhuti but he gets comforted by sleeping with his head on his sister Uma's bosom.[7] The fire is assuaged. Beloved's love is substituted by sister's love, a part of his own soul. Besides, the sense of detachment permeating the novel balances the humanistic grudge against the forces that be and terminates in resignation.[7a]

The early works of Kamala Markandaya, such as *Nectar in a Sieve* and *A Handful of Rice* present a purely humanistic perspective emphasizing the human sufferings and vicissitudes, poverty, hunger, degradation caused by nature, society, destiny or the universal forces. *The Nowhere Man* presents the pitiable plight of a South Indian lodged in London, victimised by black-white hatred and, as a consequence of a cruel stroke of destiny, suffering from leprosy in his last days and falling a victim to racial fanaticism. The dragon of racial fanaticism may endanger the future of mankind and may cause immense suffering—this is the message. *The Golden Honeycomb* (1977) has a historical and political rather than humanistic perspective. However, the predominant motive of humanism colours the human spectacle in *The Pleasure City*[8] (1982) in which a multinational is building a pleasure resort for the affluent on the sea coast displacing fishermen of a village. A truly 'Deserted Village' theme, like one used in *Nectar in a Sieve* (1954) is being used here also. However, some well-off people have a humanitarian attitude and are desirous of helping the displaced fishermen. But the most powerful humanistic touches belong to her early works.

Deepest humanistic note is audible in Bhabani Bhattacharyas earliest work, *So Many Hungers*.[9] The human sufferings and tragic events caused by the World War and the man-made famine in India will continue to ring responsive chords in sensitive readers for long. The Bengal farmers and their women, their hunger and displacement from the villages, the masses moving to Calcutta, the deaths from hunger are most unforgettable and powerful scenes in fiction.

The humanistic appeal of Anita Desai is not so powerful as she deals with the psychological problems of isolated individuals of the upper class and the middle class. Sufferings in her works are not caused by nature or invisible powers. Most of them are caused by unsympathetic and unresponsive human beings.

The sufferings of Nanda Kaul and Raka arouse keen responses in the readers because both suffer partly from destitution—Nanda Kaul is love-impoverished and deserted in love by her husband. Raka is a victim of the inhuman treatment meted out by her father to her mother Tara—her emotional imbalance is caused by the sight of her mother's misery. Ila Das is a victim of barbarous cruelty by a villager guided by blind greed and sex hunger. Thus, the sight in *Fire on the Mountain*[10] arouses humanistic appeal. In *Clear Light of Day* humanistic note partly turns into feminist note. The sufferings of Bimla Das and the Mishra sisters arouse great sympathy and sometimes mild anger against Raja and the Mishra brothers who are self-centred and given to enjoying life although the sisters suffer for them. It is Bim and the Mishra sisters who struggle very hard to sustain their respective families. But Bim's sufferings are voluntary and the result of her choice and character and these add to her stature as a woman and take away the pungency of feminist anger. Common people are guided more by awe and respect for heroic figures rather than bare sympathy.

Baumgartner's plight in the novel *Baumgartner's Bombay*[11] is pathetic. Victim of Nazi hatred of the Jew, he is by circumstances, forced out of Germany and comes to India for shelter and for some kind of business arising out of his parental trade of artistic furniture. But the iron claw of Nazism, and greed lead to his murder in his own house in Bombay. A German Aryan tourist whom he entertains in his own house kills him during night for hatred and for greed. The novelist allows freedom to the reader to draw his own conclusion.

Mild notes of humanistic sympathy are aroused by the plight of Uma who suffers a lot in the novel *Fasting Feasting*.[12] She is an unfortunate girl as nature has given her only unattractive facial features; besides she is gifted with almost below average intelligence so that she cannot get through her examinations and has to prostrate herself on the feet of her school mistress for promotion. As a result of her poor features and intelligence she is rejected by many families for marriage. She is rejected by Syals; Goels grab her dowry and reject her hand. Finally she is married to an old, already married, groom with four children.[13]

Besides she suffers from fits and some fear that she is possessed. She is married and divorced[14] and becomes a human wreck with a stoop[15] in so young an age.

Feminist anger is aroused against her parents who do not allow her to work as matron of the dormitory.[16] We feel unhappy over the plight of a female child in a Hindu family being treated indifferently as against the male child who dominates the family. Uma is exploited by her own parents and has to serve them almost as a servant. She has no independent identity and cannot use the family phone or go to Bombay for the treatment of her eye.[17]

The character of Mira Masi, the typical Hindu married woman widowed before going to her husband's arouses humanistic and feminist sentiments in the reader. She is unwanted everywhere and suffers immensely in life and turns religion into panacea for her sufferings.

Another case arousing humanistic sympathy is that of Anamika, Uma's cousin who is the daughter of a prosperous lawyer Bakul uncle in Bombay. Anamika is sharp and talented mentally, physically very attractive, who distinguishes herself as a student by winning a foreign scholarship to Oxford.[18] The novelist's comment on her is "Wherever Anamika was, there was moderation, good sense and calm."[19] But by a strange mischance she is married to a man who is heartless and sees his mother mistreat and beat her—"Anamika was beaten regularly by her mother-in-law while her husband stoodby and approved or, at least, did not object."[20] The rumour is—"she had a miscarriage at home, it was said, after a beating."[21] As a result she is damaged and flawed as a woman and cannot bear children. She could be sent back to her father's. Anamika, such a brilliant girl, becomes permanently frustrated. The result is she commits suicide. "Then she poured the kerosene over herself. Then she struck a match. She set herself alight."[22]

The cord of humanistic sympathy is strung, again, by the case of Melanie who is the daughter of a prosperous American family, the Pattons; but she is a victim of discrimination in America like a girl discriminated against a boy in India. Arun,

Uma's younger brother, who has gone to America for higher education sees a strange similarity between Melanie and Uma.

Then Arun does see a resemblance to something he knows: a resemblance to the contorted face of an enraged sister who, failing to express her outrage against neglect, against misunderstanding, against inattention to her unique and singular being and its hungers, merely spits and froths in ineffectual protest.[23] Melanie is given to relish over-eating of candies and then vomiting and becomes a neurotic case, later cured by a psychiatrist. Thus girls in both the Continents, in America as well as India, are the victims of human—social and parental indifference. Humanistic sympathy is aroused by Uma who is a victim of misfortune and hostile or indifferent destiny.

Shashi Deshpande, a woman novelist of the younger generation, is preoccupied with the interest of women and their state in Indian society and large traditional joint families. Supremacy of male children and men in Indian families arouses a mild sense of anger and feminist anger in most of her novels. Mistreatment of women and their sufferings generate mild anger and humanistic concern. Her humanism leads to a sense of rebellion against tradition. She balances her opinions of women as victims of male apathy or cruelty by showing sometimes men as victims of female cruelty. In most of the cases sufferings of married ladies of the higher middle class are brought into light.

A very pathetic incident arousing a lot of sympathy in the readers in the novel *That Long Silence* is the suicide of Kusum, Vanitamami's niece who had gone crazy and jumped in a well. Her death is welcome to many: "But it was a good thing in a way. She was of no use to anyone after she went crazy, nobody needed her."[24] Right from the beginning of her life Kusum carried the aura of defeat. She suffered all along and her suffering seeped into Jaya, the narrator heroine's soul.

Sufferings are inherent to women, so Nayana the female servant thinks that birth and life of girls are always a burden: "Why give birth to a girl, behuji, who'll only suffer because of men all her life."[25] Jaya realises she has no liberty. "And I knew I was not free. I could feel the burden of his wanting, the burden of his clinging."[26] Woman, as the female human species is to play a servile role of waiting, and not doing things of her own accord: "Wait until you get married. Wait until your husband comes. Wait until you go to your in-law's home. Wait until you have kids."[27] Woman's eternal dependence on man is the misery of a woman—this is Jaya's misery. Jaya is the model of feminist sympathy for the plight of women. Mohan thinks women in the past, Jaya's mother for instance, were tough and she finds them miserable.

"He saw strength in the woman sitting silently in front of the fire, but I saw despair. I saw a despair so great that it would not voice itself. I saw a struggle so bitter that silence was the only weapon. Silence and surrender."[28] In the novel women are shown as bundles of sufferings with Jaya's mother victimised by her father's temperamental explosions in which the food served to her, lacking in fresh chutney is thrown on the wall and the mother has to drudge again for cooking fresh food late in the night. Vimala's ovarian tumour leading to a lot of bleeding inspires a good deal of pathos in the readers about which the doctor declares, "It's too late for surgery too late for anything."[29] Living, doing drudgery, enduring are the lot of Jaya's mother, particularly of Nayana and Jeeja, the maid servants. Jeeja thinks the purpose of her life was "to go on living" and "enduring."[30] But the feminist ire is partly assuaged when Jeeja finds no grounds for anger against her parents who married her off to a man with a job and who marries another woman because she could not provide him children. Jeeja asks, "With whom shall I be angry?"[31] She can be angry only with her destiny and no human being. The tone of feminist bitterness is mollified when Jaya expresses the fact that women have 'awful power' over men. She realises that her ajjis had tremendous power over their families. She also realises the mental damage, caused by her to Mohan—"He had been utterly crushed by the things I had said."[32] However, in novel after novel, the spectacle of women ejected by their husbands inspires feminist sympathy among the readers. Nayana and Jeeja the lower class women are victims of their husband's cruelty, so are Jaya and Kusum—"And so here we were, both of us rejected by our husbands, our families, failures at everything."[33]

The centrality of Shashi Deshpande's novel *The Binding Vine* is the pathetic condition of a mother whose lot is misery and agony; she suffers because she loves. The condition of women is again miserable in this novel. After Anu, her daughter's death, Urmi has a hysterical breakdown. "I begin to bang my head against the wall. I can hear the dull rhythmic thud. There's nothing else. No pain at all."[34] Her inner pain is so great that it explodes into her thudding her own head against the wall. We recall in the earlier novel *That Long Silence* Jaya's mother hitting her own face with her hands after she feels she has done something shameful and she dies after a week. Thus mothers become self-agonizing monsters of suffering and impose punishment on themselves. Another case arousing great humanistic feeling is that of Shakutai, deserted by her husband, putting in drudgery to sustain her family. As if this is not enough another misery comes in the form of her daughter Kalpana's rape[35] who is hospitalised with injuries and the news becomes public. She faints at the news of her daughter's accident[36] in the hospital. Shakutai's misery will be increased if the news of her daughter's rape comes in the press as it will bring permanent ignominy to her and no man will like to marry such a girl.

Shashi Deshpande tries to build a case of feminist disgruntlement in showing the life of Mira, the poet, and her own mother-in-law whose writing shows a "clear thread of an intense dislike of the sexual act with her husband, a physical repulsion from the man she married."[37] Mira was married at 18 by the first man who 'saw' her. Perhaps she was angry at leaving school.[38] But the incident that inspires genuine humanistic feelings is her death at childbirth from excessive bleeding—She died a few months later, having bled to death within an hour after her child was born.[39] Her body turned black from bleeding and the husband does not even look at it. Her life was pathetic in so far as there was no emotional give and take between herself and her husband—"But loneliness was, perhaps, a part of Mira's being."[40]

Every mother's state is pitiable and pathetic—"Parenthood makes you vulnerable."[41] The very process of procreation and nursing makes one a victim at the hands of freaks of nature, disease or society. Thus, the very existence of man on the earth is a subject of humanistic reaction against the scheme of things. Human existence becomes a subject of fear gradually. A genuine case of humanistic sympathy and feminist ire is Kalpana's rape and the resultant sickness; her mother being rejected by her husband has to make both ends meet and earn all money for family expenses. As if the cruelty of her husband's deserting her is not enough, society punishes her with the rape of her daughter. The very earthly existence is the cause of Dukha, sufferings, for which Buddha left the world but the common man cannot. The very birth of Kalpana was unwanted—"I didn't want the child, I didn't want Kalpana, I wanted her to die."[42] But she was born. Shakutai has only one comfort in life, it is her betel and tea—"But this (betel)—and tea—are the only pleasures left in my life."[43] Another case of pity is that of Sulumaushi who has white spots and is never touched by her husband.[44]

Like in Anita Desai, the sense of rebellion aroused in certain women characters by life situations in the novels of Shashi Deshpande is often balanced by acceptance and surrender. In Anita Desai's *Where Shall We Go This Summer?* the female protagonist rebels against the life of Bombay and ways of her own husband, but surrenders to tradition symbolically by walking in the footprints left by her own husband on the sand of the seacoast. Similarly Sumi's rebellion against her husband's desertion is assuaged by her last meeting with her husband Gopal who seems to have taken Sanyas in Shashi Deshpande's latest novel *A Matter of Time*.[45] Feminist anger is aroused against the male species of mankind who desert their wives to live alone freely ditching the wives to drudge for the children and the family and even earn their bread. This seems an unpardonable cowardliness in man and shows the helplessness of woman who cannot desert home and responsibility in the Indian scheme of life. This arouses universal sympathy for the state of woman and raises her character.

As in Anita Desai, so in Shashi Deshpande the females feel a pang of heart at the greater respect and love shown to a male child and better treatment given to him in the family. Sumi is aware of this partisanship in behaviour right since the past—

"Sumi saw it then, the adoration of the male child. It must have been this way in the stable in Bethlehem, in Nanda's house on the bank of Yamuna in Gokul. The male child belongs."[46] Because the female child by custom has to leave her parents' home for her husband's she does not belong.

A highly philosophical sense of humanistic disgruntlement is aroused even at the transitoriness and instability of human love. Gopal, Sumi's husband found 'Ananda' bliss in the love of Sumi in Hegde's bachelor home—"And I got it, a glimpse of the purest joy, the purest metal, untouched by any base alloy."[47] But then Gopal realises, "I thought—the bliss is only for a moment. We can never possess it."[48] So human life is miserable and hence Gopal feels a tiredness and deserts Sumi. In traditional Indian society the begging bowl is taken by one who takes sanyas, in this novel on the other hand the begging bowl comes to the hand of Sumi who has not given up life, she will have to do the drudgery and the household management. Sumi says, "I've begun to think that what Gopal has really done is to take sanyas. But look what's happened—it's I who am doing that."[49] This is the pathetic situation of womankind, she can never get rest from toil and travail whereas man can.

Gopal feels tired of life, of the desire to stick to life meaninglessly even when he finds it empty; unlike Buddha he feels no compassion for the world and no meaning in life.[50] His awareness of life's meaninglessness carries him to embrace sanyas—thus humanism and spiritualism are mixed. Aru has a feminist accusation to make—every man is a betrayer and every woman is a sufferer.[51] Sumi finds love necessary to sustain life[52] without which a man withers in life hence the need of marriage for companionship. What pains Sumi is the lack of this companionship at night after Gopal's desertion.[53] Gopal's desertion arouses humanistic feelings because of this—"But for Sumi, the feeling of being abandoned remains."[54]

Sumi is reconciled to this predicament. She has arranged for a home and a job. All the relatives are ready to help. A new life is to be begun. Gopal's desertion is no more a problem. The girls are reconciled to the new state. Sumi's father Sripathi who never spoke to his wife after the loss of the mentally retarded son at the station has returned to his home. Life is normal. The bright dawn of a new life for the family can be imagined but destiny wills otherwise. Sumi is making an outing on her motorbike and invites her father for a lift. They meet with an accident and expire. The entire family is plunged in a mourning. This cruel punishment inflicted by destiny, turning Sumi's life into a tragedy, stirs humanistic feelings against the universal order.

Humanism acquires multi-coloured prismatic hues in Arundhati Roy's novel *The God of Small Things*. In the novel humanism acquires socialistic, communistic, feminist, equalitarian, deterministic, pessimistic, rebellious, libertinistic and supernal colours.

The most pathetic scene in the novel is the untimely and unexpected death of Sophie Mol, Chacko's child from his divorced wife, at the age of nine by drowning. It is grotesque and tragic in the same manner as Lucy's death in Wordsworth's *Lucy* poems. It arouses deep pathos in the reader as it seems to be caused by some unknown universal scheme. The novelist manages to elicit the readers' sympathies for Estha and Rahel, the unwanted twin children of Ammu, who is divorced and there is no guardian or caretaker for them. Ammu's death at 31, when most persons begin life in the real sense, after being divorced and ousted from her own parents' house, and in search of means of livelihood or subsistence of the children[55] as she has no legal right[56] for her parents' property which belongs to the sons and not daughters in India arouse humanist and feminist anger. Very pathetic and arousing humanistic sympathies is Rahel's marriage to Larry McCaslin of Canada, who goes to Boston and is deserted because during love-making she has strange looks—"But when they made love he was offended by her eyes."[57] He mistook the looks for "indifference and despair." After being divorced she worked in New York in a gas station and returned to India when her brother Estha was re-returned by his father. A Miss-Hanisham type pathos is aroused by Baby Kochamma whose desire to love Father Mulligham did not fructify, and with a "Bruised and almost broken"[58] heart she was forced to resort to latter-day decorations, use of jewellery and watching of television.

The entire spectacle of Ammu's life, marriage, birth of children, divorce, ousting from parents, life after her latter-day romance with Velutha, her search of job, sickness, termination of job, attempt to get a fresh job and death in sickness while seeking job—all these arouse a humanistic pity and sympathy. The first pathetic part of her bad luck is that her father has no dowry to offer for her and therefore no marriage offers come.[59] With her father's retirement and without benefit of college education she returns with her father from Delhi to Ayamenem where she has only to help her mother and wait. To escape the boredom of Ayamenem she visits a distant aunt at Calcutta with her mother's consent. It is here that a twenty-five year old assistant manager of a tea state, drunk on "eight large pegs of whisky" proposes to her.[60] She accepted the proposal—"she thought that 'anything,' anyone at all, would be better than returning to Ayamenem."[61] Such a marriage with an alcoholic is bound to fail. The alcoholic husband wishes her to gratify the manager sexually which she refuses and is beaten by her husband and hits him back.[62] Rahel and Estha were born at the time of India's defeat on China's hand (*i.e.*, 1962) and she left her husband when children were also the victims of beating bouts. She returns to her father with the added burden of two unwanted children to bring up. She now has the bad luck of a woman without a man.[63] She is blighted with the gloomy awareness that there will be no more chances for her.[64] A feminist anger is aroused at the Indian social and legal system where married daughter has no place in parents' house and divorced daughter has no place anywhere.

The case of Mammachi is still more pathetic. She untiringly goes on sweating and drudging to maintain the Paradise Pickles. When Chacko interferes it incurs loss. She is eternally ill treated and beaten by her husband who is 17 years senior to her—"Every night he beats her with a brass flower vase."[65] Mammachi has many ridges from the beatings. Her beatings are stopped when Chacko returns from Oxford.[66] His Pappachi's beatings and also talking to Mammachi stop simultaneously. Later she is reduced to a blind mother widow.[67] Thus the states of all the three women in the novel, Ammu, Mammachi, Baby Kochamma are extremely pathetic and gloomy and arouse humanistic as well as pessimistic and feminist feelings.

The plight of men who mostly dominate the scenes is no better. Pappachi, though he retires as director, gets no recognition for the Moth he discovered and hence he is permanently frustrated and becomes violent and a model of "contained cruelty." Chacko has failed to fulfil his intellectual ambitions and is unhappy as a divorcee.

But the really pathetic state is that of Velutha who is hated by all because he is a paravan, a person of low caste. He is hard working and efficient; every one is jealous of him. But he violates the social and the moral code by loving Ammu. Romance and dreamy love are crushed. He is caught and beaten by police—"Blood spilled from his skull like a secret. His face was swollen and his head looked like a pumpkin, too large and heavy for the slender stem it grew from. Inspector Thomas Mathew squatted on his haunches. Half an hour past midnight, Death came for him."[68] He paid a price too great for living; this is the irony in life. In nature there seems to exist a scheme for thwarting human aspirations and dreams. One must not trespass into the forbidden. This seems to be the important.

## NOTES

1. Raja Rao, *Kanthapura* (Delhi: Orient Paperbacks, 1970), 17.
2. Raja Rao, *The Serpent and the Rope* (Delhi: Orient Paperbacks, 1968), 403.
3. Raja Rao, The *Cate and Shakespeare* (Delhi: Orient Paperbacks, 1971), 35.
4. Raja Rao, *Comrade Kirillov* (Delhi: Orient Paperbacks), 53.
5. Raja Rao, *The Chessmaster and His Moves* (New Delhi: Vision Books), 706-07.
6. *Ibid.*
7. *Ibid.*, 708.

7a. *Ibid.*

8. Kamala Markandaya, *Pleasure City* (London: Chatto and Windus, 1982).
9. Bhabani Bhattacharya, *So Many Hungers* (Delhi: Orient Paperbacks, 1978).

10. Anita Desai, *Fire on the Mountain* (London: W. Heinemann, 1977).
11. Anita Desai, *Baumgartner's Bombay* (London: Heimemann, 1988).
12. Anita Desai, *Fasting, Feasting* (London: Chatto and Windus, 1999).
13. *Ibid.*, 92-93.
14. *Ibid.*, 95.
15. *Ibid.*, 123.
16. *Ibid.*, 143.
17. *Ibid.*, 107.
18. *Ibid.*, 68.
19. *Ibid.*
20. *Ibid.*, 70.
21. *Ibid.*, 71.
22. *Ibid.*, 150-51.
23. *Ibid.*, 214.
24. Shashi Deshpande, *That Long Silence* (New Delhi: Penguin Books Pvt. Ltd., 1989).
25. *Ibid.*, 28.
26. *Ibid.*, 29.
27. *Ibid.*, 30.
28. *Ibid.*, 36.
29. *Ibid.*, 39.
30. *Ibid.*, 51.
31. *Ibid.*, 52.
32. *Ibid.*, 82.
33. *Ibid.*, 126.
34. Shashi Deshpande, The *Binding Vine* (New Delhi: Penguin Books Pvt. Ltd., 1989), 15.
35. *Ibid.*, 57.
36. *Ibid.*, 56.
37. *Ibid.*, 63.
38. *Ibid.*, 64.
39. *Ibid.*, 136.
40. *Ibid.*, 100.

41. *Ibid.*, 77.
42. *Ibid.*, 111.
43. *Ibid.*, 90.
44. *Ibid.*, 193.
45. Shashi Deshpande, *A Matter of Time* (New Delhi: Penguin Books Pvt. Ltd., 1986).
46. *Ibid.*, 71.
47. *Ibid.*, 89.
48. *Ibid.*
49. *Ibid.*, 123.
50. *Ibid.*, 133-34.
51. *Ibid.*, 145.
52. *Ibid.*, 169.
53. *Ibid.*, 178.
54. *Ibid.*, 180.
55. Arundhati Roy, *The God of Small Things* (New Delhi: India Ink Publishing Co. Pvt. Ltd., 1997), 155-64.
56. *Ibid.*, 159.
57. *Ibid.*, 19.
58. *Ibid.*, 24.
59. *Ibid.*, 38.
60. *Ibid.*, 39.
61. *Ibid.*
62. *Ibid.*, 42.
63. *Ibid.*, 45.
64. *Ibid.*, 43.
65. *Ibid.*, 47.
66. *Ibid.*, 48.
67. *Ibid.*, 166.
68. *Ibid.*, 320.

# Chapter 9

## Salt and Sawdust: Narayan's 'Table Talk'

*M.R. Verma*

R.K. Narayan, who lived a fairly long life, continued to write nearly till his death. Though we do not get masterpieces like *The Guide, The Financial Expert* and *The Man Eaters of Malgudi* during the last phase of his writing, the works of this period too retain much of Narayan's charm. Moreover, during this period he also experimented with literary form. His *Salt and Sawdust* published in 1993, acquires a special significance in this regard. This book has been written in the form which Narayan calls 'Table Talk.' The term 'Table Talk' originated, as he tells us in his 'Foreword,' in a casual chat with N. Ram, the editor of the magazine, *Frontline*, and it was in this very magazine that his Table Talks first appeared. Defining the term, Narayan writes:

> Table Talk unlike an essay could come to life, without too definite a form, on any theme, a few lines without the compulsion of an argument or conclusion, stimulated by a passing scene or mood, or a wisp of an idea floating down from somewhere and vanishing the same way. (vii)

The flexibility of this form suits the genius of Narayan very well. This allows him to let his sensitive mind roam around and reflect on whatever takes his fancy. *Salt and Sawdust* contains not only a score of his table talks but also two short stories written in the same vein. The essence of Narayan's writing lies in his humane understanding of the comedy of life. His ironic vision quickly notices the oddities of life and his broad humanity enables him to enjoy these oddities rather than be irritated at them. The two stories, "Salt and Sawdust" and "Guru," like some of Narayan's best short stories, reveal not only his keen ironic vision but also his love for life and its oddities. About the first story, Narayan says:

> The story "Salt and Sawdust," originated from an anecdote narrated by a journalist from Holland. A Dutch lady apparently wrote a laborious bulky novel and sent it to her publisher, who after glancing through it, suggested as a joke, that she would do well to pass her time writing a cookery book. She took him at his word and produced one in the course of time. It became a best seller and continues in that rank for forty years now. (viii)

This is the sort of situation that must have appealed to Narayan's sense of humour immediately. However, though he got the idea of the story from that Dutch lady, the characters in his story are typically Indian and the background of the story his own Malgudi. As is his wont, he evokes the atmosphere with a concrete description of the scene. Veena and Swami, a childless couple, live in a one-and-a-half room on Grove street. It has a window opening on the street, a pyol beside the street door serving for a sit out, a kitchen and a backyard with access to a common well. Narayan then goes on to describe the daily activity of Swami. He gets up at five in the morning, draws water from the well, lights the store, prepares coffee and lunch for two and packs up a portion to carry with him to his workplace. It is at this stage that we realize that something is amiss. The lady of the house does not do what housewives in India are generally supposed to do—cook the meal. Later, we are led into the secret of it. Swami's early encounter with Veena's culinary skills had frightened him. Cooking was simply beyond her. Since he was a good eater who loved tasty food, he took to cooking himself. So far Veena is concerned, she is a novelist in making, and this suffices for an explanation for Swami:

> 'A novelist, probably cannot be a good cook,' he concluded, 'just as I cannot write a novel. She has not been taught to

> distinguish salt from sawdust.' He quietly took over the kitchen leaving her free to write whatever she fancied. (5)

It is in the description of the progress of the novel that we get the taste of the typical Narayan. A curious Swami asks Veena from time to time about the progress of the novel. Several days later he is informed that the heroine is 'just emerging.' Even then he does not get the name of the heroine. Another day Swami is included in the process of artistic creation. When he asks the novelist-in-making about her hero, she in return asks him what he imagines him to be. Thus with the hint from Swami, Veena's hero begins to take shape. From the hero knocking off the teeth of his adversary comes the idea of a dentist and finally Veena decides that the hero would be a Chinese dentist. It would be something original as no one has ever thought of the Chinese dentist as a hero. Swami however raises a doubt as to how a girl from South India could marry a Chinese. The problem is solved by the imaginative writer. The hero is not really a Chinese, he had only his training in China. It is in the discussion of the wife and husband about the hero of the novel that we get an idea of what Narayan means when he says that the story has been written in the manner of the table talk. The light, almost flippant, way in which the dialogue goes on underlines the very spirit of the story:

> 'Why did he go to China?' asked Swami.
>
> 'When he was a boy he ran away from home.'
>
> 'why?'
>
> 'His school master caned him one day and, in sheer disgust he went and slept on a bench at the railway platform for two days and nights. When a train passed at midnight, he slipped into a carriage and finally joined some monks and sailed for Peking in a boat.'
>
> 'Very interesting, very interesting,' Swami cried, 'How do you get these ideas?'
>
> 'When one writes, one gets ideas,' she explained, and continued, 'the monks left him at the port and vanished.' 'Were they supernatural beings? Could you explain their presence and help?'

> 'God must have sent them down to help the boy, why should God be interested?' Swami asked, 'God's ways are mysterious.' (8-9)

Essentially it is the same Narayan that we encounter in his early works, but the earlier seriousness that underlay even in comic descriptions is gone now. A new light-heartedness has crept into the style now. It is reflected in the description of the language problem. It is in the feast given on the occasion of the hero's marriage that the crux of the story lies. The description is entirely the idea of Swami since it is he who is a master of culinary art. He gives free rein to his imagination and his love for food makes the description almost voluptuous:

> The feast was very well-planned—two days running they served breakfast, coffee and idli and dosa and uppuma and two sweets and fruit preparations, a heavy lunch with six vegetables and rice preparations, concluding with a light elegant supper. Fried almonds and nuts were available in bowls all over the place, all through the day. The bride groom, the dentist, had expressed a wish that a variety of eatables must be available for those with weak teeth or even no teeth, he had all kinds of patients capable of different degrees of chewing and mastication. (19-20)

Swami not only gives a description of the different food items but also details of the spices to be used for each dish. Veena, however, does not use all the details in the novel. She incorporates only whatever she thinks proper for her novel, even then the description goes on for ten pages.

Later on, it is this very description of the feast that makes Natesh, the publisher, and Bari, the supplier of printing material, think of a book on cookery. Things would not have come to such a pass, if the publication cost calculated by Natesh and Bari had not frightened Swami. Veena who was bent upon publishing her novel had persuaded Swami that they should go to Madras in search of a publisher. Natesh who was banking upon the enthusiasm of a debutant novelist to make a profit out of the publication of the novel becomes panicky when he hears of their plan to go to Madras. His sharp business sense has made him realize of the commercial potential of a book on cookery and so he hastily proposes to Swami the publication of such a book. For this book they will have to pay nothing. On the other hand, they will be given an advance of two thousand rupees as well as a royalty of ten percent on the sale of the book. Veena, the novelist is put off by this proposal, but Natesh is careful to say that the novel would follow the book. That this never happens is only because the 'Appetizer' becomes so popular that the publisher is busy all the time preparing a reprint of it. Moreover, Veena and Natesh are also very busy lecturing on the art of cooking.

The second story in the book, "Guru" is a brilliant portrait of a miser. The idea of this story came to Narayan from a miser that he knew (viii). Unlike "Salt and Sawdust" which depends for its effect on the plot, "Guru" is a story of character where incidents have been used to unfold the character. The character of Gurumurthi is one of the best that Narayan ever created. Guru is a retired government servant who has retired not because he reached the age of superannuation but because he was forced to seek retirement or to face penal action on charges of corruption. The encounter between Guru and the District Magistrate provides Narayan an opportunity for his irony. When Guru comes back home, he tells his wife:

> That young man the collector seems to be an upstart I don't care. He demanded certain explanations, but I firmly told him that I don't care to explain and am prepared to go. I demanded all the leave at my credit and then retirement, when he found I was tough, he came down a step or two and tried to coax and cajole me to stay, but I was firm. (55-60)

The main interest of the story however lies in the description of Guru's miserliness. He married his first daughter to a person who suffered from some deformity and so was not in a position to demand any dowry. What pleased Guru more was that his daughter and her children were not in the habit of visiting him frequently, and when they came they did not stay for a long time. The maximum she could manage to stay was a week's time. Even this seemed taxing to him. So he was relieved when she proposed to go. Her mother pressed her to stay, but Guru would not listen. With much readiness he took her to the railway station, ascertaining before hand that she had money to buy tickets, and saw her off with advices to take care of herself and the children during the journey.

The behaviour of Guru seems generous when we compare it with what he did on the occasion of his second daughter's marriage two years later:

> Gurumurthi had simplified Kamala's marriage to such an extent that even Raji was not invited properly, and he spurned the idea whenever his wife reminded him to send them a formal announcement. 'All right, all right,' he said brushing her off—'leave it to me. I know when to write.' And he reflected, 'why should Raji be bothered to come with her crippled husband and the restless children, travelling all the way. Our outlook must change—a revolutionary change is needed in our society. Inviting a motley for every wedding is senseless, wonder who started this irrational practice.' (48)

Guru's daughter, Kamala, was fortunate to be married to the son of a well-known doctor, but her father's miserliness threatened to ruin her prospects of happiness. The doctor had welcomed Guru's idea of having a simple marriage ceremony to avoid wasteful expenditure, little suspecting that the amount of fifty thousand rupees saved from the wedding expenses for the groom's study in America was a promise Guru never meant to keep. The doctor kept reminding him of the promise but Guru had an excuse at every occasion. He told that the delay was due to certain government bonds, which would mature soon. The suit he had promised the bridegroom could never materialize because he had ordered imported material from a firm in Madras. When Guru tried to dodge the issue of the diamond ring for the groom by saying that the goldsmith was causing the delay, Kamala came out openly against her father. He, however, remained unperturbed. An agitated Kamala finally left her father's house and with her mother's consent went to join her husband. Guru was happy that he succeeded in marrying both his daughters off with minimum of expenditure.

Even his forced retirement did not worry Gurumurthi since he had acquired enough wealth by his corrupt means to be many times sufficient for his miserly way of living. His wife, though now always bickering and taunting him for his parsimony, had compromised with her lot. Things would have gone on the same way had Guru not thought suddenly of adopting a son who would light his funeral pyre and perform the rites. Raghu, the third son of his brother Samba, was the child he had decided to adopt. Saroja, his wife, vehemently opposed the idea but Guru would not listen to her. She kept quiet till the adoption ceremony was over, but soon after that she left her husband's house to go to her mother's house. Raghu, the adopted son, also did not live very long with his new father and stealthily ran away to his natural one.

In both the stories it is the reversal of the situation that evokes humour. In "Salt and Sawdust" the woman who cannot tell the difference between the salt and the sawdust becomes a famous author of a cookery book. In "Guru" the miser Gurumurthi is dismayed when he comes to know at the end of the story that the boy whom he had adopted in the hope that he would look after him in his old age and who had run away from him just after a few days of adoption was now legally entitled to inherit his property.

Section III of the book is devoted to table talks. These table talks, twenty in number, were written at different times. While "Looking for Magsaysay" was written in 1960, the other one dealing with Magsaysay, "In the Philippines," was written in 1993. They are also quite varied in nature. While pieces like "Parrots Ltd.," "The Judge" and "Man Hunt" verge on the farce, others like "On Ved Mehta" and "Teaching in Texas" art quite serious in nature. In length also they vary very much. On the one hand we have pieces like "Vayudoot," "The Enemies," "On Language" which are short consisting of three or four pages, on the other hand, there is "Looking for Magsaysay" which runs into nearly forty pages. In all of them, however, one thing is common—Narayan's wit, his warmth and his sense of humour.

Of these table talks "Reflections on Frankfurt" is quite remarkable as in it Narayan sums up what he considers to be the general criticism of his work. Written in 1986 it is about a rumour he heard in Frankfurt while attending the book fair to which Indian authors and publishers were invited that his name was being considered for the award of the Nobel Prize that year. In this table talk, he speculates on what might have passed in the committee room if his name had actually come up for consideration and then dropped. The whole speculation deserves to be quoted in full as it presents a brilliant summary of the general argument against Narayan's work as well the subtle derision with which he considers this criticism:

> 'For half a century Narayan has been building up a world of his own and peopled it with a variety of characters who have ceased to be fictional but are recognized and loved in any part of the world by Narayan's readers,...it is an achievement which should be treated as a contribution to world literature' argued one.
>
> 'To a certain extent, yes,' said the arbiter. 'This author's work is diverting, amusing and readable, but possesses none of the element that go to make great literature.' 'What are those elements of great literature?' All great literature must echo the soul of man. The struggles, and anguish in the soul of the individual must be reflected in the work, against the background of historical and social convulsions of the countries in which the individual finds himself tossed about as a helpless victim. All the grimness of existence must find a place in a writer's work. Above all, a certain degree of obscurity and difficulty of idiom in the text enhances the stature of a literary work.
>
> Applying these tests, Narayan's work fails. His writing is too simple and too readable requiring no effort on the part of the reader. Mere readability is not enough. A reader must be put to work and must labour hard to get the meaning of a sentence; only then can he feel triumphant at having mastered a page. Narayan's further defect lies in his light hearted tone under all circumstances. This is a grave defect, humour is all very well up to a point, but it is not everything in literature. Humour has a tendency to stimulate frivolity. Our Founder and Benefactor, Alfred

Nobel, you must remember, invented dynamite, which is no joke, and it would be inappropriate to award the prize in his name to a writer who is uncommitted to the serious and sinister problems of existence.

'Narayan' has produced quite a body of work to fill up books shelves and shows promise. He has created a new map called Malgudi in which his characters live and die. Story after story is set in the same place, which is not progressive a rather stagnant background, Narayan's stories fail to reflect the dynamism of India's civilization or aspirations.

'We hope some day Narayan will develop into a full-fledged writer deserving our serious consideration.' (122-24)

Another table talk that deals with Narayan's own works as well as the works of Mulk Raj Anand and Raja Rao is "Teaching in Texas." This is an account of Narayan's teaching stint at the University of Texas where he was invited as a Visiting Professor. This experience gave Narayan an insight into the reader's mind. He describes how people of a different cultures respond to the description of Indian culture.

## REFERENCE

All references are from *Salt and Sawdust* (New Delhi: Penguin Books Pvt. Ltd., 1998).

# Chapter 10

## Tradition and Contemporaneity in the Novels of Raja Rao

*Kavita Agrawal*

Raja Rao is called 'a child of Gandhian age.' He is a remarkable novelist among 'The Big Three.' The other two are Mulk Raj Anand and R.K. Narayan. The former is still alive while R.K. Narayan died in the year 2001. Raja Rao is a great Sadhak and the central themes of his novels are 'Vedic Vision' and 'Advaita.' He deals about Atman and Brahmin in his novels. Mulk Raj Anand once wrote that we do not get any solution of our problems only by "Clinging blindly to Sankara's Advaita of the ninth century. Our problems are different. How do we solve them? Can Sankara's answers serve us today."[1] His words are challenging questions. But we have to understand that Raja Rao is a religious man and his novels are imbued with the real problem of 'dukha,' the cosmic sorrow that Buddha sought to eliminate from the world. No doubt, his first novel the *Kanthapura* is purely devoted to India's contemporary problems. It has Gandhian philosophy of Truth, Non-Violence and Satyagrah to oust English people out of the country.

The five novels of Raja Rao from the point of view of their traditional values to the contemporary context are most important. Raja Rao is essentially a great philosopher-novelist. He is "the weaver of tales that are difficult to read sometimes but which are destined to live with you for a long time."[2] For him philosophy is a passion and the novel is only a means of its expression. His novels are his real voice. The expressions of his philosophical experiences and beliefs have been given in his five novels. In everyone of these novels he has minutely examined a particular school of philosophy *vis-à-vis* other schools of philosophy with a view to bringing out a clear-cut distinction between the particular schools and the other, and this within the framework of the art of the novel.

Thematically, Raja Rao is somewhat different from Mulk Raj Anand and R.K. Narayan. Mulk Raj Anand is a writer preoccupied with the intense desire to eradicate the ills and evils of Indians social life and to replace them by the element of modernity and progressiveness. As such, he has little interest in the political events and usually does not treat them in his work. R.K. Narayan is a regional novelist, who portrays the men and manners of Malgudi in a comic vein, highlighting at the same time the basic universal human value and the slowly changing social scene of South India. But Raja Rao is essentially a philosopher-novelist. He is a metaphysical novelist whose concerns are primarily religious and philosophical. In his novels he takes the themes of Gandhism and Karma philosophy, Advaita philosophy, Vishistadvaita, communism, etc. throwing sufficient light on the other lesser-known schools like Judaism, Taoism, Confucianism, Buddhism, Jainism, Jewism, etc. His first novel *Kanthapura* is a significant approach to Gandhian politics. His first novel *Kanthapura* is devoted to Gandhian philosophy. "The tremors of Gandhi's impacts on a South Indian village are recorded here in the chatty language of an elderly widow, and we see everything through the film of her memory, sensibility and temperament."[3]

The novel is a mixture of fact and fancy, poetry and whimsy, history and legend. It is the story of how a small, sleepy, south Indian village is caught in the whirlpool of the Indian freedom struggle movement. Raja Rao in the foreword of *Kanthapura* himself indicates that the novel is a kind of sthalapurana or legendary history, which every village in India seems to have. "These local sthalapuranas are modelled on the ancient Indian Puranas—those compendia of story, fable, myth, religion, philosophy and politics among which are Upapuranas or minor

Puranas, which describe holy places and the legends associated with them."[4]

It is mainly a novel of action and its theme centres around organized national struggle for independence from the yoke of the British rule. The novelist with the Gandhian study for freedom also takes the social problems of the untouchables and of the economic betterment of the downtrodden. Raja Rao with the addition of Harikatha and Jayanthis gives the religious touch in the novel. The event is given the colours of a Puranic myth and "the past mingles with the present, and the gods mingle with men to make the reporty of your grandfather always bright."[5]

Moorthy, the protagonist, is Gandhian man and Bade Khan, the representative of the bureaucracy, has no value before the iron-Gandhian man. The villagers are unafraid of the government. A woman says:

> What is a policeman before a Gandhi's man? Tell me, does a boar stand before a lion or a jackal before an elephant?[6]

The villagers consider Gandhi as Siva. They sing the Bhajan:

> Siva is the three-eyed and swaraj too is three-eyed self-purification, Hindu-Muslim unity, khaddar.[7]

The novel has the philosophy of selfless action, "Indian struggle for freedom is rightly chosen as a replica of the great war of the *Mahabharata* and *Kanthapura* becomes a veritable Kurukshetra where the war between the forces of freedom and slavery, love and hatred, truth and untruth, and thus it is fought both in the inner world of the spirit and in the outer world between the British Raj and nationalists."[8]

*The Serpent and the Rope* is Raja Rao's second important novel. It is extremely diverse in form. Here Raja Rao quotes from an array of languages, including Sanskrit, Hindi, French Italian, Latin and Provencal; but only the Sanskrit quotations are translated. There are long interludes and stories, such as Grandmother—Lakshmamma's story of princess who becomes a pumpkin and Ishwar Bhatta's "Story of Rama." While *Kanthapura* is the struggle for freedom and devote for Nishkam Karm Yoga. *The Serpent and the Rope* passes to the philosophy of knowledge, an epic of ideas. The protagonists—Madeleine and Ramaswamy, meet not merely as persons for emotional 'give and take' alone but Madeleine receives the truth that Ramaswamy carries with him. The physical and emotional planes of reality merge into the spiritual thought, a willing conversion of the intellect. Ramaswamy pleads that Indian Culture has ever been spiritualized and we can triumph by converting the minds into a spiritual unity and get universal brotherhood. The protagonist asserts "Truth is the only substance India can offer and that truth is metaphysical and not moral."[9] The novel is not only a religious book but it also takes its readers round various places of the world—Benares, Sobornne, Axie, Paris, Bombay and London—but always we are brought back to the truth of the self, embodied by Benares or Brindavan. The protagonist rightly says, Benares is everywhere where you are, says an old Vendantic text, and all waters are Ganges. To realize this is to be a true Cathar, "The rest is heresy."[10] Similarly Brindavan is the embodiment of the self, purged of all accessories and attachments. The novelist has its chief object of the novel a delineation of the path of knowledge as a means of liberation and knowledge is the realization of the real as distinct from the unreal. "The world is," "either unreal or real—the serpent or the rope. There is no in between-the-two-and all that's in-between in poetry, is sainthood."[11] Thus Raja Rao blends the religious and cultural tradition with the contemporary social and political realities in *The Serpent and the Rope*.

Raja Rao's third novel, *The Cat and Shakespeare* is the sequel to *The Serpent and the Rope*. The novel is very short but very important because it shows what happens after a seeker's veil of illusion has been removed by the Guru. Its theme may be summed up in Hamlet's words to Horatio towards the end of the play. "There is a divinity that shapes our ends Rough-hew them how we will." A similar view of grace is embodied in the novel in what Nair, the man, who is united to Truth, calls "the way of the cat." The "way of the cat," simply, is the notion that just as the Kitten is carried by the scruff of its neck by the mother cat, man is completely at the mercy of the Divine; consequently, the only way to live is to surrender oneself totally to Divine grace, as the helpless kitten surrenders itself to the mother cat. The novelist mingles religious theme with the contemporary materialistic-world of present society. Raja Rao tells his readers that embrace traditional morals and have faith in the Almighty. "Nair lives this philosophy and is responsible for teaching it to his ignorant neighbour, the narrator Pai. Pai is like the innocent hunter in the story who unknowingly heaped leaves on a Shivalingam and was rewarded with a vision."[12]

The title of the novel is symbolic. The cat as the mother symbolises the Cosmic Creator—the mother of all beings and also their protector. She is the giver of life as well as of all things to all the living creatures who are her children. If once we surrender to the Almighty Mother we are saved from taking the responsibility of our lives upon ourselves, and life becomes joyful and harmonious. Shakespeare stands for the temporal existence while the cat stands for the Almighty. Lord Krishna in the Bhagwad Geeta says, "surrendering all duties to Me, seek refuge in Me alone. I shall absolve you of all sins; grieve not."[13]

In the novel Govind Nair tells his friend Ramakrishna Pai:

> The kitten is being carried by the cat. We should all be kittens carried by the cat...I like being the kitten.... Ah, the kitten when its neck is held by its mother, does it know anything else but the joy of being held by its mother?.... But I say the kitten is the safest thing in the world, the kitten held in the mouth of the mother cat.... I often think how noble it is to see the world, the legs dangling straight, the eyes steady, and the mouth of the mother at the neck. Beautiful but yourself be free from all modern tensions and worries.[14]

The first three novels—*Kanathapura, The Serpent and the Rope* and *The Cat and Shakespeare* are called a 'philosophical Trilogy' of Raja Rao. The novelist takes temporal life in relation to the eternal reality. "*Kanthapura* is the national struggle for freedom but it is linked with the highest spiritual idea of satyagrah." *The Serpent and the Rope,* the mundane planes of the reality of love—physical, moral and intellectual—melt into all-absorbing flame of non-duality. In the novel his characters bathe in the purest water of the Ganges for the emergence of a true Cather. Madeleine, ultimately renounces even love for the attainment of the highest goal of her life. *The Cat and Shakespeare* presents the drama of life as the grand play of the Mother-cat-prakriti—the absolute power of Almighty—"whose kittens we all are, emphasising that our redemption from life—the big ration shop—lies in our kitten-like surrender to the care and protection of the mother cat."[15]

All these novels constitute philosophical realities. *Kanthapura* stands for selfless action, *The Serpent and the Rope* represents for the self-knowledge and *The Cat and Shakespeare* advocates for self-surrender.

Raja Rao's fourth novel, *Comrade Kirillov* is the story of a divided mind. The novel is deeply committed to an intellectual perspective revealing the varied impacts of the contact between the East and the West. Through this novel Raja Rao has brought sustained insights to his task of probing the nature and consequences of various kinds of encounter between the eastern and western mind. In *Kanthapura* we encounter political, in *The Serpent and the Rope* it is purely internal conflict, which is produced by a metaphysical change in attitude; in *The Cat and Shakespeare* there is a beautiful combination of realism and fantasy. But in *Comrade Kirillov* there is the inward conflict, which operates on an altogether different dimension of the divided consciousness of a man torn between two pulls. Kirillov is a Brahmin by birth but adopts the principles of Marx. So there is a great conflict, both in his mind as well as in his heart. He is an "Inverted Brahmin" but he has placed the material ends of his life over the spiritual. The main story, narrated by Raja Rao, is a more than ninety-three pages in large type to which are appended twenty-seven pages of the diary of Kirillov's wife Irene, and a concluding seven pages by the narrator, the effect is of a slight, sketchy novella, Kirillov, Padmanabhan Iyer, leaves India for California to propagate theosophy but, after a period of disillusionment, becomes a communist. From California he moves to London where, marrying a Czench immigrant, Irene, he settles down to the life of an expatriate intellectual. Like Rao's other protagonists, "Kirillov starts as a seeker of Truth, but after becoming a communist, he is increasingly revealed by the narrator to be caught in a system which curtails his access of Truth."[16] His wife, Irene, recognizes in her diary that her husband is biologically an Indian Brahmin and only intellectually a Marxist.

In the last few pages of the novel, the protagonist is shown to be a man of contradictions; attacking and worshipping Gandhi simultaneously, deeply loving traditional India but campaigning for a communism revolution. The narrator (R) in the novel tells about Kirillov's intellectual vision. There is numerous interesting discussion on communism in the novel, which is valuable as the social document. Moreover, there are other successful relations, which are given by the narrator. Kamal is the son of Kirillov and Irene. But there is also a tragedy in the end of the novel. Soon after Kirillov's return from India, Irene dies in childbirth, followed by her newly born daughter. Kirillov leaves for Moscow and is last heard of in Pecking. The novel ends with the narrator taking Kamal, now in India, to Kanyakumari. No doubt, in this small novel Raja Rao wants to say that Kirillov has a divided mind. The traditional sublime view of India is contrasted with the materialistic world of the West. Ultimately the protagonist realises the importance of Indian culture and the Hindu views of life.

Raja Rao's last philosophical novel *The Chessmaster and His Moves,* which appeared twenty-eight years after Rao's last major book, *The Serpent and the Rope.* It embodies his renewed, untiring search for the Absolute. This voluminous novel is, in fact, a stupendous mass of philosophical discussions and thoughts.

The hero-narrator, Shivarama Shastri, a philosopher-mathematician, is endowed with a massive intellect that is constantly in quest for the Absolute. The novel encompasses the region beyond man-made geographical, social, linguistic and cultural barriers, some of the thoughts of eminent seers, sages and thinkers have been presented by Raja Rao in this novel. The richness of thought and the language of the novel are amazing. The locale is as vast as the universe itself. The novel is a particular version of Advaita that has some major sources.

One is the philosophical practice of Sri Ramana Maharshi and the other is the sunyavada of Buddhist philosopher, Nagarjuna. Allied to the former is, of course, the philosophy of Rao's Guru, Sri Atmananda, while Nagarjuna's thought, obviously, is derived from the Buddha. *The Chessmaster and His Moves* is really anti-novel, a novel to end all novels. "It is not the realization of the self that is sought as in the earlier works, but a dissolution of self. While Moorthy, through right action, illustrates Karma Yoga, Rama, Jnana Yoga or the path of knowledge, and Govindan Nair, a type of Bhakti Yoga, a complete self-surrender to the Divine, Shivarama Shastri represents the power of negative dialectics, the attempt not to achieve something, but to vaporize one's self into nothing. Here, the familiar dichotomies between the male and the female, vowels and consonants, India and the West, the Brahmin and the Kshatriya, the sage and the saint, logic and devotion, truth and the world, all hang on the opposition between zero and infinity."[17]

The principal characters are Shivarama Shastri, son of Rao Bhadur Shivasankara Shastri, Laxmi Shastri, Uma Ramachandra Iyer—sister of Shivarama Shastri, Jayalakshmi—daughter of Sunder Ajit Singh, the Maharaja of Vilaspur, Raja Surrender Singh, Raja Ashok Sinha of Dharmapur, Suzanne Chantereux, Jean-Pierre Vauxgrand, Mireille, Ratilal Jhaveri, and Jean Abou. Though the main thematic thrust is on the search for the Absolute, perhaps for the first time in Indian English fiction eminent personalities of varied fields and disciplines like mathematics, politics, theology, philosophy, metaphysics, mythology, etc. have been given a place in the plot. Raja Rao has blended contemporariness to this traditional theme with the addition of the views and references of Pt. Jawaharlal Nehru, Ravindranath Tagore and Mahatma Gandhi. He has also taken the principal historical characters, they are: De Gaulle, the maker of Modern France, Reuben, Einstein, Hegel, Pythagoras, Moliere, Hitler, Lord Shiva, Lord Ganesa, Maa Parvati, Maa Ganga, Tagore, Sri Shankara, Attlee the ex-Prime Minister of England. The novel covers all subjects under the sun, ranging from God to common subject on this earth, from the sublime to the filthy lucre, from violence, to non-violence, from monarchy to democracy, from fascism to anarchism, from Hinduism to other religious 'isms', etc. This novel is written in the stream of consciousness technique. But the basic theme of this novel is the search for the Absolute. The novel is divided into three parts, which may be called the trilogy of thoughts. The three books are entitled as: *The Turk and the Tiger Hunt, The Goblets of Shiraz,* and *The Brahmin and the Rabbi.* The three parts of the book have symbolical meaning. Shiva is three-eyed, and so is the Chessmaster like Ramaswami of *The Serpent and the Rope,* Shivarama Shastri, the protagonist of *The Chessmaster and His Moves* is also a great scholar with a true Brahminic psyche and sensibility. The father of the protagonist writes to him long letter to take the shelter of Indian purity. The letter is full of philosophical remarks:

> Haridwar was cold, but the ripples of the river gave one truth and breath. The Himalaya, one sensed, was some vertical reality, a certitude, that power was affirmative, and affirmation, a sort of play, in a manner, a dance, Shiva's footsteps.[18]

Shivarama Shastri is deeply impressed with his father's letter. The deep-rooted Indian spirituality in him impelled to make a comparison between the Himalayas and the Alps, highlighting the essentially metaphysical nature of the former. He thinks that Alps never gave one the breath of holiness but the Himalayas seemed the nameless teacher.

The protagonist moves from metaphysics to the realm of broader humanism to universal brotherhood. Even in woman he searches for the power of Absolute. His sister Uma fills him awareness for Indian spiritual power. He learns that this is the country where giving is taking and where we truly create the new entity. Raja Rao blends spiritual significant with modern values of life. The protagonist is in search of 'non-duality':

> Heaven is a place where all is joy and peace—anand and shanty. Endless joy, that is Anandam. And unending joy is, says Shankara somewhere, is peace. And peace is where there is no duality. So heaven is non-duality.[19]

In the novel *The Chessmaster and His Moves,* the protagonist discusses women and the intricacies and aesthetics of sex without reservations, emphasizing the need of sex in human life and then taking it to sublime heights of philosophy. He calls to his memory the glorious cultural past of his country and the immortal old Sanskrit poets like Kalidasa, Bhartrhari and Amaru, who have sung the beauties of women without inhibitions and with pride in Indian manhood and alike. He says: "A nation whose chief gods were Shiva and Krishna, Shiva, whose symbol the noble phallus, and Krishna the great lover of gopis—it's strange how we've forgotten the temple of being, which is our body, and for whose proper use, the sage Vastsyayana wrote the *Kamasutra*, while the great Sri Shankara wrote the *Saundaryalahari nisargaksinasya stanatabharena klonmajuso....*"[20] The novelist gives importance to healthy sex because it has hidden mysteries and aesthetic values. He also emphasizes on the need of marriage. He considers marriage as the best station of human existence. Even our great gods, Shiva and Vishnu, were married to Parvati and Lakshmi respectively. Raja Rao tells his readers that marriage is like building a shrine in your backyard. But the mason who will build it must be right one and the proper time must come.

The last book of the novel, *The Goblets of Shiraz,* is devoted to the famous Persian astronomer-poet, Omer Khayyam, who meditated on the mystery of existence and making, had conceded drinking and merriment till the last moment of life. The novelist is rich with his philosophical vision. He has goblets full of sublime thoughts and philosophy with its allied branches like metaphysics, aesthetics, religion, myths, politics, morality, etc. He aims at showing man the way to physical happiness, mental peace and spiritual bliss, which cannot be attained without perfect equilibrium in the inner and the outer self. The protagonist is a great mathematician but he is also a great scholar and draws nectar from other branches of oriental philosophy. There is a great role of women in his life. Three female characters—Suzanne, Mireille and Jayalakshmi—form a triangle around him, and the fourth character—his own sister Uma Ramchandra—throws a protective ring around him like a true Indian sister full of motherly instincts for her brother. Raja Rao thinks that for man, the woman is just a linker, one who connects things, already existent. He says that woman brings into birth a concrete object. In the same way a woman needs a concrete man, a hero, or a conqueror. Both are in need of each other. Raja Rao blends the earthly relations with the Absolute. So he gives importance to wisdom because only it can blend the two extremes of earth and heaven. He says that one can die a saint, be carried in a palanquin and be buried in salt, and his Samadhi worshipped for childbirth and marriage, but when one is a sage, one lives because one cannot truly die, death has been killed, and so long, by Truth. The protagonist belongs not only to the earthly world but he is a man of the other world also, so he seeks of non-duality through his experiments. He goes from the South to the North to the Himalayas and to the Ganga to debate and establish the principle of non-duality. And when "I have said non-duality I've said—India."

Raja Rao also gives the contemporaneity in this vast novel. He is the product of the Gandhian age and so he provides an opportunity to his protagonist to expose Gandhian philosophy of Love, Truth and Non-violence to Karim to the extent that he (Karim) is deeply impressed by his knowledge, courage and conviction. He leaves a mark of his Indianness and Brahminical aura on the Arab fundamentalist and revolutionary. Karim, a medical student in Paris, had met Pt. Jawaharlal Nehru and Mahatma Gandhi. He was influenced with them. He wanted to know more about Gandhi and Gandhian philosophy. The protagonist tells the Arab leader in detail about Gandhi and his principles:

> .... So Gandhi says let us love that man, be brother to brother. To strangle someone is easy. But to embrace him, more difficult. You do not like darkness. You live light. You do not want hatred. You want love. Your neighbour also wants love.[21]

The novel also takes the ideological confrontation between Michael, a Jewish scholar and a linguist and Shivarama Shastri, the Brahmin philosopher. The protagonist, with perfect mathematical precision, proves to him that Hinduism means

Truth and dispels Michael's doubts that Gandhian philosophy was against the Jews. He is successful in convincing Michael that knowledge is Truth and Truth leads one to the Absolute. A Brahmin is one who knows Brahman, and he recognizes and sees Brahman in all human beings. He also says that we become mathematical entities. When a man is no man, yet a man, he is a real man, the superman, one understands. He tells him about the importance of Karma. In the last pages of the novel the protagonist is successful in convincing Michael that it is knowledge, which shows the path of Truth, and only Truth can lead one to the Absolute. Even Jews when they accept it become noble, pious and sincere like Hindus. In the Home of God there is no Hindu or Jew. Only the Karma forms our identity.

Raja Rao has also focused his attention on Jainism in his last epic novel *The Chessmaster and His Moves*. In other four novels he did not take this branch of religion. The roots of this religion go far back to antiquity. The followers of this religion have faith in the teachings of 24 Tirthankaras, spiritual leaders. Lord Mahavira, the last but the most significant Jain Tirthankar, has contributed substantially to the thought and philosophy. It is interesting to note that the Jains do not accept the overriding authority of the Vedas. But Hindus and Jains have the close relationship. Thus indirectly the Jains are influenced with the Vedas. Again it is more interesting to know that Jains do not believe in the existence of God. They look to the Tirthankaras for guidance and knowledge. They believe that there are souls in all things, the moving and the unmoving. At last the protagonist is successful in convincing Ratilal, a Jain, that Truth can never be explained through words. It can only be realized. The debate of both the scholars ends on a note of the victory of Vedanta and Vedantic logic, the only surest means to comprehending and realizing the Absolute. Thus various schools of philosophy, Indian and Western, have been presented in this novel in a very scholarly way and the protagonist is successful in proving the superiority of Vedanta over other schools of Indian philosophy like Buddhism, Jainism, Jewism, etc.

*The Chessmaster and His Moves* has highlighted certain problems for its readers. These problems have been presented in his earlier works also in a slight way. *The Chessmaster* is neither an admission of defeat nor an affirmation of success; here we don't see either the failure or success of Advaita. It is ambiguous book in which neither zero nor infinity wins. The Chessmaster moves beyond these positions to a kind of indeterminacy. Shiva, Rao's spokesman, is no longer always right. Nor does he pretend to be in full control of his metaphysical project. There is always the more powerful presence of the Chessmaster behind the movements of the characters in the book. Of course, any notion of a personalized Chessmaster or prime mover is just another version of the God that Shiva, the rationalist mathematician, would deny as the quintessence of the horizontal. But this is one of the apparent contradictions of the book, which will only be resolved in the second volume of the trilogy, after the protagonist, Shivarama Shastri, encounters the Guru.[22]

Raja Rao's other creative works after his epic novel *The Chessmaster and His Moves* are *On the Ganga Ghat* (1989), a collection of stories, published by Vision Books, New Delhi, *The Meaning of India* (1997) again published by Vision Books, New Delhi. His biography on the life of the Mahatma, *The Great Indian Way: A Life of Mahatma Gandhi,* is also published by Vision Books, New Delhi. He is still busy in writing his creative works, but so far no new publication has come out in the market. We hope to see them in future. All the latter works after *The Chessmaster and His Moves* have his thoughts and vision, which this great Sadhak has already given in his five great novels about which I have already discussed. Therefore there is no need to repeat their themes again.

In his five novels Raja Rao has introduced Indian culture and the Hindu views of life to the Western readers. These works are a part of the total Indian literature, which starting with the Vedas, has continued to shed its soothing light in all vicissitudes of history, religion and politics and culture. Never before Raja Rao, has India been interpreted to the West so well by a writer of fiction. In his five great novels he depicts the realities of social and family life of the South India and also the role of religious tradition in the lives of her people. In *Kanthapura* he deals with the political upheavals and Mahatma Gandhi's influence. Indian philosophy, specially Vedant, is treated as subject matter in *The Serpent and the Rope*. *The Chessmaster and His Moves*, *The Cat and Shakespeare* and *Comrade Kirillov* are an evolution of the efficacy of Communism.

Raja Rao has given full scope to his characters to establish their identities as social beings and as typical members of Indian society by involving them in actions, situations and experiences, which are valid in the Indian context. He has included in his novels the texture of India's religious conventions and beliefs. He has woven all these so well into the fabric of his writings that the values and the experiences which are prevalent in our society and which his characters represent look valid from all points of view and imports an everlasting reality and human interest to their milieu. Raja Rao acts as an able and interesting interpreter of the philosophy and religious beliefs of the Indian society in his short stories and novels.

Raja Rao's writings are fictionalized versions of the eternal and glorious religious heritage of India. Raja Rao has not only become the preserver and propagator of India's religious heritage, but has also become an interpreter of these eternal values to the glorious Indian tradition of the Western world. In his works he has masterly blended religious and cultural traditions of India with contemporary social and political realities of the West. It is because although he lived abroad, he never ceased to be an Indian in temperament and sensibility. On the whole Raja Rao's life and writings have evolved in the direction of increasing openness and his creative works are a fine blending of India's religious and cultural traditions with the contemporary social and cultural realities of the West. But one thing we have to keep in mind that Raja Rao has departed boldly from the European tradition and has indigenized it in the proper way of assimilating material from the Indian literary tradition. In the end I quote the words of Kathleen Raine: "Raja Rao is much more than an apologist for India who also loves and understands the best in Europe; he is a universal writer who brings the water of the Ganga to heal the ills of the modern world."

## NOTES AND REFERENCES

1. Mulk Raj Anand, *An Interview with Makarand Paranjape.*
2. Raja Rao, *The Chessmaster and His Moves* (New Delhi: Vision Books, 1988), 11.
3. K.R. Srinivas Iyengar, *Indian Writing in English* (New Delhi: Asia Publishing House, 1973), 386.
4. Raja Rao, *The Chessmaster and His Moves* (New Delhi: Vision Books, 1988), 1.
5. Raja Rao, "Foreword," *Kanthapura* (London: George Allien and Unwin, 1938), 6.
6. *Ibid.,* 39.
7. *Ibid.,* 42.
8. Narsingh Srivastava, *The Mind and Art of Raja Rao* (Bareilly: Prakash Book Depot, 1980), 28.
9. Raja Rao, *The Serpent and the Rope* (Delhi: Hind Pocket Books, 1968), 350.
10. *Ibid.,* 383.
11. *Ibid.,* 335.
12. *Ibid.,* xiii.
13. *Bhagwad Geeta,* xviii-66.
14. Raja Rao, *The Cat and Shakespeare* (Delhi: Hind Pocket Books, 1971), 10-12.
15. Narsingh Srivastava, *The Mind and Art of Raja Rao* (Bareilly: Prakash Book Depot, 1980), 36-37.
16. Makarand Paranjape (ed.), *The Best of Raja Rao* (New Delhi: Katha Classic, 1998), xiv.
17. *Ibid.,* xvii.
18. Raja Rao, *The Chessmaster and His Moves* (New Delhi: Vision Books, 1988), 11.
19. *Ibid.,* 271.
20. *Ibid.,* 341.
21. *Ibid.,* 419-20.
22. Makarand Paranjape (ed.), *The Best of Raja Rao* (New Delhi: Katha Classic, 1998), xiii.

# Chapter 11

# The Concept of Humanistic Values in the Novels of Arun Joshi

*Rashmi Gaur* and *Shivani Vatsa*

The Indian English novel is a unique amalgamation of Indian content and western form. It is an integral part of Indian reality being deeply rooted in the Indian soil. The Indian English writers in the post-independence period started turning away from the past focussing their attention now on contemporary issues. The cleavage of the country on religious-political issues, communal riots leaving millions of people either dead or homeless even after the colonial rulers had left, poverty, social injustice, class inequality—all these along with the rapid industrial and technological development created an atmosphere of general distrust and resulted in superficial existence of man. Arun Joshi delves deeply into the crises of the contemporary Indian life and establishes the supreme significance of humanistic values in the life of the modern man who is under the vicious impact of industrialization and modernization.

During industrial revolution striking changes took place in England and in other parts of Europe. The advancement in the field of science and technology came as a boon to the mankind making his life comfortable by most of the repetitive and laborious work being now done by the machines. Also the stupendous progress in science helped man to gain control over the environment and reach unprecedented levels of development. Industrialization, automation, communication revolution, urbanization, etc., have posed innumerable challenges for human beings. The revolution in communication technology has transformed the whole community into a global village. Science and technology have made a tremendous impact on health and hygiene conditions and have been helpful in controlling many dreaded diseases. The invention of steam boats, railways, Arkwright's spinning-frame and later on, electricity, etc., changed the whole world into an industrial society. It gave a boost to the standard of living of the people but it also gave rise to new problems. It led gradually to air pollution, water pollution, noise pollution, depletion of natural resources, expansion of slums, industrial unrest and to many psychological and social problems. The industrialized civilization has become ultra-materialistic and the moral values have taken a back seat. The spoils of scientific revolution are many. Man has almost been transformed into machine and, at the pace at which he is getting himself involved in the formidable industrialization, he would soon find his life devoid of all the charm, form or taste and changed into dull and insipid life surrounded on all sides by the artificiality. It is no denying that the scientific and technological revolutions had its own merits but its catastrophic impact on the society and the individuals is at the same time quite alarming. The reason for this ruinous state of civilization is due to the sheer lack in ethical standards and moral considerations.

The modernization and automation pose a threat to the individuals of the post-industrial society of the bourgeois world. Individuals inhabiting the highly modernized society are being transformed into 'thinking machines.' Mechanization has not only unleashed men from monotonous, dreary work and labour, but has also deprived him of satisfying labour, and creative and productive work. The work being controlled by the machines, the present work force remains idle leading to the nullification of individuals talents, and creative potentialities. Actively thinking, talented individuals are transformed by uncontrolled automation into a robot bereft of identity, lonelier and alienated from his fellow-beings. Arun Joshi in his works exposes the undue pressures by the modern civilization on the individuals which leave them as mere automations with no sensitivity. He depicts the subsequent degradation of the individuals in Indian milieu since their pre-independence stage, profoundly affected in cultural norms, value system, beliefs and attitudes.

The protagonist of Arun Joshi feels smothered by the malicious effects of the progress of science and technology. Billy in *The Strange Case of Billy Biswas*, feels himself "pinned down there, like a butterfly" (*SCBB*, 47). Human being depressed by the automation in the modern society has lost the feeling of his identity and awareness of his individuality. Being turned into a mechanism where his creativeness counts for nothing, man undergoes deep personality crises. Joshi depicts the dehumanization of the life of society resulting in alienation and isolation of the individuals from their fellow-beings. The brutal and inhumane post-industrial society, cold towards the alienated human beings, annihilates and destroys the individuals. The individual leads a meaningless life with his faith obliterated and psyche crippled by the tremendous advances of science and technology in the modern civilization. The protagonist of the novel, *The Foreigner,* Sindi Oberoi is a restless and uprooted character who wanders restlessly in an inept and sordid world. He reflects helplessly on his meaningless past and is equally apprehensive of his meaningless future. He feels uprooted and lost like a "foreigner anywhere" (*FOR*, 29) and endeavors all through his life not to get involved with anybody or anything. He is obsessed by his loneliness which gets accentuated by his withdrawing from the society around him. Sindi goes on hopping from one country to another because he finds his life meaningless and rootless. He realizes the futility of human achievements and purposelessness of his life at the bare age of twenty-five:

> And yet all shores are alien when you don't belong anywhere. Twenty-fifth Christmas on this planet, twenty-five years largely wasted in search of wrong things in wrong places. Twenty-five years gone in the search of peace and what did I have to show for achievement: a ten-tone body that had to be fed four times a day; twenty-eight times a week. This was the sum of a lifetime of striving. (*FOR*, 80)

The various symptoms of alienation: powerlessness, meaninglessness, normlessness, cultural-estrangement, self-estrangement and isolation are all revealed in the novels of Arun Joshi affecting inter-personal relationships by making people insulate themselves from others. Billy, a sensitive individual, is disenchanted from the contemporary society. His inner restlessness and sense of alienation is enhanced by his failure to establish meaningful contact with his wife Meena who in fact lacks the feelings of "empathy" and "sufficient idea of suffering" (*SCBB*, 185). Tormented by the proliferation and prominence of inhumane values in the contemporary society—greed, avarice, hollowness and hypocrisy—Billy leaving behind his family and filial obligations disappears in the Saal forests of the Maikala hills. He now looks for solace and tranquility in the primitive world, which is still replete with the old humanistic values. Billy feels himself alienated from the civilized men:

> I see a roomful of finely dressed men and women on downy sofas and while I am looking at them under my very nose, they turn into a kennel of dogs yawning (their large teeth showing) or snuggling against each other or holding whisky glasses in their furred paws. (*SCBB*, 96)

He has a dislike for the elite class and its character and to him all the people around him are "hung on this peg of money" (*SCBB*, 97) and are nothing more than a "heap of tinsel" (*SCBB*, 141). The novelist expresses his distaste for the money-mindedness of the people leading to the degradation of their souls. Man's internal life in the contemporary society has been displaced, externalized and trivialized. He leads a life purely on superficial plane indulging himself in the vices and tricks of the spiritually uprooted but scientifically and technologically advanced civilization. Ratan Rathor, the protagonist of *The Apprentice* and child of a freedom struggler succumbs to the worldly comforts and pleasures. Joshi, through the portrayal of Ratan emphasizes the contrast between the values prevalent in the pre-independence and post-independence times. Tryth, honesty, hard labour and character have been replaced by falsehood, cunningness, flattery and immorality in the present civilized society. All the values have become subjugated to money. The contemporary man has lost all his sense of values and norms. A simple youth, Ratan with high degree of sense of values, character and morality is transformed by the contemporary value deficient society into a cunning, nefarious and unscrupulous man. James Martin cites the statement of Abraham Maslow, an American psychologist, in his work *Technology's Crucible*:

> ...the ultimate disease of our time is valuelessness.... This state is more crucially dangerous than ever before in history. (JAMES, 72)

The humanistic values prevalent in the ancient times have gradually degraded and vanished from the society. The ancient civilization replete with the values of honesty, faith, generosity, tolerance, patience, fortitude, naturalness, feeling of brotherhood and innocence has given way to modern civilization lacking the valuable humanistic values and consequently leading to the deterioration of the individuals.

Ratan confesses that he has become a "master faker" (*APP*, 27) in "Money's Kingdom" (APP, 73). Arun Joshi through the speech of Ratan illustrates the degenerated, valueless and corrupt modern society:

> A bribe could get you a bed in a hospital, a place to burn you dead. Doctors, had a fee to give false certificates, magistrates for false judgements. For a larger sum of money politicians changed sides. For a larger sum they declared wars. Bribery was accepted by factory inspectors, bank agents and college professors; by nurses; priests and chartered accountants; by all those who acted in the public interest. Men took bribes to facilitate the seduction of their women. (*APP*, 108)

The mad rush of modern man to amass more and more wealth has resulted in the selfish nature of the man with no meaning for human values, ideals and morals. Man has become self-centred looking after his own interests rather than that of the whole society. *The Gherao,* one of the short stories from *The Survivor* delineates the money-minded nature of the Principal's son and daughter-in-law who attach more importance to wealth than to human relationship. The Principal says, "I have a son but he does not answer my letters. My daughter-in-law says she does not ever want to see my face again. And all because I did not give them the ten thousand rupees which is all that I have" (*SUR*, 27). The blind pursuit of wealth by contemporary man has alienated him from his authentic-self and moved him farther away from the wealth of humanistic values. Another story, *The Eve-teaser* emphatically brings before us the deteriorating state of the human values. The story is about two youths, Ram and Shyam who being "children of their times"—times of moral degradation—"teased young bodies, issued cat calls when the agony within their breasts became unbearable and drank in by lung-fulls the heady odours of female flesh" (*SUR*, 45). The aspect of moral degradation has also been hinted at in the story *The Servant* where the servant of Mrs. Khanna visits brothels of Bombay to satisfy his sexual urge. Also modern man seeking sexual gratification outside marriage clearly points towards the moral downfall of humanity. Ratan in *The Apprentice* starts visiting prostitutes and ogles at the women around "openly, willfully" (*APP*, 74). He is transformed into a womanizer and indulges in intimate physical relations with the prostitutes. Thus the glorious heritage of man is shattered and he has become an immoral being in the contemporary corrupt and morally deteriorated society.

Joshi finds that even religion has become fossilized and irrelevant in the ultra-modern civilization. The priest of the temple is ready to bribe anyone including Ratan himself to save the skin of his son, a contractor who having used the substandard material in the construction resulted in the collapse of many roofs and was now facing the punishment. The main cause of the decline of religious beliefs is the spirit of skepticism fostered by science and condemnation of religious attitudes.

Arun Joshi presents an India permeated with corruption which is the consequence of lack of values in our society. God, in the modern society, can be propitiated by gifts in black money to his temples, where the priests themselves are corrupt. The lack of humanistic values in the present civilization has replaced sacrifice by self-interest, honesty by fraud and deception, courage by fear, morality by corruption and ideals by deals. Through the portrayal of various characters in *So Many Hungers!* Bhabani

Bhattacharya, much like Joshi, portrays the dehumanization of man in a mechanical society, where they suffer from rootlessness and meaninglessness and feels alienated from the "self." The selfish and debased Grand Master in *The City and the River* to fulfil his personal desires alienated himself from the love of his public and plunges the whole city in the whirlpool of corruption, anarchy and chaos.

Arun Joshi's novels are a true mirror of the present-day Indian society with its cynicism, hedonism, loss of faith, confusion of values, dependence on logic and reason and anxieties. The tremendous progress in the field of science and technology has given rise to skepticism where man wants to have evidence for each and everything. This undue reliance on reason and logic has made modern man more bewildered and confused with diminishing faith in religion, traditions and customs. Individuals in the contemporary world are hedonists, blinded by the worldly pleasures and comforts. His ceaseless lust for material comforts and bodily pleasures seem to be endless. Bhaskar, influenced by the western culture, is incessantly tormented by undefinable hunger, a restlessness, incertitude, discontentment and an inherent sickness. He in his feverish quest to find peace and solace from the world of automation discovers a haunting emptiness and void and gets mentally shattered, morally deteriorated and physically impoverished. Joshi observes a significant influence on the pattern of human thinking and gullibility in the clash between faith and doubt, and belief and reason in the contemporary milieu. Reason, observation, classification, verification and scrutiny which constitute the scientific method, have subtly influenced the pattern of human thinking, man is more and more inclined to reason about the events and concepts before he makes up his mind to reject or accept. This has, though infinitesimal, but far-reaching consequence on man's approach and adherence to age-old values of life. Passive faith has been replaced by critical questioning. Som Bhaskar is puzzled between the scientific reasoning of the philosophers—Jung, Freud, Spinoza and Darwin whom he studied in his university—and the faith and trust of his mother and wife Geeta. He is tormented because his rational and scientific self attracts him to Darwin and his primitive self forces him to accept faith, trust and endurance. His analytical and skeptical mind rejects the world of Benaras, Lal Haveli and Anuradha as "bores, frogs struck in their ancient marshy well" (*LL*, 113). Bhaskar is haunted by a recurrent dream in which he sees himself flying in a plane towards a mountain. He is sitting in the front but the man sitting in the back has all the gears of the pilot. Then suddenly the sky is full of mist and fog and it starts raining blurring the way. When Bhaskar looks back he is surprised to see Aftab sitting behind him. The plane flying at a fast speed is about to crash into the mountain when Aftab escapes unharmed and Bhaskar is left alone screaming and shuddering with terror. The dream symbolizes Bhaskar's inability to get spiritual fulfillment which is beyond his reach. The dream suggests that one must forsake and liberate oneself from the fetters of selfish desires and must rely on faith, trust, endurance and love to reach the levels of spirituality. Som, thus with scientific temper, materialistic outlook and reliance on reason suffers at the hands of contemporary society. G.D Joglekar in his paper on *Science and Spirituality* says:

> Science, the word used in the most general sense to indicate natural science, and technology are the two wheels of the vehicle of development. They provide us material benefits but not cultural and higher values of life. (PODDAR, 177-78)

The treatment of the river by the Grand Master in *The City and the River* too, emphasizes the prominence of skepticism in the modern times in contrast to the faith of the boatmen. For the Grand Master, the river is just a stream of water. When the astrologer, tries to make him understand the boatmen's point of view for whom the river is "a symbol of the divine mother" (*CTR*, 21), he brushes aside the thought as a mere superstition. The river has a symbolic significance in the novel. The great river is "Times's consort and Time itself" (*CTR*, 61). It speaks only to those who are pure and innocent at heart. The 'city' stands for humanity inhabiting the mundane world with no knowledge of humanistic values and spiritually uprooted. Scientific temper and rational attitude thus have given rise to increased skepticism and doubt. Consequently man is now more baffled and confused with erosion of his faith on trust, values and reliance.

*The Survivor,* a collection of short stories by Arun Joshi though deals with different issues yet it projects through its various characters, the need of humanistic values in the contemporary civilization and man's torment in the gradual absence of it. *The Homecoming* tells us about a soldier who after his return from the war finds himself as an alien:

> His mother was very keen on his marriage. So was he, in a way until before the war. During the war he had killed ten men, led assaults that ended the lives of many others and he had seen several hundred dead, gashed, charred, bloated, hacked, shot through with their hands behind their backs. He had seen bodies gorging the viaducts of canals, flaking off like stale cake. Once he saw a hockey field strewn with the skeleton of boys. That was the first time he had seen dead people, aside from the corpses that he had seen carried around for cremation. His family were well-to-do and there had not yet been a death. So he had not seen a dead body before and now he had seen hundreds of them. And he had been wondering about marriage. What was the meaning of one man's marriage; one man's life. He had been wondering what life was all about. Who, he had been thinking could possibly be running the world such thoughts filled his head with confusion as he sat about or played cards or went out with his father for a game of gold. (*SUR*, 99)

Arun Joshi as in his earlier novels delineates the torturous impact of longing for wealth, in *The City and the River,* that dehumanizes modern man. Sindi in *The Foreigner* and Ratan in *The Apprentice* are corroded by the degrading influence of money culture. The greed for possession of unlimited wealth blinded Som Bhaskar in *The Last Labyrinth* who frantically involves himself in collecting the shares and expanding his empire. The mad rush for wealth and materialism has blinded man and denied him tranquility and solace. The novelist expresses his concern for the modern man who is turning out to be more materialistic and his lust for materialism indulges him in endless pursuit of wealth and power. Joshi, in his novels, delineates the barrenness in the life of the individuals, a result of its passion with power and self, with no feeling of compassion, understanding and love for fellow-beings. The nature of the modern existence, in *The City and the River* is revealed by the dominance of steel, glass and marble in its architect, and the total absence of vegetation and flowers in the city. The road that links the palace with the government houses is wide and well-paved but is "treeless and without flowers" (*CTR*, 31). With the coming of the winter, below the snowline the landscape becomes covered with flowers and the flowers bloom along the banks of the river. But in "the city's newly laid parks and along its well-straightened avenues and on the seven hills...in spite of the chief horticulturist's strenuous efforts and to the Grand Master regret, neither grass nor flowers grow" (*CTR*, 136). The aridity and infertility in the city stand for the barrenness in the life of the modern man: devoid of compassion, empathy, tolerance, love, faith, honesty, selflessness and morality.

The want of values pose a threat to the moral fabric of the whole human society and has led to the proliferation of hatred, greed, corruption and anarchy in the contemporary society. In *The City and the River* there are references to hoarding of food material and adulteration of oil which lead to the death of Bhoma's parents. The following words spoken by Grand trader to Dharma reveals the bribery prevalent in the city:

> We only want to know where a commodity is available and if, available whether it will create a shortage if brought in large quantities thus raising the price above the level at which it was bought...of course, we also have to know where ware-houses are available, who is to be bribed to prevent raids on these ware-houses and soon. And now, sir, I must give you a final word of advice.... You must take bribes. A police officer who does not take bribes come under suspicion. (*CTR*, 106)

Arun Joshi has dealt in length, in his novels, with the deterioration of values in the contemporary society. In *The Apprentice* Ratan makes a decided denial of having anything to do with the clearing of defective war material and accepting the bribe which had ultimately led to the death of his friend, Brigadier. His life is a story of succumbing to the temptations under the threat of insecurity, anxiety, fear and restlessness. His was the case of a man who had lost his identity in becoming one with the process of career and business and knew that "deep down...I had lost significance as an official: as a citizen; as a man" (*APP*, 70). The alienated man has moved farther from his age-old values and morals. The novels portray characters totally engrossed in the materialistic comforts and desires and thus neglect the interest of the entire civilization and think only about their own ambitions, interests and desires. The result is, then, nothing but meaninglessness and hollowness in the life of the individuals.

Many eminent novelists like D.H. Lawrence, Somerset Maugham, Samuel Beckett, Graham Greene, Bhabani Bhattacharya and many more have exposed the predicament of the individuals in a society fast depleting with the humanistic values. Lawrence in *The Rainbow* reveals the man's dilemma in establishing his own personal identity in the modern society. The desirable values of faith, loyalty and trust disappeared from the lives of the colliers and cracks began to appear in the conjugal lives of the colliers. In his another novel, *Women in Love,* Lawrence again through the portrayal of character of Gerald depicts the crisis of the civilization. Gerald, the friend of Birkin and son of the industrial magnate, Mr Crich loses touch with his 'self,' and is thus unable to respond to the feeling of others. Graham Greene's Querry in *A Burnt Out Case* and Samuel Beckett's protagonist in his novel *Murphy* experience the dehumanization in the materialistic world. They both have utter dislike for the contemporary phoney civilization and desire for basic human emotions which have almost perished in the materialistic way of life. Bhabani Bhattacharya too in, *So Many Hungers!*, "an impeachment of man's inhumanity of man" (SI, 414), deals with the lack of humanistic approach during the famine havoc brought about by the war. The colonial rulers evicted the villagers from their land, drained the countryside of rice and wrecked the boat as a response to the war. Their response to starvation was callous revealing the inhumane civilized human beings. The great ones came and talked only about "Japanese foe and the might of India's own palton" (BB,

136-37). Instead of providing food to the villagers who had walked "the three hour way to Rangamati banyan and the three hour way back on scorching sun and five thousand fake words in their empty stomachs" (BB, *ibid.*).

But among the contemporary writers, Arun Joshi has profoundly taken up the theme of need of humanistic values—truth, honesty, charity, love—in the life of the confused individuals and which alone can sustain our civilization. He, himself being a technocrat, has emphatically revealed the dehumanizing impact of technology on the moral fabric of the individuals.

It is true to comment that human race is today in the midst of one of the greatest crises of history. Through the delineation of the predicament of the characters, Arun Joshi reiterates the need of humanistic values in the life of the individuals caught in the whirlpool of discontent, frustration, disenchantment and utter dejection. The individuals find themselves in a maze and are confused with the erosion of the values in the wake of progress of science and technology, and the corrosion of man's inner-self in an overwhelming upsurge of materialism. Arun Joshi represents a world where people have lost their values, traditions and patterns of life, morality and emotions. The predicament, the novelist feels, is due to the utter destruction of the humanistic values in the society with the startling developments in science and technology. There is a conflict between ancient traditions and the emerging new ethos. Man is a blend of baseness and nobility, of intelligence and folly. Arun Joshi hopes man to be saved from the corruption present in his own nature. He expects man to make an effort to solve the conflict in himself, diminish the hateful emotions and increase love, faith, fellow-feeling, concern, tolerance, trust and moral values. Arun Joshi feels a desperate need for moulding our society in the path of development of humanistic values.

## WORKS CITED

Bhattacharya, Bhabani. *So Many Hunger!*, Delhi: Orient Paperbacks, 1978. All textual references arranged as BB.

Iyengar, Srinivas. *Indian Writing in English*. Delhi: Sterling, 1980. Textual reference arranged as SI.

Joshi, Arun. *The Strange Case of Billy Biswas*. Delhi: Orient Paperbacks, 1987. All textual references arranged as *SCBB*.

—. *The Foreigner.* Delhi: Hind Pocket Books, 1968. All textual references arranged as *FOR*.

—. *The Apprentice*. Delhi: Orient Paperbacks, 1993. All textual references arranged as *APP*.

—. *The City and the River.* Delhi: Orient Paperbacks, 1994. All textual references arranged as *CTR*.

—. *The Survivor.* Delhi: Sterling, 1975. All textual references arranged as *SUR*.

—. *The Last Labyrinth*. Delhi: Orient Paperbacks, 1992. All textual references arranged as *LL*.

Martin, James. *Technology's Crucible*. London: Prentice-Hall International Ltd., 1987. All textual reference arranged as JAMES.

Poddar, Arabinda, ed. *Man, Science and Society.* Shimla: Indian Institute of Advanced Study, 1970, Vol. 9. All textual reference arranged as PODDAR.

# Chapter 12

# Journey Beyond Death: A Symbolic View of Sri Aurobindo's Savitri

*O.P. Budholia*

Sri Aurobindo ranks among the great personalities of modern India. A Mahayogi, a politician, a social reformer, a prose writer, a critic, a story writer, a dramatist and a linguist, Sri Aurobindo holds a unique place among the Mahakavis of the world. He has an extraordinarily supple intellect, a breadth of mind so extensive that there is scarcely an important field of human interest which escapes his notice. Nurtured entirely in the first twenty years of his life on European literature, Sri Aurobindo inflames native inhibitions for his later writings. He is truly a renaissance man who makes a happy combination of the Yogi of Mahatma Gandhi and the artist of Rabindranath Tagore.

*Savitri,* a magnum opus of his poetical works, becomes an odyssey of modern India. How did he breathe in for the writing of *Savitri* is difficult to say? However, it seems appropriate to quote partially his own letter written to Sri Man-Mohan Ghose in 1899 for his strong liking of a character like Savitri. This letter shows the growth of the seed in the inner countries of his mind for the immortal character of Savitri:

> ...are Rama, Sita, Savitri merely patterns of moral excellence? I, who have read their tales in the swift and mighty language of Valmiki and Vyasa and thrilled with their joys and sorrows, cannot persuade myself that it is so.

> Surely Savitri that strong silent heart with her powerful and subtly indicated has both life and charm; surely Rama puts too much divine fire into all he does to be a dead thing—Sita is too gracious and sweet, too full of human lovingness of womanly weakness and womanly strength.... Are these not here sufficient materials of beauty for the artist to weave into immortal vision.[1] (60)

Savitri a woman of life and charm, and Sita with her womanly weakness and strength invite the enkindled creativity of Sri Aurobindo's mind. This odyssey of modern literature is immediately concerned symbolically with an evolutionary process of human psyche. In fact Sri Aurobindo concentrates himself to outline Savitri's character with such a depth of an artist as she stands to face any difficulty that arises in her upward march to self-realization. Here in this paper, an effort is made to reveal those spiritual aspects of Savitri by which she calls on Yama, Lord of Death, overcomes Him and returns back to earth for professing love as the supreme *motif* of human life.

Sri Aurobindo studied the original epics of Valmiki and Vyasa. The story of Savitri occurs in the *Vana Parva* of the *Mahabharata*. In the *Mahabharata*, this story has been told in seven cantos by Rishi Markandeya to the exiled King Yudhisthira. Aswapathy, king of Madra, retires in seclusion for eighteen years in order to perform austerities as a representative of humanity. He gets a boon from Mother Goddess during his self-realization for her incarnation in his house. The Goddess in the form of Savitri appears as a worldly daughter of Aswapathy. The story of *Savitri: A Legend and a Symbol* has been divided in to Three Parts having 12 Books of 49 Cantos spread over nearly 24000 (twenty-four thousand) lines.

The Keynote of *Savitri* thus lies in symbolism. Sri Aurobindo himself remarks about the symbolic theme of Savitri in the following words:

> Satyavan is the soul carrying the divine truth of being within itself but descended into the grip of death of ignorance; Savitri is word, daughter of the Sun goddess of the supreme truth who comes down and is born to save; Aswapathy, the Lord of the Horses, her human father is the Lord of

Tapasaya, the concentrated energy of spiritual endeavour that helps us to rise from the mortal to the immortal planes; Dyumatsena, Lord of Shining Hosts, father of Satyavan is the Divine Mind here fallen blind loosing its celestial kingdom of vision, and through that loses kingdom of glory.[2]

This quotation of Sri Aurobindo reveals that there are many symbols, images and myths which are interlinked together in order to highlight the evolutionary standpoints of Sri Aurobindo's vision. Sri Aurobindo does not like an escape from the earth to heaven. He likes to transform the earth into a heaven. He desires, amidst all fluctuations, to make earth an evolutionary place with a psychic entity as its centre. So, he shows many fluctuations first in the spiritual Sadhana of Aswapathy and next in the journey of Savitri. There are two movements in the Sadhana of Aswapathy: at the first stage he remains intoxicated with his personal emancipation, resulting in several impediments as Sadhaka; but gradually, he develops disinterestedness in his Sadhana and becomes engrossed in the welfare of humanity and thus he feels a "motionless still"—the self-realization of his soul.

Amidst such a state of trance, Mother Goddess promises him:

> O strong forerunner I have heard thy cry
> One shall descend and break the iron Law
> Change Nature's doom by the Lone Spirit's Power
> A limitless mind that can contain the World.[3]
>
> [*Savitri*, 346]

The epithet "Strong Forerunner" describes an extension of Aswapathy's Sadhana of super consciousness through Savitri, "to change Nature's doom" becomes indicative of removing all kinds of fear-psychosis and "a limitless mind" delineates the over-head concept of Sri Aurobindo even before the arrival of Savitri on the earth. From time immemorial, it has been the effort of human beings to overcome the fear psychosis either of life and death or worldly pain and suffering. The advent of Savitri on earth symbolises over coming of every kind of fear-psychosis. She is a complete human being. Like Milton's defence of justifying the ways of God to man, Sri Aurobindo too delineates the birth of Savitri with a divine radiance. Christ a God-in-man, brings the emancipation to the suffering humanity. Savitri too stands for removing all Karmic attraction and repulsion of scenes and situations:

A mightier influx filled the oblivious clay;
A lamp was lit, a sacred image made
A meeting ray had touched the earth
Bridging the gulf between man's mind.

[*Savitri*, 352]

Savitri is "a mystic acolyte" who is trained in "Nature's School." She sails the boat of her journey against the currents. She is a self-poised character who begins her life after death. She grows in the house of Aswapathy upto a maiden goddess—like (devarupini). Her father instructs her: "Seek and choose a husband for yourself." She starts her journey with this purpose and ultimately she finds one in the form of Satyavan. She chooses him as her husband in spite of the warning by divine sage Narada for the short span of Satyavan's life. Now onwards, she broods over saving her human existence and her journey becomes a spiritual journey. Sri Aurobindo during her journey reveals her human aspects too. The human weaknesses according to Sri Aurobindo can only be overcome when a man performs austerities. Prof. R.K. Diwakar remarks beautifully about the Yogic Process of Sri Aurobindo: "Man is in essence his consciousness, not his body or life or biological mind."[4]

Savitri is a fully realized character. She reacts after hearing the prophecy of Narada and at the same time listens silently the inner voice of her conscience. She realizes nucleus for her future life in austerities:

O spirit, O Immortal energy
Arise,
O soul, and Vanguish
Time and Death.

[*Savitri*, 470]

It is through penances and austerities she can triumph time. She at once begins her psychic journey to realize the untrodden regions of human psyche. Sri Aurobindo concedes an ever presence of the brute in the inner countries of human mind. In *Savitri*, the cantos entitled: "The Entry in Inner Countries" and "The Triple Soul Forces" of Book VII, Sri Aurobindo portrays the character of Savitri like an ordinary human being. She too witnesses the presence of the brute inside her mind when she undergoes Freaudian complex of ego and libido. She brings in to being the womanly weaknesses when she realizes inside her mind:

> ...the fire and mystery of forbidden delight drunk from the
> World-libido's bottomless well
> And the honey-sweet poison wine of lust and death.
>
> [*Savitri*, 492]

The recognition of attraction and repulsion is the essence of Karmayoga. Like Milton's statements of universal validity as "The mind is its own place, and in itself/ can make a Heaven of Hell, a Hell of Heaven,"[5] Sri Aurobindo too reveals, "our minds have made the World in which we live" (*Savitri*, 500). Thus, Savitri soon overcomes the brute inside her mind and emerges as a being of super consciousness. She proceeds now into "a brilliant ordered space." These two worlds correspond with Freud's concept of 'Id' and 'Super ego.'

Being aware of her inner conscience and spiritual glow, she finally "had arisen up from, body, mind and life/ she was no more a person in a world/ she had escaped into Infinity." There is a fine parallel between this super consciousness of Savitri and the concept of "Purusha" in Srimad Bhagwad Geeta. Sri Aurobindo mentions the realized soul of Savitri as:

> She was the single self of all these selves
> She was in them and they were all in her
> What seemed herself was an image of the whole.
>
> [*Savitri*, 557]

In the same manner, Sri Krishna reveals his cosmic form before Arjuna thus:

> There is nothing else beside Me, Arjuna,
> Like clusters yarn-beads formed by
> Knots on a thread, all this is threaded in Me.[6]

As the time would have it, she meets her fate when Satyavan dies in the forest. She recollects her spiritual energy and faces the dark forces in the form of Death. God of Death tries to persuade her not to insist on the release of Satyavan's Soul. He tries to make her understand that her passions and earthly desires covet her to check the Law of Nature. But Savitri negates it and says:

> My love is not hunger of the heart
> My love is not a craving of the flesh;
> It came to me from God, to God returns.
>
> [*Savitri,* 612]

Love is the nucleus in Sri Aurobindo's *Savitri*. Love bereft of human desires and lust triumphs over death. This is yet another symbolic aspect of *Savitri*. Again, there is a fine parallel between T.S. Eliot and Sri Aurobindo in their concepts of higher love. In *Four Quartets,* T.S. Eliot describes:

> For liberation not less of love but expanding
> Of love beyond desire, and so liberation
> From the future as well as the past.[7]

When Death enquires of Savitri about her spiritual power by which she intends for restoring Satyavan's Soul. Savitri reveals her spiritual powers before the God of Death, Yama. Lord Yama realizes the "third mysterious eye" in Savitri. She is now in the possession of the powers of creation and distinction. Death as such withdraws its evil forces and restores the Soul of Satyavan. This "dire universal shadow" vanishes now into the "Void," leaving Satyavan rejuvenated for the love of man on the earth. This withdrawal of Yama symbolizes a Triumph of love (Savitri) over the dark forces (Death) for the restoration of Soul (Satyavan). Finally she meets the person she adores:

> And Satyavan and Savitri were alone
> But neither stirred: between these figures rose
> A mute invisible translucent wall
> In the blank moments pause nothing could move
> All waited on the unknown inscrutable Will.
>
> [*Savitri,* 668]

Savitri, after conquering Death, develops that state of equanimity by which a man arrests desires and sensual pleasures.

T.S. Eliot also refers to the same temper for attaining the state of Timelessness and desirelessness:

> Desire itself is movement/ Not in itself desirable;
> Love is itself unmoving,
> Only the cause and end of movement,
> Timeless and undesiring.[8]

Desire entraps man in scenes and situations causing the prime source of suffering. Savitri throws away all temptations for the inhabitance in Heaven and comes back on the earth. To her and to Sri Aurobindo:

> Earth is the chosen place of the mightiest Souls;
> Earth is the heroic spirit's battle field
> The forge where the Archmason shapes his works.
> Thy servitudes on earth are greater, King,
> Than all the glorious liberties of Heaven.
>
> [*Savitri*, 686]

The evolutionary process in Savitri carries a plan of transforming human in to divine, earth into heaven and human love as the base for conquering the forces of darkness and ignorance. Savitri, a saviour of human soul, represents an absolute power (Shakti) and Satyavan represents human soul (Atman). So, this unity of Satyavan and Savitri symbolizes Satyam (Truthfulness), Shivam (Goodness) and Sundaram (Beauty). This unity also symbolizes an evolutionary process as first-born of a new supernal race set in the World to refashion human nature and earth nature.[9] Sri Aurobindo in the chapter entitled "Eternal Mate" of Book XII, plans the dialectic transformation of mind in to super mind:

> He (Satyavan) is my soul that gropes out of the beast
> To reach humanity's heights of lucent thought
> And the Vicinity of Truth's sublime.
> He is the *god* head growing in human lives
> And in the body of earth being's forms:
> He is the soul of man climbing to God
> In Nature's surge out of earth's ignorance.
>
> [*Savitri*, 703]

Sri Aurobindo is also successful in his vision for portraying the human passions and desires in Savitri. In spite of her spiritual height, she promises Satyavan to her womanly passion:

> She closed her arms about his breast and head
> As if to keep him on her bosom Worn
> For ever through the journeying of the years
> So far a while they stood entwined their Kiss
> And passion—tranced embrace a meeting point
> In their commingling spirits one for ever
> Two-souled two-bodied for the Joys of Time.
>
> [*Savitri,* 721]

And she follows Satyavan to the house of Dyumatsena her father-in-law for a greater dawn to come on the earth.

On artistic level, the poem meets a clique of detractors. There is a critic who goes to the extent of describing that he finds "Only poor false poetry, unoriginal in imagery and void of true wording and true vision."[10] The charge of unoriginality is replied by Sri Aurobindo himself as, "I was not seeking originality but for truth and the effective poetical expression of my vision."[11] Thus, the vision dominates the form of the epic. Sri Aurobindo never claims for the originality of the theme because he is dealing with the original "Upakhayan" (legend) of sage Vyasa from *The Mahabharata*. His originality lies in interpreting this legend in modern context. The imagery of the poem is concrete. The images like "Green-gold Sward" (Book V), "Swift round," "The hermit thatch" (Book V), "Vermilion caste mark," "Stone-eyed with mechanic dreams," "Golden Ecstasy," "Winged poets," "Sylvan home," "House of Clay" (Book XII) bring forth the Keatsian world of concrete images.

With regard to the vision of the epic, I would like to quote a modern critic of Literature and Linguistics from Israel—Mr. A.B. Yehoshua. Mr. Yehoshua recently visited Book Fair at Delhi on February 16, 1998. When he was interviewed by Ratnottam Sen Gupta for the future of poetry, he replied him thus: "Literature is not food for entertainment but ideology for the soul." Again, he pointed out that "Western realism with eastern mysticism," presents stark facts for open heart surgery to reveal "the veiled mysticism of the soul."[12] Sri Aurobindo is the poet who always advocated for the cause of the world vision. This is the reason he accomplished the universal Town—Auroville at Pondicherry. In fact his world vision is acceptable to all alike.

The creation of Auroville brings forth the universal vision of *Savitri,* for it is meant to be the alchemy of a new spiritual faith emerging as a constant aspiration for Life Divine on the earth. Sri Aurobindo is an encyclopaedic poet who expresses a kind of spiritual experience in *Savitri* which very few people would aspire or admit to aspiring to. His spiritual Odyssey—*Savitri* has also modern relevance for its soothing effects to the tension tormented men in this high-tech and dangerously ecological imbalanced age.

## NOTES AND REFERENCES

1. All textual quotations are to Sri Aurobindo's *Savitri: A Legend and a Symbol.* Published in Sri Aurobindo Ashram, Pondicherry. Fourth revised edition, 1993. Part and Book nos. are mentioned inside the article.
2. *Sri Aurobindo's Circle* (Sri Aurobindo Ashram: Pondicherry, 1974), 71-75.
3. *Mother India* (Sri Aurobindo Ashram, Pondicherry, June 1971), 312.
4. R.R. Diwakar, *Mahayogi: Life Sadhana and Teachings of Sri Aurobindo* (Bhartiya Vidya Bhavan, Bombay, 1976), 260.
5. Milton's *Paradise Lost* Books I and II (M. MacMillan, MacMillan & Co. Ltd., London, 1901), 8.
6. *Srimad Bhagwad Geeta* (Gita Press Gorakhpur), Ch. VII Sloka VII.
7. T.S. Eliot's *Four Quartets* (Oxford University Press, New Delhi, Seventh impression, 1986), 55.
8. *Ibid.,* 20.
9. K. Raghavendra Rao, quoted from M.K. Naik edit "Prospective on Indian Poetry in English" (Abhinav Publication, New Delhi, 1980), 61.
10. "Letters on Savitri," *Savitri: A Legend and a Symbol, op. cit.,* 794.
11. *Ibid.*
12. *The Times of India* (New Delhi: Monday, February 16, 1998), 13.

# Chapter 13

## Khushwant Singh: The Painter of Panjabi Consciousness

*Ambuj Kumar Sharma*

Khushwant Singh ranks among India's distinguished men of literary acumen who have achieved an international reputation. His versatility as a novelist, short story writer, historian, essayist, journalist and editor, has enriched the Indian English writing. In an era when Indian English writers' horizon seems to be confined to novel and short stories only, there Khushwant Singh emerges as a towering success in fiction writing along with a historian of Sikh history, biographer of Sikh leaders and many articles revealing a range of thought and reeling as wide as any to be found in the writings of the most significant Indian writers.

Though Khushwant Singh's personality is the direct outcome of western education and culture but at heart, he is a Panjabi, a Sikh. His writings show great imprintings of Panjabi consciousness. His writing has grown out of the grass roots of the social milieu. There are three kinds of environment which influenced Khushwant Singh, the man and the writer. As a child, he was brought up in the village of his birth in Panjab. He mentions in his autobiographical essay, "My roots are in the dunghill of a tiny Indian village."[1] Then he went to a school in Delhi and Lahore and graduated: "I grew up in an Indo-Anglian atmosphere of New Delhi."[2] He is the product of British education which made him, a cultured humanist. "I am the product of both East and the West," he writes, "I am, if I may coin the word, an orio-occidental."[3] In a lecture delivered at Expo 1967 in Montreal, Canada, he hints at things which are implicit in his creative endeavour. The Punjab countryside: urban Indo-anglian Delhi; and the liberal sophisticated atmosphere of London are the three most dominant influences on the writer. Though exposed to the ideas and attitudes of the West, Khushwant Singh, at heart, is an oriental who has retained his Panjabi self and Indianness.

Singh's novels centre on Punjab and his real experience provides him the necessary setting and understanding of men and situations in rural India. His exploration of the experience of rural India is the basic fact of his creative effort. The process of exploration of this fundamental experience is also the mode of his quest for identity, the manner of realising what he really is: his inner most personality.

Khushwant Singh has shown his Panjabi literary consciousness in his writings. His novels—*Train to Pakistan* and *I shall not Hear the Nightingale*, are an artistic exploration of varied facets of Sikh consciousness. They are documentaries given the shine of fiction. It is not to point out that they are pamphlets on Sikhism, for Singh does not write like a missionary or a propagandist. Instead, they are the works of an artist who, only at times, becomes over-zealous in his ideological concerns. His portrayal of the Sikh way of life is characterised by his instinctive understanding of the Sikh psyche which finds expressions in glorious Sikh virtues of valour, heroic-sacrifice and fearlessness. Written from the Sikh viewpoint about the experiences of Sikhs, both the novels are a fictional re-creation of an intensely-felt experience. No wonder, the Sikh sensibility gets communicated through his Sikh protagonists who are drawn from life itself.

*Train to Pakistan* is obviously one of the exquisite novels of post-partition Indo-Anglian fiction. This novel is clearly an effort at fictional re-creation of socio-historical reality of the partition period experienced by the Punjabis in general and Sikhs in particular. *Train to Pakistan* was originally entitled *Mano Majra*. This is the name of a place which is the centre of action in the sequence of events leading to the final disaster. It is situated half a mile away from river Sutlej which, historically speaking is the Ganges of the Sikhs, Mano Majra is shown as a bastion of Sikh culture. It is obvious from the manner in which the novelist chooses to give not only the topography of the village but also its demography. Mano Majra, truly is a representative Sikh village of the Punjab. It has about seventy families, out of which main inhabitants are Sikhs who are regarded as a martial race of instinctively warm-hearted and laborious people. Khushwant Singh describes the human geography of the village:

> The only Hindu family in the village is that of the money-lender, Lala Ram Lal. The others are Sikhs or Muslims about equal in number. The Sikhs own all the land around the village, the Muslims are tenants who share tilling with the owners. There are a few families of sweepers whose religion is uncertain.[4]

Mano Majran Sikhs have an abiding faith in the 'Akal Purakh' and are religious in their observance of religious rituals. Gurdwara, i.e., the Guru's house, is the place where they converge as a congregation on all important occasions to seek spiritual solace and moral strength. It is thrown open, round the clock to anyone in need of peace and tranquility. Every Sikh is expected to preserve its dignity by maintaining its sanctity and piety. Mr. Singh paints a graphic picture of the Gurdwara which is the hub of all the village activities—spiritual, social or secular:

> He saw the flag-mast draped in yellow cloth with triangular flag above the conglomeration of mud huts. On the flag was the Sikh symbol in black, a quoit with a dagger running through two swords crossed beneath.... At the end opposite the entrance was a large hall in which the scripture, the Granth, lay wrapped in gaudy silks under a velvet awning.... Beside the well stood a four foot brick column supporting the long-flag-mast with the yellow cloth covering it like a stocking.[5]

Meet Singh, the Sikh priest, addressed as "Bhaiji" by the villagers, welcomes Iqbal with the characteristic Sikh greeting "Sat Sri Akal" to the Gurdwara. He exhorts the stranger with a smile: "This is a Gurdwara, the Guru's house—anyone may stay here. But you must have your head covered and you must not bring in any cigarettes or tobacco, nor smoke."[6] The descriptive details about the Gurdwara are intended to evoke the atmosphere of the Sikh village. So is Bhai Meet Singh's exhortation for the preservation of the sanctity of the Guru's house, for sure, a part of the novelist's desire to air the tenets of Sikh religion—may be for the benefit of those who are ignorant of its essentials. It is evident from the novelist's treatment of the subject that he is firmly committed to Sikh religious beliefs which find expression in his novels.

His Sikh characters, though sketchily drawn, are highly representative of their social types. They highlight different facets of the Sikh way of life. Some of them like Juggut Singh, Iqbal Singh and Meet Singh are blessed with symbolic undertones. Their very names are suggestive of their nature which is vindicated by their actions. Out of all the six Sikh characters—Juggut Singh alone symbolises the sikh tradition of valour, heroic action, rebelliousness and, in a way, sacrifice. He, being a rustic, also represents vengefulness, impulsiveness and above all, the abiding faith in religion, the hallmark of the Sikh peasantry.

Though a hot-blooded youth and steeped in illiteracy, he is full of simplicity, sincerity and steadfastness. He is the Guru's true Singh who is dauntless and has the courage to sacrifice his life for a cause, be it the love of a woman or a social cause. His love for Nooran, the Muslim weaver girl, proves him worthy of the gospels of the great Gurus who waged a crusade against man-made hindrances of caste and creed. His request to Bhai Meet Singh for a prayer to invoke the Guru's blessings for the success of his humanitarian mission reflects his staunch faith in the tenets of Sikhism. Though a professional bandit, a highwayman, he uses the Sikh temple like a devout Sikh as a means of moral strength and spiritual solace for his troubled psyche. His spontaneous act of courage and supreme sacrifice elevates him and his love, prevents the massacre of the innocent, and unwittingly though, upholds the dignity of the '*Panth.*'

Contrary to Juggut Singh, Comrade Iqbal is a westernised Sikh who violates the piety of the Gurdwara. His stay abroad has made him alien to the Sikh culture to the extent that he has the guts to take whisky in the Gurdwara itself. It is a little short of a wilful attempt at the desecration of the Sikh temple. He is a Sikh by compulsion. Religion is a matter of mere convenience for him and the Gurdwara, a succour for self-preservation. Fortunately, the gullible priest takes him at his word even though he, in his obsession to look progressive, had got his long haircut and beard shaved, let alone the five 'Kakas' (Five Ks), the traditional emblems of the Sikh faith, at least in a communal atmosphere when he could be taken for a Muslim and crushed to death by the irate, revengeful Sikh mobs:

> Iqbal realised that it was the company of Jugga and the constable, who were all Sikhs that really saved him from being stopped and questioned. He wished he could get out of this place where he had to prove his Sikhism to save his life.[7]

He regards the external trappings of Sikhism as irksome, yet he would fain wear them for self-preservation. The fact is that he is a self-seeker whose only religion is self-aggrandisement. He is, in fact, a foil to Juggut Singh in many ways. If Juggut Singh is a fictional affirmation of the glorious Sikh tradition of heroic action and sacrifice, Iqbal is a metaphor to suggest its very negation. Iqbal as his very name suggests, is instead an affirmation of self-glorification, name and fame. He symbolises the educated elite among the Sikhs—those who have deviated from their religion and culture into academic moorings—which have incapacitated the spirit of action in them. They have been inflicted with moral paralysis. Unwilling to stick their necks out of their cocoons, they remain, immersed in self-oriented, wishful thinking. Though such people exist in every community, the world over, Iqbal comes handy to the novelist who has used him as a fictional ruse to suggest his personal agony at the savagery practised by all communities and his own inadequacy in preventing it, and to air his views on Indians' obsession with sex, their pretentions of spirituality and their insistence on ritual-oriented religion.

The creator has reflected his own dilemmas in Juggut Singh's character. He embodies the desire image of the novelist who says, that he would have in some ways liked to have played the role of Juggut Singh. He is, in fact, as much a foil to Iqbal as he is to the Sikh leader from the city, the one who holds the mock-prayer in the Gurdwara to invoke the Guru's blessings for the success of his sinister mission. Juggut Singh's spontaneous act of supreme courage and sacrifice gains significance when contrasted with Iqbal's mere intellectualization of the tainted milieu and his supercilious indifference to everything except his own self. His abiding faith in the Sikh religion is brought into perspective when contrasted with the sacrilegious act of the Sikh rabble-rouser whose finer sensibility and better self have been consumed by the fire of ethnic hatred and justifiable vengefulness to the gift from Pakistan which Mano Majra receives by way of two trains full of murdered Hindus and Sikhs by the blood thirsty Muslim Marauders. The Gurdwara actually becomes a sanctuary for the Sikh refugees from Pakistan, and the Sikh rabble-rouser uses it as a launching pad for the ghoulish drama of genocide camouflaged as a crusade. It is here that the plan for the mass murder of a train loaded of innocent Muslims is devised and the mock-prayer for its success held. The piety of the Gurdwara thus violated by the misuse of its holy premises is ironically restored later by Juggut Singh who is condemned by one and all as a bandit. For once, he acts heroically in an environment afflicted with hatred or inaction. It is for this reason that he seems to have been "conceived by the novelist in the tradition of Sikh Guru martyrs who have preached action—heroic of course—as a means of salvation."[8] Though he is prompted primarily by the desire of revenge on his rival Malli, it is his heroic action of self-sacrifice that makes it a noble revenge. As Harrex appropriately comments that Jugga, "lives up to the Sikh suffix Singh,"[9] and proves himself to be a Gur-Sikh. Thus we notice that Khushwant Singh has explored three different facets of the Sikh consciousness in the trio—Juggut Singh, Iqbal and the young Sikh leader who provokes the mob to violence.

Since a major part of action in the novel takes place in the Gurdwara, Bhai Meet Singh's character can be considered as pivotal. He is portrayed as a typical Granthi of a village Gurdwara:

> He was short fat and hairy.... And he was untidy. He wore his turban only when reading the scripture. Otherwise, he went about with his long hair tied in a loose knot held by a little wooden comb, combing his long beard with his fingers. Almost half of the hair was scattered on the nape of his neck. He seldom wore a shirt and his only garment—a pair of shorts was always greasy with dirt.[10]

The Granthi's portrait, though graphic and representative in character, is far from being a sympathetic one. It does not inspire respect or affection. A peasant turned priest who has taken to religion as an escape from work—"an easy way of earning bread with the offerings at the Gurdwara."[11] Except for a few Sikh prayers which he has learnt by rote, he is ill-equipped for the challenging job. He is neither learned in Sikh scriptures nor is he, like the class he represents, fully acquainted with the glorious traditions of the chequered Sikh history. The ill-informed, superstitious-minded man that the Bhai is, Juggut Singh finds it rather difficult to cajole a prayer from him in order to thwart the heinous strategy of the communalists. His words to Juggut Singh are quite clear:

> You never came to the Gurdwara any other time. Now when the scripture is resting and people are asleep, you want me to read the Guru's word—it is not proper...what have you to do with meaning? It's just the Guru's word.[12]

The reluctant Bhai does mumble out a prayer, but not without a fuss. Khushwant Singh has used him as a metaphor to satirise the rustic Sikh Granthis in particular and Indian priestly class in general—a class which, far from giving any enlightenment, feeds the teeming millions in India on the glib talk about spirituality and other-worldliness. The novelist seems to enjoy an ironic dig at the Bhai's failure. The priest's helplessness lies in his lack of courage. He symbolises the helplessness of the priestly class in India where religion is seldom separated from politics. Apart from his deficiencies and inadequacies as a priest, Meet Singh is not without virtues of class he represents: warmth, open-heartedness, religious mindedness and humility. A friend to all irrespective of their caste, creed or religion, he lives upto his name. Meet Singh is the very embodiment of the Sikh tradition of purity, sanctity, religious tolerance and brotherhood. Khushwant Singh's portrayal of Bhai Meet Singh reminds us of Joseph Addison's essay *Sir Roger at Church*.

Khushwant explores yet another facet of Sikh consciousness, i.e., Sikh militancy. Sikh militancy came into being as a reaction against—Muslim racial chauvinism and fanaticism. The Sikh Gurus, who stood up in defence of their faith, had to suffer persecution at the hands of the then Mughal emperors of India. The consecutive martyrdoms of the Gurus steeled the nerves of the Sikhs whose hurt psyche led them to the path of militancy. Khushwant Singh has used Malli and the self-styled Sikh leader as a metaphor to suggest the militant trait of Sikh consciousness. Both the characters represent the instinctive vengefulness of the hot-blooded Sikh youths who must avenge the wrongs done to them whether by an individual, a class or a community. This militant trait of Sikh character is highlighted by the revenge-motif in the novel. In Malli, who has taken to banditry and criminal ways of life, the desire for revenge against individuals and society is prompted by a sense of deprivation and jealousy; in the self-styled young "Sikh leader," on the other hand, it is actuated by the sense of hurt caused by the brutalities and barbarities let loose on the Sikh community by the Muslim chauvinists in Pakistan. Jointly, the two take pride in spilling human blood. Their militancy as shown in the novel, is nothing short of Communalism.

In contrast to the militant stand of the two Sikh characters, Lambardar Banta Singh symbolises the rustic good-heartedness, communal amity and the voice of sanity which may be silenced but can never be destroyed:

> If you decide to stay on, you are most welcome to do so—we will defend you with our lives.[13]

Thus the novelist has acquainted the readers with the tenets characteristic of the Sikh way of life.

Khushwant Singh's art is revealed in not merely probing deep into the real but transporting the real into symbol and image. His art is a creative endeavour of portraying the Sikh consciousness authentically.

*I shall not Hear the Nightingale*, the second novel by Khushwant Singh is yet another attempt to explore the Sikh consciousness. Though this novel is developed with the underlying theme of East-West encounter during the years of Quit India movement. According to Khushwant Singh, this novel is based on a true incident which took place in his own family during Quit India Movement. The characters of this novels are somewhat exaggerated or lampooned. In fact, it was his father who was the hero of the episode as he was expecting to be knighted but the writer chose to make his mother the heroine for Freudian reasons (the oedipus complex). Written from Sabhrai's point of view, the novel eulogises the Sikh matriarchal tradition. Sabhrai is the idealised vision of the novelist's mother, grandmother and mother-in-law all the three virtuous women juxtaposed in one:

> Ever telling the beads of rosary, always chanting 'The True, The True the Great Guru,' regular in visiting the Guru's house, meticulous in performing Sikh religious rituals like reading the Granth and preparing parshad for the Congregation on the first of every month and other religious occasions. Though Sabhrai regards her husband as a God in whose arms she would like to die, she is spiritually wedded to the Guru. She does not show any panic at the prospect of death of which she gets an intuitive awareness, she tells Shunno, 'Don't talk. Send for my family. My time has come.'[14] Later in a sedate tone she tells her husband:
>
> 'I don't need a doctor. Let me go to my Guru with your blessings...what is all this noise? You want me to go with the noise of crying in my ears! Say the morning prayer—all together. And do not stop till it is over.'[15]

Having survived the worst moments of crisis in life which could not unnerve her, she retains her poise in death too, and is at complete peace with the world while having to leave it at the call from the Great Guru.

As a mother, Sabhrai emerges as a class apart. She is a unique character in the whole range of Indo-Anglian fiction. Alive or dead, she possesses a halo of unearthly brilliance around her. She does belong to the old world and has an old-world dignity and charm about her. It is this trait in her which evokes respect from the English District Magistrate, John Taylor, who remarks, "She has the dignity of an ancient people behind her. Without knowing her I have respect for her."[16] She is unlike other members of the family, who are the typical products of the modern world. They represent its culture sophistication, divided loyalties, self-centerdness, opportunism, servility and sex-hunger. Like the Wazir Chands, Jimma Singhs and the Peer Sahibs, they symbolise the tainted milieu, the spiritual waste land whose only hope lies in charity, compassion, faith, selfless service and spirit of sacrifice.

Sabhrai believes in the power of prayer. Her night-long vigil at the Golden Temple to invoke the great Guru's guidance in the hour of her anguish, restores her calm and helps her regain her spiritual poise. The agony of her soul is healed by her unshakable, unflinching faith in the Guru who is her real guide in life. The Guru, in all his resplendent glory, appears to her in her vision. Overwhelmed by her awareness of the warrior Guru's unique sacrifice, her chilled veins are infused with warm blood, and she starts reciting His stirring lines:

> Eternal God, who art are shield
> The dagger, knife, the sword we wield
> To us Protector there is given
> The timeless, deathless lord of Heaven.

Endowed with the Guru's grace and spiritual grandeur. She now conveys the Guru's injunction to her son that he who betrays his fellow beings is "no longer to be regarded as a sikh."[17]

In reality, Sabhrai has translated the Guru's teachings in her life. As the guiding spirit of her family, she retrieves the lost souls with her moral uprightness, piety and spirituality. It goes to the credit of Khushwant Singh that despite her mystic traits Sabhrai is not reduced to a personified abstraction. On the other hand, she is a full-blooded, vital character. Her maternal concern for the safety of her daughter Beena and her daughter-in-law Champak, who, she has a hunch, may choose the primrose path in Madan's company, finds a mystic expression in the holy verse from the Adi Granth which she quotes in her letter to them:

> O, Black Buck why lovest thou
> The pasture of fenced-in-fields?
> Forbidden fruit is sweet but for a few days
> Then leaves one sorrowing.

Her concern for her son Sher Singh, couched in credible human terms is no less when she says, "Where is my son, my moon, my little Ruby? Where is he? Why don't you tell me?.... You are only concerned with yourself. Don't you want to save your child's life?"[18]. Her maternal compassion does not remain confined to human beings. It spills over to her son's dog Dyer, too: "Hey Dyer, what's happened to you? Who's hurt my little son? Did not Sher take you to the doctor?"[19] The fact, however is that the mother in Sabhrai seems to be always at war with the mystic in her.

The character of Sabhrai resembles so much with that of grandmother in Khushwant Singh's short story *The Portrait of a Lady* where apart from looking after her grandson, she takes the responsibility of feeding the stray dogs in the village and after shifting to city, in the absence of dogs, she starts taking care of the sparrows' diet. She derives an extraordinary satisfaction out of this act of hers which is no less than any prayer. Like Sabhrai, she too has translated Guru's teachings in her life and like Sabhrai, the death scene of grandmother too is rendered in a very touching manner and creates a feeling of vacuum in the members of the family as well as the readers.

*Train to Pakistan* and *I shall not Hear the Nightingale* are complementary in as much as together, the two constitute Khushwant Singh's composite attempt at portrayal of the Sikh way of life. Viewed as such, Sabhrai's character compliments Juggut Singh's. Together, the two characters bring the novelist's attempt at an exploration of Sikh consciousness to the fine finish. Both Sabhrai and Jugga symbolise two complementary Sikh traditions—secular and spiritual. Juggut's virility sets off the impotence of Sher Singh who, ironically enough, seeks manly crutches in the warrior Guru's picture.

The Sikh element is the most central aspect of Singh's novels, which are fictional histories of the Sikh way of life, Sikh religion and glorious Sikh traditions. Novelist's concerns are largely humanistic and so are his sympathies. The novels are an attempt at artistic exploration of the various facets of the Sikh way of life. He has never been less than honest, and most importantly has never betrayed the expectations of his readers.

## NOTES AND REFERENCES

1. K. Singh, *Khushwant Singh's India* (Bombay, 1970), 212.
2. *Ibid.*
3. *Ibid.*, 213.
4. Khushwant Singh, *Train to Pakistan* (Bombay: IBH Publishing Company, 1967), 2.
5. *Ibid.*, 30-31.
6. *Ibid.*, 31.
7. *Ibid.*, 142.
8. S.C. Harrex, *The Fire and the Offering* (Calcutta: Writers Workshop, 1977), 180.
9. *Ibid.*
10. Khushwant Singh, *Train to Pakistan,* 69.
11. *Ibid.*
12. *Ibid.*, 151-52.
13. *Ibid.*, 111.
14. Khushwant Singh, *I shall not Hear the Nightingale* (Bombay: IBH Publishing Company, 1983), 231.
15. *Ibid.*, 233.
16. *Ibid.*, 230.
17. *Ibid.*, 209.
18. *Ibid.*, 190.
19. *Ibid.*, 189.

## GENERAL READINGS

Singh, Khushwant, *Not a Nice Man to Know* (New Delhi: Viking Penguin India, 1993).

—, *Truth, Love and a Little Malice: An Autobiography* (New Delhi: Penguin Books India, 2002).

# Chapter 14

## Search for Human Values: A Study in the Partition Novels

*Lalji Mishra*

The Partition of the Indian subcontinent on the communal basis into the sovereign states of India and Pakistan at the dawn of her freedom, after a long period of slavery and tryst with destiny, on August 15, 1947 created a hell of human killings on the earth which was marked as "one of the bloodiest upheavals in the history of human race"[1] and shocked the mankind with notes of "anguish and dismay at man's wolfish cruelty to man in the name of religion."[2] The birth of a new nation was actually the creation of two nations out of a single people which resulted in an endless tale of destruction, massacre, loot, rape inconceivable inhuman cruelties. The exchange of train-loads of dead bodies of refugees as "a Gift from India" and "a Gift from Pakistan" dominated the contemporary scene with notes of barbaric cruelties, communal fury and religious frenzy. It also produced the scenario of homelessness, footlessness, the perpetual dishonour and irreparable loss of shame and condemnation of displaced people.

The reckless speed at which partition was accomplished with little regard to an ordinary transfer of population between the two new states led to a holocaust. The total tandav (dance of death) of the partition carnage was against the spirit of freedom fighters and that of Gandhi's belief in man and the nation. He had no desire to earn the freedom of the country at the cost of violence, blood baths, catastrophes and untruth. The opportunist-leaders led to the communal rancour and as Nayantara Sahgal in her novel, *The Day in Shadow* depicted that people found "an appropriate time to bury Gandhi and write a new page of history."[3] People welcomed freedom is liberty to plunder, to kill, to molest and to project man in a position of displacement, hatred and unsealing insult. Such gruesome facts but not fictions are recorded in the annals of history which played a vital role in "turning contemporary history into literature."[4]

A great national experience provides a great reservoir of literary milieu and motif to the contemporary writers of any country. As a result, we can witness the impact of the greatest historical events like the French Revolution, the American Civil War, the Russian Revolution and the two world wars which provided the rich materials for great fictions like *A Tale of Two Cities, War and Peace, All Quiet on the Western Front, A Farewell to Arms, From Here to Eternity, Doctor Zhivago* and *The Naked and the Dead.* Similarly, the partition provided a number of Indian English novelists the basis for their fictional experiments. Some of them took such national experience as a theme, while others took the partition indirectly, as a background to their personal narratives.

The theme of partition has been a compelling experience with the irresistible creative urge to several Indian English writers of fiction like Khushwant Singh, Malgonkar, Balchandra Rajan, Attia Hosain, Raj Gill and Chaman Nahal. They have dealt with the theme of partition with new perspectives like their counterparts in Urdu literature. Bhairab Prasad Gupta in *Sati Maiya Ka Chaura*, Yashpal in *Jhootha Sach*, Bhisma Sahani in *Tamas,* Kishan Chaunder's *Chaddar* and "Peshwari Express," Vatsyayan Agyey's "Sharnarthi," Ramanand Sagar's *Aur Insan Mar Gaya,* Masoom Raza Rahi's *Topi Shukla, Adha Gaon* and *Oase Ke Boond,* Hoyatullah Ansari's *Lahu Ke Phool,* Abdullah Hussain's *Udas Naslen,* Kartar Singh's *Ujala Anchal,* and Qurrat-ul-Ain Haidar's *Housing Society* and *Aag Ka Darya* and Kamleshwar's *Laute Hue Musafir* portray the problems arising out of partition of Indian subcontinent and the exodus of refugees which give birth to refugee literature. Apart from it, R.N. Tagore's *Kalantar,* Tarashanker Bandopadhyaya's *Uttarayan,* Narayan Gangopadhyaya's *Lal Mati* in Bengali literature, Surinder Singh Narnla's *Dil Darya* in Punjabi literature and Chuni Lal Vardhaman Shah's *Kantak Chhayo Panth* and *Ankut Dhara* jointly written by Jaimal Parmar and Niranjan Varma in Gujarati literature depict the communal riots and their magnitude and intensity of calamities with painful tremors throughout the country at the time of partition in India.

The horrors of partition with its throes and predicaments have been the content of Indian English writers and we can find out the wounds and scars of partition still fresh in the hearts of people even after several decades. The religious madness with racial hatred and separatist politics have transformed man into beast when human values were recklessly thrown to the winds, men became homeless, lonely and alienated and stranger to their background. But even in the stormy night of bloodbaths, people maintained their notes of brotherhood and love.

We can witness the peculiar identity of human beings struggling for the cause of love, and human values even at the time of partition holocaust and communal frenzy. Khushwant Singh's *Train to Pakistan* (1956) portrays the massive slaughter of innocent people during partition and that of communal harmony. Even after the ghastliness and the total insanity of partition prevailing in the Indian sub-continent, Mano Majra is an obscure, placid, sleepy and tiny frontier village which stands out as an oasis of communal harmony, where villagers reciprocate their mutual respect and love for Muslims and Sikhs equally. They do not know if "the country is divided into Hindustan and Pakistan" (20). The *Lambardar* of Mano Majra addresses refugees from Pakistan, "This is your village as much as ours," and convinces them, "As long as we are here, no body will dare to touch you. We die first and then you look after yourselves" (110).[5] Juggut Singh, a Sikh by birth and popular as an inglorious *badmash,* sacrifices himself for his Muslim love, Nooran and saves the life of so many people like a brave humanist.

Balchandra Rajan's *The Dark Dancer* (1958) set in the background of partition offers a still nobler picture of life. Kamala readily gives away her life to save a Muslim woman. It impresses upon our minds that hope, beauty, truth and goodness will survive the crimes, cruelties and large-scale devastation brought about by the partition. Manohar Malgonkar's *A Bend in the Ganges* (1964) gives us an epic presentation of Indian Independence and its aftermath with its hostility, violence and that of communal harmony. Debi with an imagination of a happy and settled future with a Muslim girl, Mumtaz, as his wife, is hacked to death and his piercing cry denotes the cry of outraged humanity.

Attia Hosain's *Sunlight on a Broken Column* (1961) condemns her own community for the demand of partition resulting in harrowing scenes of violence. Laila, the narrator-heroine, appreciates the sincere efforts of the Hindus in protecting millions of Muslims, left helpless in India by the Muslim creators of Pakistan out of their communal rancour. *The Rape* (1974) by Raj Gill gives a vivid description of gruesome crimes and collapse of human values. Dalipjit, the hero, is terribly shocked by his father's raping his beloved and by terrible scenes of suffering on both sides. But the human nature triumphs over the baser animal nature and he concludes, "The Muslims killed the Hindus and the Hindus massacred the Muslims in a bid to live, and not to die"[6] and finds it out as an absurd belief. Chaman Nahal's *Azadi* (1975) portrays the family of Lala Kanshi Ram with a placid, easy and happy life before partition who has lost everything during gloomy partition. But he displays a wonderful belief in forgiveness and adds, "We have sinned as much. We need their forgiveness."[7] It shows his noble heart rich with human values.

We can, thus, find out that characters in partition novels present the eternal conflict of good and evil and these two faces come out on the surface as symbols of bold belief in human values and that of evil notes. The inglorious *badmash*, Juggat, in love of Nooran, the muslim woman, dies like a brave humanist in *Train to Pakistan*; Kamala in *The Dark Dancer* sacrifices herself in order to save a Muslim prostitute from the brutal clutches of Hindu miscreants; Debi in *A Bend in the Ganges* possesses a desire in his heart to marry the Muslim girl, Mumtaz, but he was hacked to death by the orthodox muslims which aroused the outraged humanity; *Sunlight on a Broken Column* displays the Muslim woman, Laila, the narrator-heroine, who condemns the defenders of Pakistan who left them to suffer in India but they were saved by Hindus; Lala Kanshi Ram in *Azadi* even after loosing everything in Pakistan has a great love for helpless Muslim refugees who were unnecessarily and faultlessly victimised, Lala Kanshi Ram appears as an idol of forgiveness and reconciliation with opposites; Dalipjit in *The Rape* feels ashamed of his father raping his beloved and cultivates the atmosphere of harmony as an exponent of love. They are not characters but characteristics and of human love, the milk of human kindness and that of human values.

In brief, we can say that the partition novels represent the great strength of human love even after the horrors of partition holocaust, the endless catastrophes and inconclusive miseries which plundered their happiness and filled them with notes of tragic throes and predicaments. The novelists, therefore, display their characters as the sensible, humane and generous messengers of human love and they stand as the torch bearer's to the homeless refugees who have the fractured consciousness and the broken hearts. The note of human love is not an end but it is a beginning to an end and the process will continue till human beings live on the earth.

## NOTES

1. K.K. Sharma, "The 1947 Upheaval and the Indian-English Novel," R.K. Dhawan (ed.), *Explorations in Modern Indo-English Fiction* (New Delhi: Bahri Publications, 1982), 30.
2. *Ibid.*
3. Nayantara Sahagal, *The Day in Shadow* (Delhi: Vikas Publishing House, 1971), 186.
4. C. Paul Verghese, *Problems of the Indian Creative Writer in English* (Bombay: Somaiya Publications Pvt. Ltd., 1971), 119.
5. Khushwant Singh, *Train to Pakistan* (London: Chatto and Windus, 1956), 20.
6. Raj Gill, *The Rape* (New Delhi: A Sterling Paperback, 1974), 296.
7. Chaman Nahal, *Azadi* (New Delhi: Arnold-Heinmann, 1976), 340.

# Chapter 15

# Psychic Dissociation of the Sequestered Self: Protagonists' Dilemma in Anita Desai's Early Fiction

*Balram S. Sorot*

Anita Desai is a novelist of psychological leanings. Her major preoccupation, in her three early novels: *Cry, The Peacock*, *Voices in the City* and *Where Shall We Go This Summer?*, is to delve deep into the inner recesses of the psyche of the fictional persona, most of whom are "fragile introverts,"[1] hypersensitive, egocentric, fanciful, impressionistic, isolated, and freakish. Mrs. Desai herself admits that she is "interested in characters who... have retreated, or been driven into some extremity of despair and so turned against, or made to stand against, the general current."[2] Unusually high susceptibility, extra refined sensibility, proclivity towards romantic-idealism and acute "right-consciousness"[3] render these characters malcontented and misfit in the modern malignant world. These people expect too much from life, fail in expectations and are disappointed bitterly. Their dejection results in their emotional and mental suffering. Most of them are young, inexperienced, dreamy, emotionally raw and psychologically unsteady. They present themselves to the reader as classic examples of split selves or dissociated personalities. From Maya to Nirode, Monisha, Amla or Sita, all undergo the state of mental or spiritual agony caused by the simultaneous existence of two or more centres of consciousness in each one of them. In other words, the neurasthenia and the feeling of a cloistered existence predominant in Anita Desai's protagonists directly ensue from the state of psychic dissociation of the sequestered self, and this becomes their perennial dilemma.

Maya, the young heroine of *Cry, The Peacock* (1963), is a vivacious, but hypersensitive, pampered, and love-lorn girl. The problem she faces is how to adjust with life, which she finds inhospitable and inscrutable. Actually, Maya is "romantic-related with ideal,...egotistical and self-indulgent, pursuing fancies and fanciful feelings...a 'toy-princess' living in a world of elusive happiness."[4] Gautama, her husband, is a practical man of the world. He does not relish Maya's eccentricity and self-indulgence. As such, he chides her:

> "Life is a fairy tale to you still. What have you learnt of the realities? The realities of common human existence, no love and romance, but living and dying and working, all that constitutes life for the ordinary man. You won't find it in your picture books. And that was all you were ever shown—picture books...."
>
> * * *
>
> "...all you ever knew was happiness. What a crime! A crime because it was a delusion. And here you are, capable of seeing nothing but delusions, imagining them to be real. How prettily you stroll in your garden dreaming of the fairies that sleep in the buds...."[5]

Actually, Maya has been a father's "pet" since childhood. When she grows up, she develops a dream-like quality in her nature, unable and unwilling to face the harsh reality of life, marriage and Gautama. Not exposed to the vagaries and adversities of life, she has been living an insulated life. Consequently, she lacks an understanding of life. At times, she acts like a person possessed; at other times, she appears to be abnormal and incommunicado. In fact, she has a complex personality; more precisely, a split-personality, that disintegrates under the weight of uncongenial environs, incompatible marital alliance and unhappy encounter with the albino astrologer. Moreover, it is Maya's grave predicament and severe defalcation that she is "forever reducing the abstract to the tangible."[6] As such, forebodings of death through the albino priest make Maya suffer fear psychosis. Dread of the stalking doom—death of either Gautama or herself at the end of four years of marriage—plays havoc with her fragile mental make-up. Since she is exceedingly in love with life, Maya gradually comes to feel that only she has the right to live. Gautama being redundant, is to die. While talking to her mother-in-law and Nila, Maya peremptorily insists:

> It had to be one of us, you see, and it was so clear that it was I who was meant to live. You see, to Gautama it didn't really matter. He didn't care, and I did.[7]

Even prior to Gautama's murder, Maya, obsessed with the idea of death and doom, gradually loses her grip over sanity. Her thoughts, words and actions become incoherent. She becomes aware of the impending insanity:

> Yes, I am going insane. I am moving further and further from all wisdom, all calm, and I shall soon be mad, if I am not that already.[8]

Maya's "mental deterioration"[9] is "the effect of self-centredness or self-pity."[10] In her state of frenzied agitation, she deduces:

> ...no, I'll never sleep again. There is no rest any more—only death and waiting.[11]

Emotionally high-strung and mentally distraught, she evokes myriad delusive and hysteric impressions through her hyperactive imagination:

> Torture, guilt, dread, imprisonment—these were the four walls of my private hell, one that no one could survive in long. Death was certain.[12]

In her early youth, Maya occasionally feels elated:

> The world is like a toy specially made for me, painted in my favourite colours, set moving to my favourite tunes.[13]

In the years that follow, she becomes forlorn and dejected. Bereft of all hope from life, she can think of nothing but stony silence and extinction:

> What if tomorrow I were a mere stone, mute, immobile, extinct? For now I knew my destiny. It was annihilation. Annihilation, I repeated trembling.[14]

As time passes, Maya herself comes to realize the schism in her psychic self, and admits:

> ...I am torn between two worlds—the receding one of grace, the approaching one of madness. My body breaks in battle.[15]

Guided by instinct, which overrides her intellect, Maya dwells in the half-light, the hazy consciousness, of the difference between illusion and reality; and consequently, fails to reconcile the two facets of life. Clash between the two juxtaposing sides of her psychic self renders her utterly nonplussed. She fails to know and discern, "What was true? What was lasting? What to believe in? What reject? Danger, danger...."[16] This heightened instinctual awareness of "danger" impels her to act in a beastly manner. She murders the element of sanity, and she lapses into the dark abyss of insanity. Thus, the psychic dissociation of Maya's sequestered self being over, she lands in the lunatic asylum—a fit resting place for her on earth.

In *Voices in the City* (1965), three major characters, namely Nirode, Monisha and Amla, become cynical, freakish and desperate because they feel abandoned and ignored in life. All of them are highly educated, intellectually gifted and ambitious individuals, yet the problem with them is that they have an "over-exacerbated sensibility."[17] The Ray progeny love life excessively, but are inapt at distinguishing the actual from the illusory. "Their creative energies do not converge on a common point of integration so that they all remain fragmented and unfulfilled."[18] Each one of them has a strong desire to open the channels of effective communication with others, but is unable to do so because there pervades "an atmosphere of emotional and spiritual stagnation"[19] around them. None of the trio is able to acquire an attitudinal objectivity and matter-of-factness since they are sentimental temperamentally, and have nihilistic as well as predatory proclivities. Jit, one of Amla's friends, is intrigued and disgusted to observe it, and says:

> I don't understand it—this terrible destructiveness in all of you. You seem to worship it.... Nothing will persuade you to forego it.... You destroy—you destroy yourselves, and you destroy that part of others that gets so fatally involved in you.[20]

The primary cause of this fatal "destructiveness" happens to be the "absence of positive faith or a sense of permanent commitment,"[21] not only in Nirode, but also in Monisha and Amla. The result is that they are utter failures in life. "Each character in the novel," says R.S. Sharma, "typifies a particular kind of activity and each activity suggests a typical failure."[22] Intermittent rebuffs and setbacks in life leave these characters dazed and confused. They suffer because all of them have disjointed selves, with multiple centres of consciousness, always operative at cross-purposes. The young Rays, esp., Nirode and Monisha, remain afflicted with the overriding sense of ennui, stagnation and sorrow, and as such, they become solitary figures for whom "aloneness alone was the sole natural condition.[23] Their lives become tangles of mischance and defeats, which reduce them to near-neurotics, maladjusted and isolated like three remote and obscure islands in the vast ocean of Calcutta populace. Eventually, one of them, Monisha, ends her life in the prime of her youth; the other two—Nirode and Amla—survive and experience death-in-life.

Nirode Ray, the bright boy of the Ray family, loses his parents untimely: his father is snatched away by Death, and his mother, by Cupid. He finds himself abandoned, rootless and redundant, and grows abnormal psychologically. He becomes cynical to and acrimonious against everything in life. He feels that he has to wade through the marshy land of life on his own. He has an intense "desire for self-esteem,"[24] and therefore, is deeply disgusted and dejected when he encounters failure after failure. He slithers into a state of helplessness and futile waiting, deeply conscious of his own insignificance in and irrelevance to the scheme of life. Anita Desai faithfully records Nirode's sense of defeat and worthlessness:

> ...he drifted, a shadowy cipher, and his life consisted of one rejection following another. He loathed the world that

> could offer him no crusade, no pilgrimage, and he loathed himself for not having the true, unwavering spirit of either within him. There was only this endless waiting, hollowed out by an intrinsic knowledge that there was nothing to wait for.[25]

Since Nirode has lost his anchor of hope, faith and emotio-spiritual strength owing to his alienation from his mother, he grows into a psychically imbalanced person with "instinctive pessimism"[26] and an abject disinterestedness in everything around him. Very often, he remains sitting or standing "in the slumped attitude of a lifeless creature just let down from the gallows."[27]

Being psychologically vulnerable, he suffers terribly after every jolt and rebuff of life. He becomes a social recluse and calls himself an "outlawed hermit crab,"[28] while his younger sister terms him as "an unshelled snail, a flightless bird."[29] Just as Maya, in *Cry, The Peacock*, is engrossed in her childhood memories and suffers an oppressive father-fixation; Nirode also keeps over-clinging to his past and his mother, and consequently, is unable to acquire the normal mental equipoise, or psychic balance. As time passes, he becomes so frustrated that he often thinks of annihilating himself:

> Better to leap out of window and end it all instead of smearing this endless sticky glue of senselessness over the world. Better not to live.[30]

Prof. R.S. Singh very aptly analyses Nirode's propensity for ending his life, in the words:

> For the lack of any 'positive' in his personality, he was condemned to be cynical, nihilistic and restless....[31]

Actually, the misery and suffering, the inability to correlate and communicate, the acute sense of alienation and the desire for self-extermination in this "psychic outlaw,"[32] rootless intellectual and "misfit hero,"[33] directly emanate from his sequestered self, which makes him feel: "I am a leper, diseased with the loneliest disease of all."[34] Monisha, too, is a psychically fragile person, with a hyperactive imagination and great expectation from life. Sense of emotional insecurity, which creeps early into Monisha's psyche because of her mother's irresponsible behaviour towards her, later on, is permanently etched on her consciousness due to the callous and apathetic behaviour of her husband and the other family members. As a result, Monisha comes to acquire an abnormal personality. She withdraws into her private inner shell when she finds her husband uncaring and unresponsive. The emotional hiatus between herself and others renders her an exile in her own home. She realizes it and analyses the underlying cause thereof:

> I think that what separates me from this family is the fact that not one of them ever sleeps out under the stars at night. They have indoor minds, starless and darkless. Mine is all dark now.[35]

The real cause, however, of her psychic dissociation lies in her inability and unwillingness to connect, to relate with the world: "I will involve myself in nothing anymore."[36] Finding life "only a conundrum"[37] she is bitterly disheartened to see its inscrutability, gets gloomy and pessimistic day by day.

Fear of losing her conscience and sanity increasingly haunts Monisha. "As in Nirode, in Monisha also, fear is the inspiring force of life, not love."[38] The fear-psychosis makes her emotionally impaired and choked. Consequently, she turns into a "shrunken, etiolated, wasted thing,"[39] almost 'invisible' to the world. Her abnormal, fractured self does not let her establish a healthy, meaningful communion with life. Hers is a silent, a private, but an acute suffering, with a painful realization: "Traceless, meaningless, uninvolved—does this not amount to non-existence, please?"[40]

Monisha appears to have "a partial resemblance with Maya"[41] in that she, too, is a parent-fixated person, like Maya. This unhealthy 'fixation' is partly responsible for tragedies in their lives: in Maya, it operates through over-indulgence, while in Monisha, through non-indulgence. The former's deep interest in life and the latter's total lack of interest in it; the subsequent killing of her husband by one and the terminating of her own life by the other; one can explain all this in the light of the parent-child relationship in both the cases.

Monisha's unmitigated privation and suffering cause her complete disenchantment with life, hurt her extra-refined sensibility and loosen her grip over life, and when her over-susceptible and badly bruised psyche cannot effectively grapple with, and take on the harsh, hostile reality of day-to-day existence, she takes on her own self by committing suicide.

Like the other Ray progeny, Amla is also "largely self-afflicted, self-driven, self-condemned to crash in defeat and disaster."[42] She is a commercial artist, whose life embodies non-fulfillment. She, too, has to suffer the total disillusionment in life. Though she survives, yet she remains frustrated all through. Whenever she attempts an alignment with someone, it is only partially successful because the streak of "terrible destructiveness,"[43] so typical in the Ray family, does not let Amla strike a harmonious relationship within or outside her family, nor can she pursue some higher ideal of life. She drifts like a rudderless boat on the turbulent waters of life, tossed violently every now and then, struggling merely to keep afloat. Lack of a meaningful emotional communion with her mother, or with Nirode and Monisha, render Amla psychologically lacerated and weak, and ultimately, she is left gasping in bewilderment, with the realization:

> Yes, I'm surviving—I suppose that is just what one would call this state of existing, just breathing and eating and going around with a perpetual headache and stomachache.[44]

Mrs. Desai, in a way, looks back to her first novel and its heroine, Maya, while creating Sita, the principal character in *Where Shall We Go This Summer?* (1975). Prof. Tripathi rightly asserts about Sita:

> In possessing more than ordinary organic sensitivity she is younger sister of Maya, the heroine in *Cry, The Peacock*.[45]

Besides this, Sita grows with a morbid notion that she "came into the world motherless."[46] She dotes on the memory of her father, like Maya, holding him as her ideal. Again; hers is also an incompatible marriage like that of Maya, and Raman, her husband, is almost Gautama reincarnated. A hardcore realist, calculatin, prosaic, business-oriented person, he is "not worth much thought or introspection. Not an introvert, nor an extrovert, a middling kind of man..."[47] whereas Sita is "imaginative, poetic and romantic,"[48] with a pronounced "proclivity for drama, for theatre, for emotion."[49] An introvert by nature, Sita hardly has anything common with Raman. There is a wide psycho-emotioned gulf between the two, and she has nobody to share her thoughts and feelings with, nor anyone to connect to.

Uncared, marginalized and almost unconnected (except for Jiwan), as a child, and "a woman unloved, a woman rejected"[50] after marriage, Sita develops a cleft psyche. An acute sense of denial gnaws at her inner self, and makes her rash, temperamental, psychologically insecure and alienated. The novelist aptly describes Sita's "wanting and not being given what she wanted."[51] As such, she prefers to live in an atmosphere of "twilight, shade and silence,"[52] suffering the morbid fear-anxiety syndrome in the inner world of her soul. Sita fails miserably to adjust with life because of a preponderance of dreaminess in her temperament, which becomes evident in her "phantasmagoria about the womb."[53] She fantasizes that she can withhold her child-birth, and declares:

> I mean I want to 'keep' it—I don't want it to be born.[54]

She thinks that the world is mindlessly destructive and so, unfit for creativity: "She had refused to give birth to a child in a world not fit to receive the child."[55] This perverted view about the world and the human creativity warps and deforms her whole outlook on life. Her vision and perspective become blurred and stunted. She feels like:

> a moth that has emerged from its cocoon not into sunlight, but into a grey non-light that does not warm the damp wings or give them strength for flight.[56]

In this dimness of her awareness, Sita reckons her life merely as "a shadow, absolutely flat, uncoloured."[57]

Full of anxiety about the insubstantiality of her life, Sita desperately attempts to escape, to retreat from the mainland where

> life was a crust of dull tedium, of hopeless disappointment—but a thin crust, a flimsy crust that, at every second or third step, broke apart so that she tumbled in, with the most awful sensation, into a crashed pile of debris.[58]

Her ardent desire and feverish endeavour to reach Manori, the magic island, actually signify a feat accompli by the dreamy side of her hyperactive subconscious-self, which seeks to avoid the stark reality and embrace illusion. The novelist records:

> ...ordinary life, the everyday world had grown so insufferable to her that she could think of the magic island again as of release. If the sea was so dark, so cruel, then it was better to swim back into the net. If reality was not to be borne, then illusion was the only alternative. She saw that island illusion as a refuge, a protection. It would hold her baby safely unborn, by magic.[59]

In fact, "the island," says Prof. R.S. Sharma, "is that primary ground of being where illusion and reality are inseparable;"[60] so they are in Sita's psychic self, too.

There is "a powerful struggle between life-denying and life-affirming impulses"[61] in Sita's splintered self, and so, her will is paralyzed. In her cloyed, benumbed state of consciousness, she experiences, on the one hand, an existential anxiety that her life has been divested of all order and meaning,[62] while on the other hand, she has the disconcerting realization of her betrayal by all around her, but fails to know the reason thereof:

> Their betrayal had torn her open with such violence, now violence poured from her like blood. In it was also the shame, the disappointment;.... They had all betrayed her. Why?[63]

Sick with the boredom of "aloneness alone"[64] and with a tragic awareness of being "an island on the island,"[65] Sita is gradually disillusioned with the magic of Manori, and says:

> Manori was not a romantic island. Besides its palms, its deserted beach, its wild silence, there was that most squalid of villages, with its open drains, its mangy *pai* dogs, drunkards...the continual wash of the rain could not quite cleanse it....

> ...she was confused—where *was* the magic of the island that she had promised herself, promised the children? Was *this* it?[66]

The sea and the palms on the island, which bore a promise of wholesomeness and fulfillment in life in the beginning, turn out to be the agents of her final disillusionment, disgust and disjointedness. In the words of Prof. Tripathi:

> So the sea becomes a symbol of nostalgia when life is disgusting and intolerable...like the sea itself, the palms become a symbol of Sita's own wounded, agonizing self under the conflict between illusion and reality.[67]

The dilemma of her existence ensues from her fragmented psyche, which renders her utterly dazed and fazed, like a person marooned on an islet, unable to decide, to know the real from the unreal:

> But was she sure it was not the other way around after all? Had not her married years, her dulled years, been the false life, the life of pretence and performance and only the escape back to the past, to the island, been the one sincere and truthful act of her life, the only one not false and staged?
>
> How could she tell, how decide? Which half of her life was real and which unreal? Which of her selves was true, which false?[68]

Sita's plight becomes extremely grim when even Moses, the primitive islander, condemns her as a "mad" woman and contemptuously growls: "Let her go. Who cares?[69]

In the final run, it emerges that Sita's traumatic experiences, delusions, agonies and "madness" are the handiwork of her deformed psychic self. If she does not go mad like Maya, or does not hang herself like Monisha, her life is not very happy, nor fulfilled either. She, too, like Amla and Nirode, is condemned to pass through the dregs of life, living almost *no life*, when the nobler values or higher ideals are lost to her.

Mrs. Desai, with her subtle "cognitive-perceptional powers yoked with a hypersensitive emotive faculty,"[70] has created these extremely sensitive characters whose thoughts, reactions and wavering defy the norms of conformity and adequacy. These fictional persona view themselves as much wronged than wrong-doing in a "bad" world. They suffer the pathological coexistence of several distinct personalities, dissentient with or antithetical to each other, resulting in their isolation and neurosis.

## NOTES AND REFERENCES

1. R.A. Singh, *Cry, The Peacock: A Study* (Bareilly: Prakash Book Depot, 1992), 13.
2. Anita Desai in her interview with Yasodhra Dalmia, *The Times of India* (Sunday Bulletin), April 29, 1979, as quoted by S.P. Swain in his article, "The Alienated Self of Maya: A Study of Anita Desai's *Cry, The Peacock*," *JIWE*, ed. G.S. Balarama Gupta, Vol. 20, Nos. 1-2, Jan.-July 1992, 43-44.
3. J.P. Tripathi, *The Mind and Art of Anita Desai* (Bareilly: Prakash Book Depot), 1986, 7.
4. *Ibid.*, 13.
5. Anita Desai, *Cry, The Peacock* (New Delhi: Orient Paperbacks 1980, 6th imprint, 1993), 115 (All subsequent quotations are from this edition).
6. Sudhakar Ratnakar Jamkhandi, "The Artistic Effects of the Shifts in Points of View in Anita Desai's *Cry, The Peacock*," *The Journal of Indian Writing in English* (Special Number on Anita Desai), ed. G.S. Balarama Gupta, Vol. 9, No. 1, Jan. 1981, 42.
7. *Cry, The Peacock*, 215-16.
8. *Ibid.*, 108.
9. S.R. Jamkhandi, *JIWE*, Jan. 81, 40.
10. *Ibid.*, 41.
11. *Cry, The Peacock*, 98.
12. *Ibid.*, 102.
13. *Ibid.*, 36.
14. *Ibid.*, 103.
15. *Ibid.*, 177.
16. *Ibid.*, 86.
17. Peter Alcock, "Rope, Serpent, Fire: Recent Fiction of Anita Desai," *JIWE*, Vol. 9, No. 1 (Jan. 1981), 18.

18. R.S. Sharma, *Anita Desai*, New Delhi: Arnold-Heinnemann, 1981, 51.
19. J.P. Tripathi, *The Mind and Art of Anita Desai*, 29.
20. Anita Desai, *Voices in the City*, New Delhi: Orient Paperbacks (1965), 1982, 175 (All subsequent references are from the same edition).
21. R.K. Srivastava, "Voices of Artists in the City," *JIWE*, Vol. 9, No. 1, Jan. 1981, 50.
22. R.S. Sharma, *Anita Desai*, 49.
23. Anita Desai, *Voices in the City*, 24.
24. J.P. Tripathi, *The Mind and Art of Anita Desai*, 34.
25. Anita Desai, *Voices in the City*, 64.
26. *Loc. cit.*
27. *Loc. cit.*
28. *Voices in the City*, 190.
29. *Ibid.*, 126-27.
30. *Ibid.*, 18.
31. R.S. Singh, *Indian Novel in English*, New Delhi: Arnold-Heinnemann, 1977, 172.
32. D.S. Maini, "The Achievement of Anita Desai," *Indo-English Literature: A Collection of Critical Essays*, ed. by K.K. Sharma; Ghaziabad: Vimal Prakashan, 1977, 222.
33. M. Mukherjee, *The Twice Born Fiction*, New Delhi: Arnold-Heinnemann, 1974, 202.
34. *Voices in the City*, 61.
35. *Ibid.*, 139.
36. *Loc. cit.*
37. *Ibid.*, 125.
38. J.P. Tripathi, *The Mind and Art of Anita Desai*, 35.
39. *Voices in the City*, 139.
40. *Ibid.*, 140.
41. B.O. Vyas, "Viscid Voices of the Inner Kingdom," *JIWE*, Vol. 9, No. 1, Jan. 1981, 7.
42. K.R. Iyengar, Srinivasa, *Indian Writing in English*, New Delhi: Sterling Publishers [1962], 1990, 469.
43. *Voices in the City*, 175.

44. *Ibid.*, 182.
45. J.P. Tripathi, *The Mind and Art of Anita Desai,* 74.
46. Desai, Anita, *Where Shall We Go This Summer?*, New Delhi: Orient Paperbacks [1975], 1982, 84. (All subsequent textual references in this article are from the same edition.)
47. *Ibid.*, 47.
48. *The Mind and Art of Anita Desai,* 74.
49. *Where Shall We Go This Summer?*, 109.
50. *Ibid.*, 133.
51. *Ibid.*, 132.
52. *Ibid.*, 82.
53. *The Mind and Art of Anita Desai,* 64.
54. *Where Shall We Go This Summer?*, 35.
55. *Ibid.*, 139.
56. *Ibid.*, 76.
57. *Ibid.*, 147.
58. *Ibid.*, 58.
59. *Ibid.*, 101.
60. R.S. Sharma, *Anita Desai,* 100.
61. Atma Ram, "A View of *Where Shall We Go This Summer?*", *JIWE,* Vol. 9, No. 1, Jan. 1981, 79.
62. *Where Shall We Go This Summer?*, 86.
63. *Ibid.*, 97.
64. R.S. Singh, *Indian Novel in English,* 164.
65. Atma Ram, *JIWE,* Vol. 9, No. 1, Jan. 1981, 74.
66. *Where Shall We Go This Summer?*, 102-03.
67. *The Mind and Art of Anita Desai,* 77.
68. *Where Shall We Go This Summer?*, 153.
69. *Ibid.*, 157.
70. *The Mind and Art of Anita Desai,* 3.

# Chapter 16

# Concept of Violence: A Critique of Kamala Markandaya's Novels

*Alka Rani Purwar*

The word violence, however abhorrent it may be, has always been in the core of human thought and action. In spite of all denunciation, violence continues unabated and has become a part of everyday affair. The ongoing violence has created a vicious circle in which the entire world in general and the Indian Republic in particular has been caged. Ever since the origin of human life on this earth, violence has been used in some or other way. Even our great Holy Epics like *Ramayana* and *Mahabharata* speak the language of violence. In a sense, scriptures have shed more violence than weapons throughout the world. As a result, violence took permanent place in the long surviving caste and communal systems which even today badly affects life all over the world.

When violence is so deep-rooted a phenomenon not only in India but in the most parts of the world, how can our Indian writers remain uninfected by the germs of violence?

Born in 1924, in a well-off and sophisticated Brahmin family in South India, Kamala Markandaya holds distinct and distinctive place among the novelists of Indian writing in English. Markandaya has participated actively in India's struggle for freedom and when she started writing novels, India was just at the threshold of newly-won independence. It was the time when India was facing not only the communal disturbances but also its after effects like poverty, hunger and starvation. Through violence, Markandaya has depicted either race conflicts, temperamental disparities, cultural clashes and even the inner frustration and tension of the characters. In this paper, I'm endeavouring to refer specially the three of Markandaya's novels *Some Inner Fury* (1955), *A Handful of Rice* (1967) and *The Golden Honeycomb* (1978).

In *Some Inner Fury*, the novelist has expressed the violence by dividing the human race in 'your people' and 'my people.' The novelist endeavours to grip the volcanic inner fury of the nation which destroys the illusion of harmony and relationship between different races and nations. Sometimes the writer seems to protest against the violence specially against the war which fills everyone with "shadows and fears and a sense of tragic fury gathering across the sea."[1] Through the novel Markandaya reveals her full consent for Quit India Movement and presents people fully immersed in independence movement by boycotting the foreign goods. Govind, a great supporter of violence, incites his followers to do the same and they not only set fire to the newspaper office but also put up banners in the streets having an open message of hatred and anger inscribed on them and thus preparing the mob mentally ready for the violence. Towards the end of the novel, the tension and conflict reach the climax when Mira, the heroine deserts Richards, her English lover, to join the procession of political agitators. The novel definitely concludes on a melodramatic note having blood shed, agitation, procession—the different forms of violence in abundance.

In *The Golden Honeycomb* (1977), Markandaya's 'magnum opus'[2] as Prof. A.N. Dwivedi calls it, we come across a series of violent events, pitiable strikes, baffling agitations and lockout. Rabindranath, the hero is the chief personality to infuse violence by supporting the public agitations against undue levies and treaties. He joins even a violent mob of striking industrial workers at Bombay and creates awakening among the mass. Meanwhile, the novelist has also mentioned the Non-violent Movement of Gandhiji in the forms of 'dharnas' and 'satyagrahas,' which are actually the peaceful expressions of inner restlessness and violence of the people. Again in the final phase of the story, the people grow violent and aggressive for freedom and it was their bold struggle that resulted in uprooting of the Britishers.

In both of these novels, Markandaya presents Indians full of action so far as the political field is concerned. Govind in *Some Inner Fury* and Rabi and his associates in *The Golden Honeycomb* do a lot to liberate India from the clutches of the cruel Britishers. Though mainly the novelist points out the fatalistic approach of the Indians but she never means to advocate the idea of fatalism. She, in fact, depicts it to portray the simplicity and innocence of the Indian villagers and peasants where as she actually wants Indians to be active like Western people. Therefore, we find a direct clash between the fatalism, spiritualism and idealism of the East and the pragmatism, materialism, and individualism, of the West in her novels. This clash, sometimes results also in the form of violence.

In contrast to above-mentioned violence, practised for the struggle of freedom, Markandaya has also chosen it as a strong medium to express the inner frustration, helplessness, the lurking feeling of hatred and the inner conflict of her characters. As in her novel *A Handful of Rice*, when Ravi, the hero becomes rebellious and materialistic, he loses even his latent concern and love for living creatures. In a severe fit of violence, he turns out Thangam, his sister-in-law and her none-too-good husband, the cripple Kumaran, and even commits incest with his mother-in-law. This reversal in his nature is resulted as the part of city influences on him so, the noble qualities of Ravi, in fact, dry up under the crushing pressure of violent hunger. But when his belly is full, he meditates like a sensible person. The book comes to an end with the depiction of the violent, hungry and unruly mob, intends in looting grains. Ravi also joins it demanding loudly and violently "Rice today, rice. Rice, today, rice!"[3] In this context, K. Venkata Reddy makes very apt observation, "an attempted act of violence marks both the beginning and the end."[4]

In fact, Markandaya's all absorbing intention is to highlight the progressive forces of the time and underline the tension born of the Western contact with Indian mind. In order to attain this purpose, the novelist has used violence as a powerful medium of expressing the emotional state of mind. Thus, the main concern of the writer in depicting violence is either to highlight the inner furies of the Indians which came outside in the form of national movement for the freedom of India or to exhibit the inner psychic depth of the characters to entrap the varying moods for the survival of the existence.

## REFERENCES

Dwivedi, A.N., *The Golden Honeycomb: A Critical, Appraisal, Perspective on Kamala Markandaya,* ed. by Madhusudan Prasad, Vimal Prakashan Ghaziabad (1984), 219.

Markandaya, Kamala, *Some Inner Fury* (London: Putnam, 1955), 130.

——, *A Handful of Rice* (New Delhi: Orient Paper Backs, 1966), 233.

Reddy, K. Venkata, *A Tryst with Conscience* (New Delhi: Prestige Books, 1990), 156.

## BIBLIOGRAPHY

Banerji, Niroj. *Kamala Markandaya: A Critical Study.* Allahabad: Kitab Mahal, 1990.

Bhatnagar, A.K. *Kamala Markandaya: A Thematic Study.* New Delhi: Sarup & Sons, 1995.

Dwivedi, A.N. *Papers on Indian Writing in English*, Vol. II. Delhi: Amar Prakashan, 1991.

Iyengar, K.R.S. *Indian Writing in English.* Delhi: Sterling Publishers Pvt. Ltd., 1993.

Jha, Rekha. *The Novels of Kamala Markandaya and Ruth Jhabvala.* New Delhi: Prestige Books, 1990.

Joseph, Margret P. *Kamala Markandaya.* New Delhi: Arnold Heinemann, 1980.

Markandaya, Kamala. *Some Inner Fury.* London: Putnam, 1955.

—. *A Handful of Rice.* New Delhi: Orient Paper Backs, 1966.

—. *The Golden Honeycomb.* London: Chatto and Windus, 1977. Prasad, Madhusudan ed. *Perspectives on Kamala Markandaya.* Ghaziabad: Vimal Prakashan, 1984.

Rao, A.V. Krishna and Menon, Madhavi. *Kamala Markandaya: A Critical Study of Her Novels (1954-1982).* Delhi: BRPC, 1997.

Singh, R.S. *Indian Novel in English.* New Delhi: Arnold Heinemann, 1977.

# Chapter 17

# Depiction of Women in the Novels of Bhabani Bhattacharya and Shobha De: A Contrastive Study

*Neelam Singh* and *Rashmi G.*

One of the most striking aspects of the fiction of Bhabani Bhattacharya is the importance, freedom and vivid colour that he imparts to his women characters in each of his novels. His admiration for Indian women is very high and he keeps them on equal footing with his male characters. They are not mere second fiddle to their male counterparts, rather they are fully independent, self-sufficient, have free spirit and/or aware of their rights and responsibilities. They are pure with exuberant vitality and high ideals. Their inner conscience and goodwill keep them on proper path and they even help, guide and give moral support to their partners and others surrounding them, to follow the path of righteousness and mercy. Through the female characters, the author tries to inter-link polarities, connect culture with culture, tradition with modernity and the individual with society. Thus, Bhattacharya presents a very idealistic portrait of female characters in his novels.

The novel, *Music for Mohini*, sketches the intellectual and emotional development of the heroine, Mohini, from a care-free and innocent girl-hood to the position of a wife of a thoughtful idealist, who desperately desires to play his part in the building of the country's future, and the mistress of a prominent and influential house with great traditions. Mohini is a city-bred girl given a modern education by her liberal, professor-father, meets and solves the problem of adapting herself to the lifestyle and tradition of Behula village, where she goes to live with her scholarly young husband, Jayadev. He expects her to sympathize with and to share in his scholarly pursuits and to give him the necessary moral support in his course of social re-construction. He sees her as *Gargi* or *Maitreyi*, "no household drudge, not decorative being, but an intellectual, striding besides man in a tireless quest for knowledge."[1]

She understands as time passes that she has to modify her stand and make adjustments if she is to play her role as a wife and as the mistress of an illustrious house. She knows that her married life can be peaceful and meaningful only if she adjusts herself to the wishes of her husband, shares his ideals and renders him positive help in his agenda for social reforms. She thinks:

> But she could. She must. Her husband needed her help. How could she fail him? In the great task ahead she should play her part. She would be his true partner in feeling, in faith and in dream. (129)

She cooperates with her husband and helps him to fulfil his goal of making his village the ideal one. She even establishes friendship with the kids of the village. She teaches the illiterate group of women of the village in order to eradicate the existing superstitions steeped deep in them. The village women identify the young mistress of the Big House with themselves. They exclaim:

> Their own, their joy, their joy and pride and she was so human, without any of the plumage of the rich, whose distant look bespoke that they trod the blue pathways of the sky! (150)

Thus, Mohini tries to prove worthy of her husband and establishes deep communion with him. This sharing of interest brings them closer together and puts an end to all differences existing between them. In this way she proves herself capable of being Jayadev's *Maitreyi*.

She also adjusts herself to the orthodox ways of life forced upon her by her mother-in-law. Mohini strives hard to adjust to the old ways and modes of life in the rural society and in this process she, too, changes unawares:

> Yes, the young mistress of the Big House took deeper colour from new life everyday. Slowly she fitted herself to the rural design. Her sprightliness, her quick girlish laugh, she easily subdued. The mother was ruthless teacher. (130)

Mohini sometimes feels sour about her mother-in-law's stern behaviour and old-world spirit, but with the passage of time she realizes that mother is not completely devoid of the basic qualities, like compassion and sacrifice. She, therefore, overcomes initial hurdles and develops a great love and sympathy for her:

> Yet, Mohini told herself, perhaps she judged the mother too harsh? Perhaps she saw the wrong side of this old tapestry of tradition and missed the design? Duty and compassion were not at odds in the mother; the key to the design was sacrifice which was right and privilege, not a duty alone. (173)

The struggle between the contrasting values that is so intense and fierce in the beginning gradually reduces and resolves finally into a happy compromise. It is not only the younger character who tries for mutual adjustment but the old characters also realize and try to fulfil the demands of the new age. Jayadev, as an ideal husband, always gives moral support, encouragement and provides her even the musical instrument, which his mother dislikes, in her most trying moments. He always tries to make the situation easy and comfortable for Mohini when she faces several prohibitions and restrains from her mother-in-law. She is kind-hearted, generous and true companion of her husband. She courageously faces every odds of life and life finally becomes music for her and others attached to her:

> At last, there was no discord. Life was music—a note of song for the Old Mother was in her, a note for Jayadev and his rebel gods, a note for the Big House and Behula village, torn and at cross-purpose for a while. Her life was music—the quest for every woman, her deepest need. (188)

In *Shadow from Ladakh*, Suruchi, wife of Satyajit and mother of Sumita, is the most fully developed woman character. Suruchi is really a woman of aesthetic temperament and collaborates in all reformatory activities of her husband. Suruchi though devoted to her husband and his vow of *brahmacharya*, is an incarnation of the aestheticism of Tagore. She radiates vitality and represents beauty during her stay in Shantiniketan. No wonder when Satyajit comes in contact with her as a teacher at Shantiniketan, he feels that the fullness of life of which the poet has spoken has "taken shape before his eyes, sari-draped on a reed mat."[2] Suruchi is such an embodiment of the fullness of life as Satyajit's; early-married life is a perfect union of asceticism and aestheticism. As Satyajit's wife, Suruchi is also his helpmate working side by side with him in the creation of Gandhigram, the city based upon the models of Gandhiji's percepts. "Suruchi had willingly passed through every stage of readjustment, and remained tranquil" (20). She would be his companion in ideas even if they were so very strange, shows her firm determination. She is the first person to comprehend the integration between Gandigram and Steeltown mode of living. Bhattacharya writes, "She had not accepted Gandhigram in it's entirely. But she had not rejected it, either" (273).

She believes in the Tagorian philosophy of the integration of diverse elements of life and recalls: "Integration—that was the poet's life long quest; integration of the simple and the sophisticated; the ancient and the modern; city and village; east and west" (215). Owing to her intimacy with, and correct understanding of, her husband, she knows that he does not completely discard Steeltown and it's materialism because he is aware of it's significance. But she is unhappy to see that Bhaskar is not able to realize the importance of Gandhigram and it's spiritual values for the fuller growth of human life. Naturally, she wants the integration of the two different ways of life and wishes that Bhaskar should realize the significance of Gandhigram.

Suruchi, however, does not appreciate Gandhigram's rigid adherence to the outdated morals and conventions. According to her, there must be synthesis of the old and new and the asceticism and aestheticism. She is also pained to watch the development of Sumita into an ascetic. When the elders of Gandhigram condemn the girl, Jhanak, for her misconduct, then Suruchi defends her, as she considers aestheticism to be an important content of life and opines that body is useless without spirit and both must be fed together, and not turn-by-turn, to live the life in fullest sense. Suruchi adapts herself considerably to Satyajit's wish. She becomes "part of Satyajit. The nail of his toe. A strand of hair on his scalp" (49) and realizes that Satyajit's ideals "had become part of herself. She was as much Gandhigram as he" (49). Yet, despite all this, the clash between the two contrasting forces—asceticism and aestheticism—continues to bother her and she is not able to accept or reject the ideals of Gandhigram totally.

At the end of the novel, her husband realizes the hollowness of the ascetic life he has been leading and compelling his wife to lead. He comes to realize how he has denied worldly pleasure to himself and Suruchi for long. So in the light of this new vision, he, finally, decides to make amends. His friend Bireswar suggests him to surrender himself to Suruchi. "The novel thus represents first the movement of Suruchi from graceful naturalness to cramping asceticism and, secondly, a movement in the opposite direction, namely, from inhibition to spontaneity and freedom."[3] Finally Suruchi's self-understanding and compassionate and intelligent aid to others in their own searching bear fruit.

Any study of Shobha De would remain incomplete without the 'woman subject' but she is quite different from Bhabani Bhattacharya in her treatment of the same topic. In her novels it is the woman who occupies the central place. Being a journalist, she expands her novels to the wide range of experience. Her novels give evidence of her intense awareness of women's problems. As a feminist Shobha De has worked for the complete emancipation of woman, but she is a feminist of another kind, one who projects the ideas of liberating woman through self-actualization and the understanding of self-identity. Shobha De says:

> I did write with a great deal of empathy toward women. Without waving the feminist flag, I feel very strongly about the woman's situation.[4]

In this male-dominated society, women are treated with double standard, either to be worshipped or to be burnt. Talking of women, Virginia Woolf says:

> Imaginatively she is of the highest importance. Practically she is completely insignificant.... Some of the most inspired words, some of the most profound thoughts in literature fall from her lips; in real life she could hardly read, could hardly spell and was the property of her husband.[5]

Shobha De feels that the whole question of the position of females in India is so wonderfully confused that it is impossible to take anyone's stand on it. For what they deserve as an autonomous being, they never get. From their childhood, they are made to learn how to compromise with status of a second person. Arrival of youth brings a wrong notion that they begin to see the fulfillment of their desire in their marriages because, as they wish, marriage will be a solution to their problems. But in truth, marriage shatters all their dreams and presents a very crude picture of reality before them. And this perplexing situation compels them sometimes to take such step, which is a major deviation from the established traditional norms. Through experience they come to their real self. As Shobha De believes that the woman has to be aware of her identity as a human being and think for herself. Woman should be an independent identity by being aware of the choices open to her. Shobha De has extraordinary ability to present man-woman relationship in really wonderful manner. She has superb and intimate understanding of the psyche of woman and her problems. De, through her female protagonists in *Socialite Evenings* and *Second Thought*, has explained similar issues by showing self-actualized heroines, Karuna and Maya.

Karuna, a problematic child, tries to escape from her middle-class environment and indulges into the fashionable world of modern life, which has been introduced to her by Anjali, a middle-aged prominent socialite. Karuna has a rebellious instinct and wants to initiate and regulate her life on her own. She thinks fashion world can bring a life leading to wealth, freedom, status and mainly the fulfillment of her desires. She leaves a very caring and affectionate fiancee due to the lack of his weak financial condition and marries an unexciting, uninspiring, untutored man who is not made for introspection. Soon, she realizes the failures of her marriage. Conventionally her marriage is all right because as an average Indian husband, he has provided her with a good house, and identity linked with his name and four meals a day. She thinks: "My marriage went sour because I'd married the wrong man for the wrong reasons at the wrong time"[6] and marriage has now new definition for her that she concludes, "marriage is nothing to get excited or worried about. It is just something to get used to" (68).

Karuna detests callous attitude of her husband and the unbearable condition. She says:

> We were reduced to being marginal people. Everything that mattered to us was trivialized. The message was "you don't really count, except in the context of my priorities." It was taken for granted that our needs were secondary to theirs. And that in some way we ought to be grateful for having a roof over our head and four square meals a day. (69)

In this patriarchal society, man can think about his life without woman but a woman cannot do the same. What a wife can do when she is ignored and neglected for all her feelings. Some mutely endure this situation and spend their whole life in suffocated atmosphere. But Shobha De's women are not ready for this easy acceptance. Her meeting to her husband's friend, Krish brings a feeling of revolt against her insensitive husband. In Krish, she finds a man who can give her a life to lead in fullest sense. As a result she begins an extra-marital affair to get rid of her discontented married life. She indulges herself in her own inexperienced imagination. When Karuna tries to seek Anjali's opinion in this matter, Anjali misguides her by saying:

> This man doesn't sound like husband material. It's best you have him as a lover—even a long distance one. I know your marriage isn't fantastic, but it isn't a total write-off either. If you can have both—a boring husband in the home and an exciting lover on the sidelines—perfect. (173)

So a neglected life, an inexperienced mind, a desire to live her life in fullest sense and a company of socialite like Anjali, prompts her to involve herself in extra-marital affair. But when she realizes the fact that Krish is not sincere about her and all these extra-marital affairs cannot bring a true meaning of life, she gets ready to live her life on her own terms by rejecting the idea of getting married second time. She says to her mother:

> But mother, why does security rest with a man? I feel confident now that I can look after myself. I am earning as much as any man. I have a roof over my head. I don't really have any responsibilities. I am at peace with myself. I'm not answerable to anyone.... (276)

When her husband tries to reconcile with her, she understands his duplicity and deviousness and thus rejects him. Now through her experience, she has accepted her single-woman status as an affirmation of her self.

> I still resisted them. I suppose my real concerns were different. It wasn't money or success I was looking forward to in my life at that point it was the freedom to do what I wanted. (273-74)

As a self-realized person she finds that extra-marital affairs do not fetch happiness for the women. Although Karuna is attracted by intellectual snobbery of Girish and Ranbir, she refuses a 'good life' offered by them, because it entails a loss of individuality. Karuna refuses marriage and prefers to create her own representation, which gives her a sense of freedom. Pramod K. Nayar writes:

> Karuna's act of writing her life is an attempt to write and represent it on her own terms, emphasizing and narrating her experiences.[7]

In brief, we can say, although she is not precisely gifted or trained for any profession, through her self-recognition and self-awareness as a mature and an experienced person, she establishes herself in the highly competitive world and becomes emotionally and financially independent.

*Second Thoughts*, is a sober, serious look at a modern-day marriage. A young middle-class Bengali girl Maya, born and bred in Calcutta, makes an arranged matrimonial alliance with a Bombay-based, foreign-returned Bengali boy Ranjan. Maya is highly impressed by Bombay's life, full of glamour and freedom. She thinks:

> Marrying Ranjan was like marrying Bombay, and she thought she was the luckiest girl in the locality, who had bagged a foreign-educated Bombay-based groom.[8]

But after marriage, she feels herself trapped in a neglected and passive life because of her husband's conservative nature, superiority complex and his insensitivity to all her feelings. After marriage, Maya wants to pursue a career in textile designing but Ranjan rejects that plan. Behind this decision lies Ranjan's ego and he projects himself as the lord and master and Maya has to abide by his whims and fancies whether she likes it or not. He always reminds her of her duties as a married woman. He says:

> ...a housewife's duty is to stay at home and make sure everything is tip-top. That is where her true happiness lies. You've seen my mother's house—learn from her. (56)

If Ranjan reaches out for Maya, "it was a gesture devoid of any passion. And impersonal friendly sort of gesture which always left me feeling like a well-trained dog being rewarded for his good behaviour" (251). Maya is constantly depressed because of her neglected and lonely life. Ranjan always tries to hold on tight to purse-strings to control his wife, locks STD facility on phone for her and has full control even on the use of the air conditioner. She cannot share her feelings with anyone; even she cannot bear any child because of her husband's lack of interest in physical-gratification and, on the top of that, she has nothing creative to do in that city. She feels:

> Nobody needed me, absolutely nobody. My parents no longer thought I belong to them. My husband belonged to his mother. It was unlikely that I would bear children who would belong to me. And I did not have a single true friend to call my own. (266-67)

With her husband and house she never finds a sense of belongingness. She sadly admits, "it was never a home. My home. Our home always 'the house'—impersonal, distant, cold" (227). So, when Nikhil meets her and shows his interest in all minute outlooks of Maya, she recognizes the truth that her husband is not tuned to her wavelength. Maya, who wants to listen soft and caring words from her husband, gets this gesture from Nikhil. With Ranjan she has learnt to curb her feelings but with him, she could never be light hearted. In turn, Nikhil encourages her, appreciates her and, above all, he reminds her of existence and individuality. Maya knows the restrictions of a married woman, but as a human being she wants companionship of a man in order to satisfy her emotional and physical urge. With Nikhil, her dreams and desires once again surface and she wants to express her joy and happiness. She wants to be free, alive, and reckless and go mad with joy. Amidst all this enjoyment, she feels guilty that she is betraying Ranjan. In the torrent of physical-gratification she involves herself in physical relationship with Nikhil that later proves to be a mere betrayal. As a result, she falls from her wifely pride because of hollowness and hypocrisy in married life. Circumstances compel her to change her mind and in desperation she deceives Ranjan, otherwise she is not a woman of easy virtues. Due to lack of emotional and conjugal bliss from her husband, she goes against him and tries to seek happiness and fulfillment through Nikhil but Maya's dream world shatters again. She comes to know of Nikhil's engagement. Maya, who seeks rays of hope in Nikhil, finds herself again in the dark. She has now known what she is and what she wants, and she is not sorry for what she has lost. She knows, she has no choice but to operate in the stifling atmosphere of her arranged marriage. "Two uncool people stuck together in unholy matrimony" (200), are left. Ultimately, she realizes how to survive the sultriness of Bombay along with sultriness of her marriage and she decides to dedicate herself for her household only, in the end of the novel.

When it comes to comparison, Bhabani Bhattacharya's women characters are mature and fully developed. They are the better half of their male partners and give them moral support. They have the proper understanding of their role and are aware of their rights and responsibilities. They favour the reconciliation of tradition and modernity. Bhattacharya creates the women protagonist as a finer human instrument than the male. They are always in tune with their instinctual needs and are filled with noble ideas. Thus, Bhattacharya's women characters are idealized characters. Whereas Shobha De's women characters suffer due to the lack of experience, maturity and the neglect and non-cooperative attitude of their husbands. But through their self-realization they recognise themselves better as an independent individual. The development of her women characters as realized person brings the yearning for a life of fulfillment, which comes after self-actualisation. In the process of development, they first appear in an inhibited form and later on they become fully aware of their own blooming, though slightly bruised, self.

## NOTES AND REFERENCES

1. Bhabani Bhattacharya, *Music for Mohini* (Delhi: Orient Paperbacks, 1975), 71 (all subsequent references to this edition are indicated by page no. in parentheses).
2. Bhabani Bhattacharya, *Shadow from Ladakh* (Delhi: Hind Pocket Books, 1966), 15 (all subsequent references to this edition are indicated by page no. in parentheses).
3. K.R. Chandrasekharan, *Bhabani Bhattacharya* (New Delhi: Arnold-Heinemann Publishers, 1974), 113.
4. *The Hindustan Times Magazine*, 12 February, 1995, 3.
5. Virginia Woolf, *A Room of One's Own* (New York: Harcourt, Brace and World, 1992), 45-46.
6. Shobha De, *Socialite Evenings* (New Delhi: Penguin Books, 1990), 65 (all subsequent references to this edition are indicated by page no. in parentheses).
7. Pramod K. Nayar, "*Socialite Evenings*: Towards a Feminist Romance?" in Jaydipsinh Dodiya (ed.): *The Fiction of Shobha De* (New Delhi: Prestige Books, 2000), 117.
8. Shobha De, *Second Thoughts* (New Delhi: Penguin Books, 1996), 195 (all subsequent references to this edition are indicated by page no. in parentheses).

# Chapter 18

# "To be or not to be:" The Question of Professional Women in Shashi Deshpande's *The Dark Holds No Terrors, Roots and Shadows* and *Small Remedies*

*Shubha Dwivedi*

Among Indian women writers Shashi Deshpande is specifically committed to the reorganisation of female subjectivity. Her concerns related to the feminist questions are important in the interest of an Indian feminist-praxis. Her fiction holds a great promise and helps us in finding ways in which the historical 'location' of Indian women can be interpreted in terms of their subordination accentuated by law, sacred literature and practice. Deshpande's feminist ideology stems from her belief in 'self-striven' approach towards women's empowerment or what S.L. Sharma terms as 'empowerment without antagonism' in her article of that title. She refuses to indulge in 'adversarial-orientation' or intemperate expressions towards men. She attributes profession to her protagonists as a 'strategic interest' which enables them to enter the prevailing and androcentric system and to dismantle their politics. Deshpande's treatment of issues like Indian woman's autonomy, identify, space and desire may lead to an Indian model of feminism which will be workable, honest and more violable for indigenous condition. Instead of providing tales of female victimization she seems to be concerned with the idea of 'how women can live afresh?' (Rich, 35). The present paper is divided into five parts. The first part deals with the question of profession women in Indian context and the subsequent parts depict the inter-role conflicts and dilemmas in Deshpande's protagonists of *The Dark Holds No Terrors, Roots and Shadows* and *Small Remedies*. Deshpande provides a revised version of Indian women's world as her protagonists come out of the bedrooms, kitchens and attics to articulate and reconstitute their lives through their 'feminist awareness' and introspection. Deshpande's novels record polyphonic voices behind every structure and relationship which have contributed to silent Indian women. Muted by society/patriarchy her protagonists feel crippled by a sense of inferiorization, non-entity and loss of 'self.'

Deshpande's novels encapsulate the tensions underlying women's aspirations and their cultural identities. Their urge for self-definition culminates in the identification of the areas of conflict. They are encased and suffocated in the patterns of androcentric culture and their desire to perform is taken over by the necessity to conform. These women are steeped in the conventions and customs of a patrilineal society which dislocates and alienates them from the process of being and becoming. Deshpande's novels are polemical attacks against the patriarchal world, where women are treated as a 'kind of non-man.' Like Margaret Atwood, Virginia Woolf, Betty Friedan, Deshpande also argues that male-assigned roles of wife and motherhood entrap women in the masculine plot of desire and thereby marginalise them from other socio-political economical and creative spheres of life. She refers to the plight of the women who have abandoned their identities in search of what Betty Friedan described as 'the feminine mystique' (a world confined to her own body and beauty, the charming of man, the bearing of babies, and the physical care and serving of husband, children and home). Luce Irigaray speculates that in this 'patriarchal enclosure' woman is man's 'specularised other,' where man's triumph should parallel women's failure and her function is to reflect back man's meaning to himself. And thus she becomes the negative of this reflection. Women are thereby forced into a subject less position by the patriarchal 'logic of the same.'

Her protagonists refuse to be caught in the 'masquerade' of femininity.[1] Deshpande explores the traumas and agonies of being a woman. She is concerned with women's quest for self-definition. In an interview Deshpande admits that all her characters are concerned with their "selves" and they learn to be "honest to themselves." Women's passivity and submersion in the traditional roles of wife and mothers terminates in their self-diminishment. Deshpande's women, however do not walk off this marriage economy which institutionalises the essentialist construction of the feminine self-lessness and masculine self-assertion and sexual-coquets. These women seek for an 'aesthetic space' within the restricting confines of domesticity which is provided by various professions, occupations and creative activities. The traditional criticism on Deshpande's fiction recognises her significant contribution to the field of feminist studies and the argument of my paper is that her foremost contribution lies in her delineament of professional Indian women which is a fast emerging class. The strength of Deshpande's work is her awareness of gender-disparity, sexual division of labour which start at home and which are deeply enrooted in the public and private lives.

The contemporary women are facing structural inequalities between man and woman and cultural rationalisation of these inequalities. Anil Kumar Gupta in his book *Women and Society* writes, "The discrimination based on gender differences are interlocked at every level of society from the most intimate to the most general" (8).

The present paper attempts to study the changed consciousness of middle-class educated Indian women. With their education and their social awareness these women have thrown off their conditioning and the whole psychology of oppression. They bear the burden of the past and the aspirations of the future. They desire to overcome 'dependence syndrome' and have an urge for self-definition, but also care for sensitive family relationships and emotional involvement of the self. The complex situations in the lives of professional women have changed the picture of the Indian families and have also questioned the values and politics behind matrimony.

Deshpande portrays a picture of Indian woman who is sensible, educated, attached to her roots, economically independent and yet who is different from her past image as a 'full-time home-maker,' 'an angel at home,' 'an evil counterfeit' and 'a weak vessel.' The degree of self-reliance achieved by these professional women is limited and the patriarchal society interprets their self-sufficiency as deviance from their 'femininity' i.e., "the stereotype of a woman: nervous, incompetent needing male help and support." Krishna Chakraborty in her book *The Conflicting Worlds of Working Mothers* records the dilemma of a working woman, which is created by the contradiction between their occupational pursuits and domestic obligations. "There is an unconscious fear among all including women themselves, that to after the traditional arrangement might change or even destroy the family and femininity." These professions provide economical privileges as well as creative outlets for women. They get an opportunity to erase their long silence and grapple with the questions of identity and self-assessment. Social institutions accuse them of being defiant, disobedient and egoist. Malashri Lal in her *The Law of the Threshold*, locates her feminist theorising in significations of "home" and "not home." She applies "Indocentric approach" and argues that traditionally "men pass over threshold unchallenged" whereas "for women, a step over the bar is an act of transgression" (12). Deshpande's Saru, Indu and Lata are examples of women who make complex negotiations in the space on and around the threshold.

Deshpande's narratives deconstruct the idea of 'Indian Women' generally related to a sacrificing, non-assertive, satisfied being and traces of her positioning in a system of 'difference.' Romila Thapar contemplates that the position of women in India is a "curious intermeshing of low status, ritual contempt, sophisticated sexual partnership and deification" (6). The portrait of subdued and suffering women holds the fancy of Indian men. The images of woman as the mother-protector, the inspirer and the motivating force, as the object of desire, weakling and dependent on man tends to magnify men's stature by contrast. Virginia Woolf has remarked in *A Room of One's Own*: "Women have served all these centuries as looking glasses possessing the magic and delicious power of reflecting the figure of man at twice its natural size."

This cultural colonization, which is the result of biologism and sexism retards the mental, emotional and intellectual growth of Indian women and strangles their efforts at selfhood. The ideology of patriarchy seems to be confirmed in Richardson's view that women should shine only in the domestic sphere. This state of dependence on men makes them accustomed to suppression and subjugation. Mary Wollstoncraft dwells upon men's belief that "women find satisfactory fulfillment only in motherhood" confines them to their homes, their "natural sphere," as Freud termed it. Deshpande juxtaposes her educated, strong-willed, questioning and career-oriented protagonists with the whole lot of self-negating 'feminine' characters and achieves the desired effect. The main protagonists' personal experience with accumulated knowledge leads to self analysis and here we see the progression of the female psyche through the phases of "limitation, protest and self-discovery" as Elaine Showalter posits.

Indian women's 'feminized' education, the subsidiary position of their career interests and occupational commitment in comparison with the importance of marriage in their lives have to be seen as agencies in perpetuating the male/female dichotomy. Deshpande's protagonists socialise and conform to their 'expected' role but also make choices that provide them with ideas for independence and freedom. Her protagonists' occupation as writers, doctors, singers and political activists impart them an individual space to question conventional cultural assumptions.

Through her works, Deshpande examines the 'cultural production' of femininity.[2] She seems to argue that women have been forced into a position where they must remain passive. They 'exist only to be acted on by men.' Her fiction presents a murkish picture of gender-based compartmentalization in our society and she goes to the root of hegemonical politics where women are depicted as women while theoretically 'femininity' is valued.

In *Sisters's Choice* Showalter writes that "Women like men are shaped by the country they inhabit, by their nation's language, history, literary canons, cultural mythologies, ideologies and ideals." Deshpande also refutes the idea of 'global female imagination' or 'universal sameness of femininity' based on biological or psychological fixtures. Therefore, it is important to interpret Deshpande's fiction in specific national context. Religious and cultural prescriptions continue to influence societal and individual approaches to the status of women, both within and outside the household. In India women are socialized according to the Sita, Savitri, syndrome which stresses on self-giving, asceticism obedience and self-less devotion to their husbands. The Sati dimension of femininity tends to represent woman as subordinate to her husband. The alternative form or contrary to feminine i.e., 'Shakti' of female experience has practically vanished from the thinking of women in contemporary India. *Manusmariti* has distinctly defined the role of woman as a wife, mother and daughter, she is always secondary to man. A woman who conforms to the norm is loved and protected; in opposite cases, nations of female disobedience are related with social degeneration and contribute to silencing any ideas of disobedience (39).

In order to overcome their self-alienation and subjugation by misogynistic prejudices, Deshpande's women work against 'numerous monolithic systems.' She explicates multiple differences, multiple desires utilising personal narratives and lived experiences of her heroines. Multiple voices in her novels explore the burden of private history. Her novels have a thematic framework which studies the interface between women's silence and their speech, their cultural erasure and resistance.

Deshpande analyses various patterns through which urban women try to empower themselves. In many cases external sources of financial support, their ingress in social and political system supplement their courage and confidence. Some of them have tried to sustain strength and confidence by seeking a spiritual path as well. Sociologists argue that in spite of the constitutional provision for women in India, problems like amniocentesis, female infanticide, widespread harassment of brides, rape and other forms of increasing violence against women speak clearly of women's oppression, deprivation and suffering. She points out the 'scarcity-syndrome' experienced by a large number of the working and non-working women who fail to procure a share in property, material aspects of family and control over their earnings and above all their contribution in the decision-making process.

Deshpande accepts working women both as subjects of victimization as well as agents of change. Working women appear in her novels not merely as the passive victims of an oppressive ideology but also as the active agents of their own positive constructs. Like post-modernist commitment to heterogeneity, fragmentation and difference, Deshpande also recognises 'difference' in the understanding of gender issues, which have a specific roots in linguistic, cultural, socio-economic, political, sexual and psychological grounds. She deconstructs the misnomer of unified subjectivity by delving deep into fragmented subject problems. With the dissolution of unitary subjects it becomes easier for Deshpande to facilitate feminism of difference(s). One step in this direction is her construction of women subjects within their social positions which is evident in her treatment of middle-class working women. She imparts plentiful details on the interplay between individual lives and particular social structures.

She deals with women's conditioning in relation to their choice of career. They seem to be bound within the traditional roles of caring, curing and nurturing. Through their natural capacities or qualities of compassion and nurturance the society circumscribes them to specific roles, where there are plenty of avenues for men in which we can see diversity and change.

For these women their professions have a therapeutic effect on their lives and sensibilities. Whereas these professional women, attaining reputation in their fields of arts and skills, holding prestigious positions and well-paid jobs generally tend to feel competent and productive and possess high self-esteem, they also derive interpersonal satisfaction from their family and job. The compartmentalization between home and workplace in equal order and the stress by the intolerable and vexatious demands inevitably frazzle these women and create a sense of guilt and fragmented self in them. It is quite paradoxical, yet true that Indian women feel honoured and humbled even when pressing demands are placed on them. Friedan recognised that, while women have been pulled into the public domain, men have not been enticed into the private realm. Women attempt to excel at both the traditional female sex roles and the role of paid labourer by working in "two shifts." In Indian context the domestic division of labour remains gender specific and the lop-sided division of familial responsibilities leads to the condition what Friedan termed as 'super woman syndrome.' In spite of being in a constant state of stress they try to evade from the paths of passivity, interdependence and emotional depravity which ordinary women walk through during their life-journey. By her portrayal of working women, Deshpande puts in contrast the plight of housewives who have been confined and constrained by the marriage contract which gives unlimited power to a husband and the right to demand unpaid work (housework, raising of children) and other obligations like cohabitation and forced coitus.

Sunder Rajan reveals the intersection of the politics of representation with the procedures of subjectification, in India. She accepts biological determinism as the basis of segregation in the power and status of men and women. The ideological mechanism of patriarchy is maintained by women's cooperation. Thus women themselves become complicitous in the system of oppression. The co-operation or complicity is secured by various means: denial—of access to production resources and economic dependency on the male head of the family, class privileges and honour bestowed on conforming and dependent women of the upper classes, ideologies of male superiority and/or separate spheres, and the threat or the actual use of force when required as when the ideologies and practices of patriarchies were resisted.

The identity of women is jeopardized by their husbands inside the "enclosure in patriarchy" (Pratt, 38). Their self-definition and individual development ultimately "transcends gender" in Jungian terminology. The nurturing of individuality by these protagonists is carried out differently through various professions. These protagonists dare to alter the circumscribing perspectives.

## II

Shashi Deshpande's fiction sets forth the nature and influence of Indian woman's role as a 'co-provider' on her own as well as on her husband's domestic role and on their familial and marital relations. The questions related to professional woman's role, status, power, duty, obligations and empowerment *vis-à-vis* her husband's are congenital to feminist studies and a clear assessment of professional woman's experience regarding their role-conflict, role overload marital stress, dilemma, fatigue and self-doubt can be explicated through the study of *The Dark Holds No Terrors*. Saruis caught in an emotional flux, endeavours to come to terms with her protean roles, while trying her best to integrate her true self.

Growing into woman is, for Saru, "something shameful" and "torture" (55). In her quest for gender free identity, Saru opts for the medical profession. Saru's profession gives her self-reliance and a meaningfulness in life. Smita, Saru's friend is a 'feminine archetype' as she resigns to her husband's whims, becomes Geetanjali after marriage and is subsequently reduced to a mechanical existence even after receiving medical education. Embarrased Smita, once borrows hundred rupees from Saru and utters: "You don't know how lucky you are not to have ask any one for money. If you know my problems." Saru is repelled by Smita's resilience and her self-effacing strategy to keep her husband happy. In spite of her radical and modern outlook Vidya bows down to the worn-out customs and the traditions of a conventional life for the sake of harmony. Being a doctor, Saru comes to terms with the reasons behind the inert, passive, unconcerned existence of her patients. She acknowledges that many of their ailments stem from neglect at home, over burden, loneliness, sexual abuse, physical violence and silence. She calls such women 'stupid silly martyrs:'

> Backache, headache, leucorrhea, menorrhagea, dysmenorrhea, loss of appetite, burning silently and as long as possible, because 'how do you tell anyone about these things?' Everything kept secret, their very womanhood a source of deep shame to them. Stupid, silly martyrs, she thought; idiotic heroines. Going on with their tasks, and

> destroying themselves in the bargain, for nothing but a meaningless modesty. (107)

There is a reference in the novel to a woman who, ill-treated by her in-laws drowns herself in a well. There is another woman mentioned who is tied to a peg by the family and fed in the cattle shed. These incidents of violence against women cultivate the fear of the men in women.

The physical, sexual and psychological violence against women is normative punishment for every woman who rebels against the defined codes of society. Woman's role is prescribed by Manu, "Women never deserve freedom" and yet as a wife she should advise like a minister, be a slave, have the appearance of Laxmi, pardon like mother Earth and in bed be the celestial prostitute Rambha. Despite their higher "virtues" and "attainments" they must be "inferior" to their husbands. In Saru's case economic security seems to be the part of the marriage arrangement which is more like a contract than a loving and intense relationship. Manu feels proud of being called the husband of a 'lady doctor' he is responsible for the disintegration of Saru into a 'terrified-trapped animal.' Saru's married life crumbles as she attains heights in her professional career and Manu fails to become a famous poet. Unable to accept his failure, Manu manifests his frustration in the form of sexual sadist attacks by the night. Gerda Learner rightly posits that men punish women by "ridicule, exclusion or ostracism," if they attempt to "interpret their own roles" (12-13). Saru shows remarkable restraint in order to save some peace for her family life:

> We belong to the same caste really. Both of us despise ourselves. What he does to me, he does it not so much because he hates me, but because he hates himself. And I... I hate my self more for letting him do it to me than I hate him for doing it to me. (8)

Deshpande's Saru is not radically defiant like Ibsen's Nora or Toni Morrison's Sethe. Though she has overcome the 'scarcity-syndrome' and 'identity-crisis,' she is also vulnerable, submissive and conformist to a certain extent. In spite of her repulsion for social establishment Sam has condescended to the concept of a "total female" Deshpande reworks and reshapes the 'feminine archetypes' to express her protest and her repugnance. Saru's girlhood dreams of a Prince Charming and hopes for "being the adored and chosen of a superior, super-human male. That was glory enough...to be chosen by that wonderful man" (53).

The desires to become indispensable for someone, 'to belong' and 'to be loved' make evident the 'internalised femininity' in Saru:

> As a child my fantasies, my dreams, has no relevance to the fact that I was a girl. The fact had not meant to me then what it would later. But as I grew up, they became the dreams of a total female—I saw myself humbly adoring, worshipping and being given the father-lover kind of love that was protective, condescending yet all encompassing and satisfying. There was no 'I' then, not as yet, craving for recognition, satisfaction. (53)

Saru, a professional woman dislocates the binary of husband as 'provider and protector' versus wife as 'recipient and protected.' Saru's employment is acceptable only because it supplements her husband's income. The story of Saru clearly depicts a duality deeply entrenched in the psyche of Indian society which sways societal definitions and expectations of women's public and private roles, consequently, women are expected to be both traditional and modern in domestic and public jurisdictions. Saru's economic independence makes her husband insecure. Saru tries to conform to her husband's expectations and yet Manu's male pride is wounded when an interviewer from a woman's magazine, asks Manu, "How does it feel when your wife earns not only the butter but most of the bread as well?" (182). This remark shows the dualistic approach of Indian society to woman's employment. These complex situations in Saru's life focus on the pathetic state of an Indian middle-class working woman.

> My mother had no room of her own. She retreated into the kitchen to dress up, she sat in this dingy room to comb her hair and apply kumkum, she slept in her bed like any overnight guest in a strange place. And I have so much my

mother lacked. But neither she nor I have that thing "a room of one's own". (135-36)

Through this narrative, Deshpande questions the assumption that the employment of the wife can serve as the means of her economic independence and self-actualization. At the same time the profession of women does not entail the potential to reduce the gap between men and women. While Saru's income provides a higher living standard to her family her contribution remains unnoticed. The hierarchic nature of marital roles is acknowledged by Saru in the following words:

> Don't ever try to reverse the doctor-nurse, executive-secretary, principle-teacher role. It can be traumatic, disastrous. And, I assure you, it isn't worth it. He'll suffer, you'll suffer and so will the children. Women's magazines will tell you that a marriage should be an equal partnership.

That's nonsense. Rubbish. No partnership can ever be equal. It will always be unequal, but take care that it's unequal in favour of your husband. If the scales tilt in your favour, god help you, both of you.

## III

In *Roots and Shadows* Deshpande makes a point that economic deprivation and physical torture are the instruments used to curb the spontaneous growth of a woman. Like Virginia Woolf's *A Room of One's Own*, this novel deals with the difficulties of women in general and women writers in particular. Woolf's insistence that a writer who is 'harassed and distracted with hates and grievances' (88) cannot produce any thing of enduring value is appropriate in the context of Indu. The inability to receive proper education, the limited opportunity to earn an adequate salary, the grinding demands of motherhood and domestic servitude—all contribute to the basic constraints of material life as well as of the imaginative life, as it is explicated in the following lines:

> It's a trap...that's what marriage is. A trap a cage...a cage with two trapped animals glaring hatred at each other...it isn't so wrong after all. And it's not a joke, but a tragedy. But what animal would cage itself? (59)

The mental vacuity of the women of Saru's family is evident as the authoritative and dominating male members are absent for a while:

> The house was silent, as if tired of its pretence of liveliness. A few women who had been left behind, and who had been carrying on an interminable argument in the kitchen, their voices rising and falling monotonously, were now hustled out by an authoritative male voice. (6)

The fact that money not only confers freedom, but also access to power, grace, prestige and an altogether confident and positive attitude towards one's own self and one's capabilities, is an overt statement made by the narrative. Akka, a rich, childless widow becomes a tyrant and dominates too much authority on family matters. Atya and other family members eulogize her as a leader, who assures happiness to everybody. Akka becomes indispensable to the family while the enforced subjugation and poverty of other women of the family results in their mental, moral and physical inferiority.

The predicament of Indu portrays the inner conflict of an artist to express herself, to discover her real 'self through her inner and instinctive potential for creative writing. Her creative activity combines the inner and outer voyage of self-discovery. The power of the creative act itself sanctifies her spiritual strivings for freedom. Through Indu's process of 'becoming' Deshpande works for the cause of the sexually colonised and biologically subjugated women subject. Indu's desire to 'exist' finds expression in her anxiety:

> Marriage makes one so dependent.... When I look in the mirror, I think of Jayant. When I dress, I think of Jayant. When I undress, I think of him.... Always what he wants. What he would like. What could please him.... It is not the way I want it to be. (54)

Indu is an educated 'New woman' who has the desire and the freedom to talk about things and to question the seriousness and nature of matters related to her. She thrives on emotional conflicts and oppositions. Her creativity and her observant nature makes her sensitive to issues like discrimination against girls, the trimming of their bodies, speech and mind and marital rape. She shows a lot of anger and resentment against her immediate family. Her disorientation is complete as she fails to conform to the conventions of 'femininity' because of her liberal education and job as a journalist but at the same time she strives to 'belong.' "To belong, to be wanted, needed, loved, desired and admired...how many traps there are! And I fall into all of them" (27). Her dissatisfaction with her woman's magazine is clear as she retorts, "(It believe) in taking the lure of least resistance and in increasing sales" (77). Her stories about troubled, intense human relationships are rejected by the editors of magazines because they neither instruct nor entertain nor educate and nor have a moral. Just for the sake of a handsome amount of money she continues. She left her job in a women's magazine for obvious reasons. "Women, women and women.... I got sick of it. There was nothing else. It was a kind of narcissism. And as if we had locked ourselves in a cage and thrown-away the key. I couldn't go on Where Naren asks that it would have been better for her to, write her "own stuff" she replies back in agony:

> What the hell shall I write about! tell me, Naren? women's lives and frustrations? Family life and domestic quarrels? Love without a capital L and marriage as the ultimate happy ending? Or may be I'll get bolder and write of menstrual pains and the pangs of child birth and the ecstasy of orgasm.

Indu wants to extricate herself from this kind of service in which she has no freedom and no scope to fulfill her own wishes. Evoking the two separate ambiences of woman's life Deshpande focuses effectively on the chasm between the haves and the have-nots. In order to be acceptable to the requirements of her employers she writes stories with male narrator, but fails. Deshpande herself went through such identity crisis in her career. But woman's writing alone can make this recovery. Woolf has systematically tried to point out that the distinction between men's writing and women's writing is crucial:

> But this creative power (of women) differs greatly from the creative power of men.... It would be a thousand pities if women wrote like men, or lived like men, or looked like men for if the two sexes are quite inadequate, considering

> the vastness and variety of the world, how should we manage with one only? Ought not education to bring out and fortify the differences rather than the similarities. (132)

Deshpande stresses that by writing like a woman is to explore the range of one's own sensibility without the influence of any narrow masculine pattern, and to feel entirely confident in one's own judgment and values. Jayant does not endorse Indu's idea of leaving the job and here, one is reminded of Woolf's famous conclusion that women must have five hundred pounds and a room of their own if they are to produce fiction on poetry money is important to the degree to which 'Intellectual freedom depends upon material things' (162-63).

Jayant hampers Indu's urge for self-expression which should be based on honest and fair ideals. Put Jayant believes that Indu is but a clog in the whole system of work-culture and therefore, she cannot bring about a change by raising her pen:

> What can one person do against the whole system. No point making a spectacle of yourself with futile gestures. We need the money, don't we? Don't forget we have a long-way to go. (17)

Indu's quest for an artistic self-hood is stifled before Jayant's philistine pursuit of material happiness, she hates it and herself for succumbing to monetary pursuits at the stake of her conscience. She compares herself to a fluid which has no shape of its own. Eventually, with Akka's money, she achieves her self and leaves all the shadows behind. "That I would at last do the kind of writing I had always dreamt of doing" (205).

## IV

*Small Remedies* is a saga of women emancipation. The novel is about the 'making' of a writer, singer and a social worker. Here, Deshpande envisages a hopeful future for women in their "shared experienced as women" (Pratt, 167) and the "imaginative continuum" (Showalter, 1977: 11). Madhu, Savitri Bai Indorekar, Leela and Hasina learn to know themselves and in the company of, female folks they achieve their social as well as spiritual identities. These women attain solicitude and sense of self-through their occupations and skills and continue to defy the servility of men.

For Savitri Bai Indorekar, a great singer of the Gwalior Gharana, in her music lies the aesthetic dimension of the erotic as well as her spiritual salvation. Extremely devoted to her practice she left her in-law's house and moved to Bhavanipur with her lover and Tabala master Ghulam Saab. Unlike Saru and Indu who go back to their homes with better understanding and the decision to compromise, Savitri Bai rearranges her domestic life without her kith and kin and confronts dilemmas and experience role overloads. Madhu writes about Savitri Bai:

> I can make Bai the rebel who rejected the conventions of her times. The feminist who lived her life at her terms. The great artist who struggled and sacrificed every thing in the cause of her art. The woman who gave up everything—a comfortable home, a husband and a family—for love. (166)

Madhu's aunt Leela is another non-conformist who participated in the '42 Quit India Movement, and was responsible for daring deeds. Leela is a widow, who remarries a Christian man and works for the upliftment of the women of the lower strata. Madhu narrates Leela's suffering and angst in her effort to create a space in male stratified system:

> I know that Leela was, certainly, a person who accepted wholly the consequences of her actions—Therefore, no complaints. In her work, too, though she was sidelined after years of working for the party, though she never reached the top of the hierarchy, while men who'd worked under her got there, she never complained. Only once, when a woman was selected as a candidate for a by-election, this woman the widow of the sitting member who'd been killed, only then I remember Leela saying, "It seems you've got to become a widow for them to remember that you exist."

This incident shows societal ambivalence towards women's changing roles. Madhu's desire to write an honest and true biography of Bai helps her in overcoming her sense of loss after the death of her son Aditya and her husband's distrust for yielding to a stranger in a moment of strong impulse. Arduous mental upheaval reveals her weaknesses and her strengths. Madhu leaves her home to come to terms with her identity and desire.

It is true that Deshpande presents a very conventional idea of feminism. Within the four walls of domesticity, she presents a certain image of middle-class ethos, still one can read here the theme of resistance. There is a deep struggle with the previous generation of women and distancing of mother, but this situation again creates a 'lacuna' as in the case of Saru. Saru is able to overcome her 'separation anxiety' only when she returns to her parental home and talks to her father. Deshpande recognises the importance of interaction among different generation of women. She emphasizes that women's strength lies in their acknowledgement of their desires not only sexual but creative as well. Deshpande's work exemplifies that woman need to be assertive in order to regain their mental equipoise and individuality.

## V

Shashi Deshpande is not radical to a great extent. Her protagonists do not think in terms of losing and winning because most of them are conditioned in age-old conventions. Deshpande's idea of feminism is different from her western counterpart which is an offshoot of individualism—the doctrine which is rooted in the idea that individual should take precedence over the interests of the social group, family or the state. However in India the idea strengthened by religion and culture is that individual rights should not be attained by isolating one self from family and community. Deshpande seems to believe in Sara Longwe's framework for women's empowerment i.e. gender equality achieved through women's share in material welfare, access to resources and benefits, conscientization, participation in the decision-making process, and, control over one's body and levels of power. Deshpande assesses and reassesses what exactly the Indian woman wants, and stresses that through education and self-dependence Indian women can come out of the servility-syndrome.

## NOTES

1. Karlekar defines femininity: Femininity means non-assertiveness, compliance obedience and in education, choosing options that will not conflict with these basic orientations—clearly then education

has to be manipulated to provide goals and training for girls which are substantially different from those for boys (157).

2. Kumkum Sagari and Sudesh Vaid specify in 'Recasting Women' that in Colonial India "Womanhood is often part of an asserted or desired, not an actual, culture identity."

## WORKS CITED


Chakraborty, Krishna. The conflicting worlds of working mothers. Calcutta: Progressive Publishers, 1978.

Deshpande, Shashi. "The Dilemma of a Woman Writer." Ed. R.K. Dhawan. Set III, Vol. 4.

——. "In Interview with Shashi Deshpande. With T.N. Geetha.

——. *Roots and Shadows*. 1983. Hyderabad: Dishabooks, 1992.

——. *Small Remedies*. New Delhi: Penguin Books, 2001.

——. *The Dark Holds No Terrors*. New Delhi: Penguin, 1990 (1980).

Freidan, Betty. *The Feminine Mystique*. New York: W.W. Norton, 1963.

Gupta, Anil Kumar. *Women and Society*. New Delhi: Print India, 1986.

——. *Indian Eomen Novelists*. Ed. R.K. Dhawan, Set III, Vol. 4, 9-11.

Irigary, Luce. "Speculum of the other woman." Trans. Gillan C. Gill. Ithaca: Cornell University Press, 1985.

Karlekar, Malavika. "Women's nature and access to education." *Socialization, Education and Women: Explorations in Gender Identity*. Ed. Karuna Channa. New Delhi: Orient Longman, 1988.

Lalm Malashri. *The Law of the Threshold: Women Writers in Indian English*. Shimla: Indian Institute of Advanced Study, 1995.

Larner, Gerda. "The Creation of Patriarchy." *Black Women in White America: A Documentary History*. New York: Random House, 1972.

Longwe, Sara. "Gender awareness: The missing element in the third world development project" in *Changing Perceptions: Writings on Gender Development*. Oxfam: Oxford, 1991.

Loomba, Ania. *Gender, Race, Renaissance Drama*. Bombay: Oxford University Press, 1993.

Narayan Ram, Acharya, ed. *Subhashitaratnabhandagar,* Bombay: Nirvana Sagar Press, 1957.

Pratt, Annis. *The Archetypal Patterns in Women's Fiction*. Bloomington: Indiana University Press, 1981.

Rajan, Rajeshwari Sunder. *Real and Imagined Women: Gender, Culture and Postcolonialism*. London: Routledge, 1993.

Rich, Adrienne. "When the Dead Awaken Writing as Revision" in *Lies Secrets and Silence*. New York: W.W. Norton, 1979, 35.

Sangari, Kumkum and Sudesh Vaid, ed. *Recasting Women: Essays in Colonial History*. New Delhi: Kali for Women, 1989.

Sharma, S.L. "Empowerment without Antagonism: A case for reformulation of women's Empowerment approach." *Sociological Bulletin*. 49.1, March 2000.

Shastri, Acharya Jagdish Lal, ed. *Manusmriti*. Delhi Motilal Banarasi Dass, 1983.

Showalter, Elaine, ed. *The New Feminist Criticism: Essays on Women, Literature and Theory*, New York: Pantheon Books, 1985.

——. *A Literature of Their Own: British Women Novelists from Bronte to Lessing*. Princeton: Princeton University Press, 1977.

Thaper, Romila. "Looking Back in History." *Indian Woman*. Ed. Devati Jain. New Delhi: Publication Division, 1975.

Wollstone Craft, Mary. *A Vindication of the Right's of Women*, 1792, 1.

Woolf, Virginia. *A Room of One's Own*. Harmondsworth: Penguin Books, 1975.

# Chapter 19

# Portrayal of Rural India in Kamala Markandaya's *Nectar in a Sieve*

*L.M. Joshi*

Kamala Markandaya's first novel *Nectar in a Sieve*[1] (1954), is about the rural India. It portrays the story of Rukmini and Nathan, a simple peasant couple from South India. The novel deals with industrialization and its impact on rural human life. The problems of rural India, the tragic predicament of Indian peasants have been depicted with moving realism. It focuses on the theme of hunger. The social problems like poverty, lack of family planning, beggary, the element of crime, unemployment, prostitution, zamindari system, caste and class conflict, superstitious beliefs, dowry system, low status of woman, marriage system etc., are very beautifully portrayed by Kamala Markandaya in *Nectar in a Sieve*.

The novel presents the life of simple rural people of South Indian village. The village people who are worried about the minimum basic needs and are engaged in agricultural activities. Rukmini, the protagonist of the novel, who is also the narrator, is married to a poor tenant farmer Nathan, in a South Indian village. They have a daughter named Ira, and six sons named Arjun, Thambi, Murugan, Selvam, Raja and Kuti. Meanwhile the peace of village is disturbed by the arrival of urban builder, who wants to build a tannery in the village. The evil of industrialization like inflation, ugliness grows up. Ira who is married to a farmer is deserted by her husband as she is barren. The family on the verge of starvation has no option but to assent to Arjun and Thambi joining the tannery. But due to their voice of protest they are forced to leave the work and they go to Ceylon. Murugan also goes to the city as due to terrible drought the family starves. Raja dies and Kuti falls ill. The poor girl, Ira, seeing her family starve during the famine, turns into a woman of the street and gives birth to an illegitimate child. Starvation takes away old Granny and Kuti. Rukmini and Nathan leave the village in search of Murugan, who himself has left his wife and had gone away. With the help of Puli, a young orphan, they live on charity and petty jobs. Nathan dies, Rukmini returns to her village with Puli.

As the rural people are illiterate, Rukmini as an exception, knows how to read and write. She teaches her children at home because she cannot afford to send them to school. The village that has been portrayed in this novel has two facets: One the peaceful village before the introduction of technology and the other after starting of the tannery. Agriculture is the main occupation in the village. In fact Kamala Markandaya did not depict the big landlords and agriculturists but the life of landless farmers who are also the neglected people. The landless farmers, in particular are held in the clutches of constant fear, as the land being snatched away, the failure or excesses of rains, droughts etc. Markandaya gives a very realistic and touching description of such fear "The calamities of the land belong to its alone, born of wind and rain and weather, immensities not to be tempered by man or his creations. To those who live by the land there must always come time of hardship, of fear and hunger" (181). A farmer has no hopes for the future, but yet he keeps hope, amidst fear of getting disappointment. Rukmini sums up the life of a peasant, when she says: "Hope and fear. Twin forces that hugged us first in one direction and then in another, and with one was stronger no one could say.... Fear constant companion of the peasant...fear, fear of the dark future, fear of the blackness of death" (110).

In a traditional Indian family, woman is always subordinate to the man. While the sons are considered as assets and the daughter are considered as a burden on a family. When the first born child was a daughter, Rukmini was very much disappointed "for what woman want a girl for her first born" (25). Nathan "wanted a son to continue his line and walk beside him on the land, not a pulling infant who would take with her dowry and leave nothing but a memory behind" (27). Rukmini thinks that it was a punishment for her past sins "I have no sons; only one child, a girl.... Why should it be? ...Am I not clean and healthy?" (32). In the village, much more than in city, a childless woman is considered an ill-fated one. The life of a woman who had no children at all, is more worse. Ira's husband deserts her, because she is barren. Hence, the husband in the rural area had a social sanction to discard his barren or sonless wife. It is natural that Rukmini easily reconciles herself to Ira's ill fate and consoles her. "You must not blame him, he has taken another woman" (65).

While socio-religious forces create problems of acceptability and respectability for the childless woman, absence of money for survival drives her to prostitution, as happens in the case of Ira. Prostitution is a major social problem today in both urban and rural areas. Ira wants to save her ailing brother. She is fed up of poverty and hunger. Kunthi, a village woman also takes to prostitution. Nathan calls Ira a 'harlot' and never touches even food that is bought out of Ira's earnings. Markandaya portrays the fate of the prostitutes very realistically "But the man who finds a woman in the street, raises his eyebrow and snaps his fingers so that she follows him, throws few coins that he may possess her, holds her unresisting whatever he has paid for. What cares such a man for the woman who is his for a brief moment? He has gained her relief, she her payment" (157-58).

By and large most of the characters in the novel are typically rural, Rukmini, Nathan, Janaki, Kali, Kunthi, Ira, Old Granny. Their way of life, attitudes, manners and speech belong to the countryside; Hari Mohan Prasad calls Nathan and his wife "Symbols of teeming millions, archetypal figures like Adam and Eve."[2] Superstitions and beliefs are just fruit of illiteracy. The villagers have many beliefs. It is believed that Cobra are sacred, and hence they should not be killed. Nathan, though illiterate, does not believe that. The rural people take pride in having more children, considering it not only a concrete testimony of divine blessing but also a fortune in having more hands to work on the farm. When Rukmini fails to get any child after Ira, her mother takes her to temple, then they pray together, before the deity for the son. She also gives Rukmini "a small stone lingam" (30), a symbol of fertility. The belief paves way for customs. Rukmini is faithfully devoted to her husband, does not call him by his name but address him only as husband. A garland of mango leaves is to be tied up across the doorway, as it is "a symbol of happiness and good future" (13).

Caste system is a predominant force in the Indian society. In this novel except an occasional reference to the Muslims and Cobblers, there is no mention of any other caste. Though there is reference to gods and goddesses, they do not bear any identity. It appears Markandaya makes particular reference to the Muslim woman with an intention to express her dislikes towards the purdah system. But Markandaya gives a detailed description of the class system. In the village the landlords are the most powerful in social hierarchy. Nathan has tilled the land for thirty years, he is told that the land would be given to another one if he fails to make payment. He thinks, "Money is not everything" (95).

Kamala Markandaya has not given the description of the village at the height of its glory but at its transitional period, affected particularly by the setting of tannery. Nonetheless slow change was coming to the villages where Srinivasa Iyenger feels "life has not apparently changed for a thousand years, but now with the invasion of industry and Modern technology sinister consequences issue."[3] For some people the tanner proves to be a boon "Day and night women twist rope, since they could sell as much as they made, and traders waxed prosperous selling their goods to the workmen" (42). Though a village woman, Kunthi feels happy with the change that their, "Village is no longer a clump of huts but a small town" (33). But soon the darker side start to emerge out. Rukmini does not like the change, because of its noise, stinking smell and crowds. The bird's seems to have forgotten to sing; or the noise drowns their melodious calls. Rukmini denounces the change also because the money buys less and less. In place of quiet the village has "all noise and crowds every where and rude young hooligans idling in the street and dirty bazaars and uncouth behaviour and no man thinks of another but schemes only for his Money" (66).

Industrialization has brought demoralization in the village. There is nothing but the smell of tannery, the crowds, the shouting and disturbance. Ira also turns to prostitution. The quiet life and village economics both are affected, values have lost their roots, and money is what everybody is interested in. Industrialization affects family the very basic institution of a society. As A.V. Krishana Rao remarks: "Industrialization with its main emphasis on urban development and the mechanization of the means of production and distribution necessary result in the social dislocation of the family."[4]

Nathan, a landless farmer, has to live on the mercy of the zamindar. He has suffered under the zamindari system. Nathan works for thirty years under the illusion of owning up the land and of his sons working on it with him, though they are cruelly depressed of it in the eve of their life. Whether the harvest is good or not he has to pay the Revenue of the land. He sells the utensils, two brass vessels of the tin trunk, two shirts of their eldest son whatever gains that were left, and even bullocks and seeds, so as to retain the land, to clear the dues with a hope that today or tomorrow he will own the land but when the tannery owners pay good price the zamidar sells all his land and Nathan and many more likes him have to go landless. As A.V. Krishana Rao remarks: "Rukmini and Nathan, the peasant couple in South Indian village are victims of two evils, zamidari systems and the industrial economy."[5]

The tragic picture of hunger is pointed out by Markandaya, when Rukmini divides food into 24 small parts to feed the entire family for an equal number of days. Such starvation leads to human degradation. Ira seeing her family starve during the famine turns into a woman of the street and gives birth to an illegitimate *albino child*. Hunger makes Ira a prostitute; hunger leads to suspected theft of a calfskin by Raja and his subsequent death. Starvation forces Kunthi's death. As P.P. Mehta rightly remarks: "The struggle between man and overpowering hunger before which, honour, morality and even God do not count."[6] The problem of poverty has been realistically depicted by Markandaya the adverse physical condition like drought make Nathan unable to pay his land revenue. Puli has to face poverty and go on begging because he has none to support and care for. Puli has "no mother...there is no one to worry about me... and none to worry me either, which is a good thing" (230). As N.K. Jain feels that the novel presents "an authentic picture of village life in transition, particularly of rural poverty and hunger."[7] The lack of family planning in rural India also forces the rural families to poverty as in the case of Nathan's family, Poverty and unemployment leads to many other social problems like prostitution, beggary and crime. Nathan and Rukmini too, the two simple and hardworking villagers, are forced to go for beggary, though called free food in the name of charity. Poverty along with other social problems, gives birth to offences also. Puli engages himself in petty crimes when he fails to get any alms. Murugan engages himself in gambling.

Kamala Markandaya clearly disapproves of superstitious practices of the rural people. On the failure of rain, Rukmini threw herself on the earth, prayed, offered a pumpkin and a few grains of rice to the goddess, but no rains came. The living conditions of the rural people are almost primitive. Nathan's house is a small thatched mud hut near a paddy held in the vicinity of a couple of similar huts. A garland of Mango leaves has been hung across its doorway to herald happiness and good fortune. The hut has two rooms, one of which is a kind of storehouse for grain where as the other is for virtually everything else. For lighting, the village has a wick lamps or oil filled coconut shells used as lamps. The village transport is a bullock-cart, moving in the midst of sight and sound from nature, which makes the journey enjoyable to both animals and passengers.

Thus Kamala Markandaya has given a very descriptive and realistic picture of a rural India and its problems in this novel. The problems described in the novel have a typical rural tinge. Whether it is on economic, social religious or human level, the novel belongs to Indian rural life in all its manifestations as

S.Z.H. Abidi remarks: "The social realism employed by Kamala Markandaya in this novel is very close to the observed condition of life."[8]

## NOTES

1. Kamala Markandaya, *Nectar in a Sieve* (New Delhi: Sagar Publication, 1968).
2. Hari Mohan Prasad, "The Fictional Epic on Indian Life—A Study in Theme and Technique of *Nectar in a Sieve*," *Perspective on Kamala Markandaya*, ed. Madhusudan Prasad (Ghaziabad: Vimal Prakashan, 1984), 99.
3. K.R.S. Iyenger, *Indian Writing in English* (Bombay: Asia Publishing House, 1973), 438.
4. A.V. Krishana Rao, *The Indo-Anglian Novel and the Changing Tradition* (Mysore: Rao and Raghavan, 1972), 64.
5. *Ibid.*
6. P.P. Mehta, *Indo-Anglian Fiction: An Assessment* (Bareilly: Prakash Book Depot), 1979, 255.
7. N.K. Jain, Kamala Markandaya, *Nectar in a Sieve,* "Major Indian Novels," ed.: N.S. Pradhan (New Delhi: Arnold Heinemann, 1985), 74.
8. S.Z.H. Abidi, *Nectar in a Sieve: A Critical Study* (Bareilly: Prakash Book Depot, 1989).

# Chapter 20

## Influence of T.S. Eliot in Arun Joshi's *The Foreigner*

*Siddhartha Sharma*

Right from the beginning to the very end of Arun Joshi's *The Foreigner* (1968), we find the influence of T.S. Eliot. The themes associated with Eliot's poetry are prominent in *The Foreigner*. We find the elements of alienation, rootlessness, purposelessness, and moral and spiritual bankruptcy in the novel. As S. Rangachari aptly remarks: "The themes of alienation, of rootlessness of individuals, of inanity and purposelessness of human existence, of moral vacuity, spiritual bankruptcy and apathy—the themes which are associated with Eliot's early poetry figure prominent in *The Foreigner*."[1]

Sindi appears to be a typical Eliotean character. Like Prufrock, he is a coward and for him "detachment" becomes a euphemism for non-involvement which sparks off many tragedies—especially in the lives of Babu and June. Towards the end of the novel he becomes involved (*karmayogi*) which is again a page from Eliot's *The Four Quartets*.

Arun Joshi's Boston is Eliot's Boston of *The Waste Land*—insipid, sterile, degenerate, with no hope of resurrection. Arun Joshi fails for words to highlight the hypocrisy of the modern, degenerate, spiritually dead American society and straightaway borrows the idea from Eliot's "Love Song:" "...there will be time/ To prepare a face to meet the faces that you meet." Even the ball and parties in America are, for him, quite a fraud. The show of being courteous was a sham, and the promise to meet again after the party was over, was merely a lip-service. The unreality and artificiality of the Boston community makes him feel out of place, an alien, an outsider: For him all the roads lead to alienation. Like Eliot's Harry in *The Family Reunion* he undergoes experiences of a "solitude in a crowded desert." Sindi observes: "I drank and watched the crowd bob up and down in the huge mirror behind the bar. All those faces distorted in the cheap mirror made me feel even more like an alien. Except for the bartender and me there wasn't a soul in the room who wasn't dancing or talking or beating his feet to the music. It is remarkable how you can be in a crowded room like that and still feel lonely like you were sitting in your own tomb" (24). The reference to the bundles of soggy humanity whether he be in Boston or London or India, for Sindi the show remains unchanged. For Eliot, all cities are one, all men are one. It appears to be an echo of Eliot's description of people in *The Waste Land*:

> A crowd flowed over London Bridge so many,
> I had not thought death had undone so many.

Kenya, London, America and India—all shores—are alien to him. He tells Khemka, "I have no roots; I have no system of morality" (143). He has no roots, as he himself confesses, so the question of his culture or morality simply doesn't arise. This very view—a man acquires culture only when he has roots—is subscribed to by T.S. Eliot in his famous social criticism "Notes Towards the Definition of Culture." He is like the self-isolated Eliotean characters as Prufrock, Gerontion, the Chamberlaynes, Celia, Lord Claberton, etc. He has gained a different set of experiences, and is convinced of the impermanence of things. He says to June, "Nothing ever seems real to me, leave alone permanent. Nothing seems to be very important" (107). His entire life is geared around his quest for permanence in life. When June suggests that they get married, he tells June, "we are alone both you and I. That is the problem. And our aloneness must be resolved from within" (126). It is reminiscent of Prufrock's interior monologue, "Let us go then, you and I," as the two live in their own private hells.

Sindi regards life as absurd which is akin to Eliot's view that life is a "panorama of futility."[2] It is this feeling of the meaninglessness of life that makes him withdraw from the world into the nightside of life. Earlier also he had attempted suicide when he was a college student in Nairobi as he was tired of living. Sindi had been indifferent to June and Babu which leads to their death. For Babu's death his own innocence born of his sheltered life is responsible. Eliot's shadow can also be seen in the recurrent death images in the novel, especially in the first part. He leads a death-in-life like the wastelanders. His asthmatic illness, he says, leaves a taste of death in his mouth. After his uncle's death, he says, he existed only for dying. Early in the narrative while watching a lone beauty in one of Khemka's giant parties, Sindi becomes aware of his own loneliness and feels: "Between her and me the chasm of a living world prevailed. I had a feeling that I was watching her from the edge of the world just where Death's kingdom began" (16). It is reminiscent of "death's twilight kingdom" in T.S. Eliot's "The Hollow Men." Like Eliot's strawmen, he ekes out an existence which is a veritable death-in-life.

All his weaknesses he covers with the blanket term "detachment" which is nothing but a euphemism for his non-involvement which does not accord with the sublime concept of detachment as enunciated in the *Bhagwad Geeta*. This emotional aridity and cowardice are obvious as he suffers from a Prufrockean aboulia: "And indeed there will be Time/ To wonder, 'Do I dare?' 'Do I dare?'"

Sindi's vision is a morbid one, littered with the images of death, and thereby serving as the 'objective correlative,' Khemka finds him "living but as bad as dead" (137). His feeling of the utter futility of his life can be seen in the following lines, where Prufrock-like he has "measured out with coffee spoons."[3] "Twenty-five Christmas on this planet, twenty-five years largely wasted in search of wrong things in wrong places. Twenty-five years gone in search of peace, and what did I have to show for achievement; a ten-stone body that had to be fed four times a day, twenty-eight times a week. This was the sum of a life-time striving" (92).

Like a Wastelander, he remains neutral or indifferent to almost everything. On being asked by June as to what he was thinking; he non-chalantly replies "nothing," which is reminiscent of the answer the lover gives to the lady in "the Game of Chess." Even the mechanical nature of sex between Sindi and June is suggestive of the sexual act between the lady-typist and the young man in *The Waste Land.*

Sindi's affair with Anna reminds us of the love depicted in Eliot's "Portrait of a Lady." Like Eliot's lady, Anna too, as Sindi later comes to realise did not yearn for his company but for her lost youth.

But Sindi shows exemplary courage in his capacity for regeneration when he is thrown into managing Khemka's chaotic business. At dawn it starts raining: "It was the first of the monsoons, carrying a freshness and coolness that was a welcome change from the humid heat of the previous day" (234). The shower, like in T.S. Eliot's *The Waste Land*, is a fertility symbol. It symbolizes reawakening, his rebirth, his regeneration. That afternoon the sky is clear and he goes to Muthu's wretched dwelling place. The clear sky, as Mukteshwar Pandey opines, "symbolises the light of knowledge that will dawn upon Sindi."[4] He condescends to visit Muthu's dwelling place, where Muthu asks him to take charge of the management, and further telling him that sometimes detachment lay in getting involved. Sindi is wise enough to comply with Muthu's request, as Eliot says in "East Coker:" "The only wisdom we can hope to acquire/ Is the wisdom of humility: humility is endless."[5] It is a humble admonition from Muthu to the escapist Sindi in the manner Eliot says in "The Dry Salvages:" "So Krishna, as when he admonishes Arjuna on the field of battle. Not fare well,/ But fare forward, voyagers."[6] His past has been a colossal waste which he thinks of redeeming through right action, irrespective of the consequences or failures. As Eliot says in "The Dry Salvages:" "And right action is freedom/ From past and future also"[7] and in "East Coker," "For us, there is only the trying, rest is not our business."[8] Like Arjuna, he decides to perform *nishkama karma* as Eliot writes in "The Dry Salvages:" "And do not think of the fruit of action/ Fare forward."[9]

## NOTES AND REFERENCES

1. S. Rangachari, "T.S. Eliot's Shadow on *The Foreigner*," *Scholar Critic,* edited by N. Radhakrishnan, January 1994, 2.
2. T.S. Eliot, "Ulysses, Order and Myth," *Selected Prose of T.S. Eliot,* edited by Frank Kennode, Harcourt Brace, 1975, 177.
3. T.S. Eliot, *Selected Poems* (London: Faber and Faber, 1954), 13.
4. Mukteshwar Pandey, *Arun Joshi: The Existential Element in His Novels* (New Delhi: B.R. Publishing Corporation, 1998), 53.
5. T.S. Eliot, *Four Quartets* (London: Faber and Faber, 1970), 27.
6. *Ibid.,* 42.
7. *Ibid.,* 45.
8. *Ibid.,* 31.
9. *Ibid.,* 42.